LITERATURE, LETTERS AND THE CANONICAL IN
EARLY MODERN SCOTLAND

Literature, Letters and the Canonical in Early Modern Scotland

edited by

THEO VAN HEIJNSBERGEN and NICOLA ROYAN

TUCKWELL PRESS

First published in Great Britain in 2002 by
Tuckwell Press Ltd
The Mill House, Phantassie, East Linton, East Lothian, EH40 3DG
Scotland

ISBN 1 86232 270 8

British Library Cataloguing-in-Publication Data. A catalogue
record for this book is available on request from the British Library

Typeset in 10.5/13 Garamond
Printed and bound in Great Britain by
Bell & Bain Ltd., Glasgow

Contents

Acknowledgements

The papers in this volume were all presented at the Ninth International Conference on Medieval and Renaissance Scottish Language and Literature, held at St Andrews University in August 1999 under the auspices of the St Andrews Scottish Studies Institute and the School of English, University of St Andrews. Our first debt of gratitude is therefore owed to the Director of the Institute and the then Head of School, Professor Douglas Dunn, and to the Institute's tireless secretary, Mrs Frances Mullan, for their essential contributions to the organisation of the conference, and for their moral and practical support in the production of these proceedings. SASSI also ensured that these proceedings received an initial financial subsidy, for which the editors are very grateful.

Further generous financial subsidy was granted by the Department of Scottish Literature, University of Glasgow, and also by the Hunter-Marshall Bequest Fund, University of Glasgow. It is a paradox of modern academic life that while academic staff are under increasing pressure to publish, the funds to enable publication are fewer and more jealously guarded, so the editors warmly thank Professor Douglas Gifford for supporting our applications for financial assistance. The Anderson-Dunlop Fund paid for the reproduction of the cover image which is crucial to the editors' understanding of the collection's contribution to the study of early modern Scottish literature. We thank the Trustees of the Fund, Professor Hector MacQueen and Dr Alan Borthwick, for their encouragement of our application. We are also grateful to the Royal Commission on the Ancient and Historical Monuments of Scotland, who granted us permission to reproduce the image.

Finally we would like to thank our typesetter Elfreda Crehan, for her patience, her professionalism and for her ability to come up with solutions to knotty problems.

Abbreviations

Aldis	H. G. Aldis, *A List of Books Printed in Scotland Before 1700*, (Edinburgh, 1904; repr. with additions, 1970)
ASLS	Association of Scottish Literary Studies
BL	British Library
CSP Scot.	*Calendar of State Papers, relating to Scotland and Mary, Queen of Scots, 1547–1603*, ed. by J. Bain *et al.*, 13 vols (Edinburgh, 1898–1969)
CUL	Cambridge University Library
DNB	*Dictionary of National Biography* (London, 1885–1900)
DOST	*A Dictionary of the Older Scottish Tongue*
Edin. Recs.	*Extracts from the Records of the Burgh of Edinburgh*, ed. by Sir J. D. Marwick, 4 vols, SBRS (Edinburgh, 1869–82)
EETS	Early English Text Society (O.S. – Original Series; N.S. – New Series)
IMEV	*The Index of Middle English Verse*, ed. by C. Brown and R. H. Robbins (New York, 1943)
IR	*Innes Review*
MED	*Middle English Dictionary*
NAS	National Archives of Scotland
NLS	National Library of Scotland
OED	*Oxford English Dictionary*
RPC	*The Register of the Privy Council of Scotland. First Series 1545–1625*, ed. by J. H. Burton and David Masson, 14 vols (Edinburgh, 1877–98)
SBRS	Scottish Burgh Record Society
Scots Peerage	*The Scots Peerage*, ed. by J. Balfour Paul, 9 vols (Edinburgh, 1904–14)
SHR	*Scottish Historical Review*
SHS	Scottish History Society
SIMEV	*Supplement to the Index of Middle English Verse*, ed. by J. L. Cutler and R. H. Robbins (Lexington, KY, 1965)
SLJ	*Scottish Literary Journal*
SP Henry VIII	*State Papers: Henry VIII*, 11 vols (London, 1830–52)
SSL	*Studies in Scottish Literature*
STC	*A Short-Title Catalogue of Books Printed in England, Scotland, and Ireland and of English Books Printed Abroad 1475–1640*, ed. by A. W. Pollard and G. R. Redgrave, 2nd edn, rev. and enl. by W. A. Jackson, F. S. Ferguson, and K. F. Pantzer, 3 vols (London, 1976–91)
STS	Scottish Text Society

Contributors

Keely Fisher is currently a tutor in medieval English and Scots at St Hilda's and Brasenose Colleges, Oxford. Her academic interests focus mainly on late medieval secular literature in English and Scots. At present, Dr Fisher is preparing her 1999 doctoral thesis for publication.

Morna Fleming is Assistant Rector and teacher of English at Beath High School in Fife, Scotland, and has continued writing and contributing to conferences since completing her doctorate on 'The Impact of the Union of the Crowns on Scottish Lyric Poetry 1584–1619' at Glasgow University in 1997. She has contributed a commentary on James VI's *Reulis and Cautelis* for the Scotsoun audio-cassette series, and her most recent article on the *Amatoria* of James VI has just appeared in *Royal Subjects*, ed. D. Fischlin.

William Gillies is Professor of Celtic and head of the department of Celtic and Scottish Studies at the University of Edinburgh. His research interests include Celtic literary tradition, Scottish Gaelic poetry and Highland historiography and genealogy.

Janet Hadley Williams is a Visiting Fellow in English and Theatre Studies at the Australian National University.

C. Marie Harker specializes in late medieval / early modern English and Scottish literature, with particular interests in the intersections between manuscript studies and gender studies criticism. Most recently, she has studied the role of gendered rhetoric in the works of John Hardyng, John Lydgate and Sir David Lyndsay.

Theo van Heijnsbergen is a lecturer in the department of Scottish Literature in the School of English at the University of Glasgow. His research and publications focus on sixteenth-century Scottish literature and culture.

David J. Parkinson, Professor of English, University of Saskatchewan, specializes in the literary history of late medieval Scotland. Recent publications include essays on Scottish patronage, popular entertainment, and reception of Chaucer, as well as editions of poems by Gavin Douglas and Alexander Montgomerie.

Jamie Reid-Baxter works as a translator for the European Parliament, Luxemburg, and is an Honorary Research Fellow, Department of Scottish History, University of Glasgow.

Nicola Royan is a lecturer in medieval and early modern literature in the School of English at the University of Nottingham.

Marie-Claude Tucker has just published her 1997 thesis for the University of Clermont-Ferrand under the title of *Maîtres et étudiants écossais à la Faculté de droit de l'Université de Bourges (1480–1703)*. She has written several articles on cultural and academic connections between early modern Scotland and France, and is currently also mayor of St Vitte in France.

Introduction

THEO VAN HEIJNSBERGEN AND NICOLA ROYAN

As our understanding of early modern (*c.* 1500–1750) Scottish culture increases, it becomes evident that we need to challenge and critique the images of the past and of past literatures that we have inherited, be it through popular tradition or scholarly investigation. By its title, the present volume signals its intention not only to foreground less well-known names and titles and link them to wider cultural issues, but also to re-assess authors and texts that have developed canonical status within the Scottish literary and literary-critical traditions. In so doing, the essays collected here offer new perspectives on the construction of the canon – both the method and the edifice – and of canonical critical attitudes, seeking to bring these closer in touch with the actual texts and culture involved. They do so by siting texts and authors differently in place and time, by gendering them, and by looking at them from the position of the audience or persona rather than that of the author. Until the 1980s, such new perspectives on Scottish literature and culture proved difficult to develop, especially because much of the preparatory work that normally precedes such revisions, including the provision of reliable editions with comprehensive critical notes, had yet to be done. Judging from the evidence of the contributions in the present volume, however, enough of that critical work has now been rendered to allow the revision and expansion of previous selections of critical choices, develop new perspectives, and reconfigure our understanding of early modern writing in Scotland.

Reforging a canon, however, is a continuous process; this collection does not describe a completed object or project, but rather outlines some of the new dimensions of its construction currently coming into view. The introduction summarizes and links the arguments of individual essays, and selects common strands that suggest cultural coherence(s) for a period more normally characterized as unproductive and, therefore, lacking coherence, in terms of literature. The latter term itself requires scrutiny. Preconceptions of what constitutes literature, arguably in tandem with intellectual laziness, have in the past led to the entrenched notion of the Scottish seventeenth century as a barren field, with isolated features in the cultural landscape such as William Drummond or the ballads as the exceptions that prove the rule. The essays in this volume add to the growing amount of evidence that proves this to be a proposition based on too narrow a definition of literature as creative and purely fictive writing. Instead, they propose a wider definition of literary writing, one which describes it in terms of 'letters' rather than the less inclusive label of 'literature'. This approach foregrounds one of the attractions of Scottish texts from the sixteenth to the early eighteenth centuries in their own context, namely their capacity to articulate critical perspectives that are crucially different from – and thus interrogate – those conceptualized and canonized in more received models of interpretation.

The essays also illustrate the ways in which many Scottish texts from the early modern period, taking their cue from late medieval literature, display an open-ended, porous practice of culture, across genres, languages, classes, localities, and eras. Instead of voicing a series of one-dimensional or somehow isolated cultures, these texts manifest an openness to contiguous cultural discourses such as 'folk' and 'art' poetry, or Scots and Gaelic writing, be they those of their own or a previous era, or of their own or another culture. In doing so, they establish an imaginative, synchronic continuum (socially and culturally) in their respective eras. Those continuities also work diachronically, invalidating the watershed traditionally posited between medieval and 'Renaissance', which has in Scotland often been further simplified as pre- *v.* post-Reformation literary culture. The remarkable survival into the eighteenth century of prominent sixteenth-century literary phenomena such as the flyting, allegorical dream-vision, or David Lyndsay, and of the mixture of historiographical practices as documented by several papers in the present collection, reveals an inter- as well as intra-cultural permeability that refutes the post-Union reputation of early modern Scottish culture as trivial, limited, or fragmented.

In agreement with a more comprehensive redefining of 'literature' as 'letters', the papers in the present collection, presented at the International Conference on Medieval and Renaissance Scottish Language and Literature held at St Andrews in 1999, fully engage with the varied perspectives available to readers of early modern texts.[1] Like the triennial conferences of which the one at St Andrews was the ninth, they signal the growth of the discipline of early Scottish cultural and literary studies. In particular, they respond eloquently to the introduction in an earlier volume of proceedings which concludes that *its* papers and these conferences 'engage in a re-imagining of Scotland that persistently invokes an appreciation of plurality: Scottish and European, Scottish and English, vernacular and Latin and – for what those terms are worth – medieval and Renaissance. In positive re-evaluations of the propensity of Scottish culture for mixing such things up lies the future of our subject'.[2]

Because of the historically enforced juxtaposition of 'early modern Scottish literature' with especially its English counterpart, its literary and critical perspectives have traditionally been considered 'off-centre'. In response to this, rather than trying to prove any 'centrality' or 'stability' of Scottish literature and thus running the risk of replacing one fallacy by another, it is better to argue that 'central stability' is an imaginary construction in the first place, and to emphasize that the conceptual mileage of early modern Scottish literature in fact lies in exactly such an awareness of itself as off-centre, of its texts as local inflections of international, almost 'virtual' cultural narratives.

The cover of the present book illustrates such a self-awareness, linking Scottish to European and sixteenth to eighteenth-century cultural paradigms. It shows a *trompe-l'œil* cupola, the central section of the painted ceiling of Pinkie House that James VI's Chancellor, Alexander, Lord Seton, commissioned in 1613.[3] Its deliberately off-centre perspective, as if one is standing slightly to one side while gazing upwards into the illusional lantern, presses home the possible absence of stability, but that exposure of the illusory nature of art's capacity to impose fixity on the flux of life at the same time draws attention to the purposeful art of the skewed perspective itself.[4] It effectively demonstrates that a perspective need not be central in order to illuminate a larger structure. Whether this is an expression of 'Renaissance' confidence, baroque nervousness, or mannerist sensibility – a debate more likely to address modern anxieties regarding art and culture rather than Seton's – is a moot point; more importantly, the painting in any interpretation playfully exposes the artificial nature of any fixed centre, a proposition no doubt relevant to the contemporary Scottish cultural psyche after the departure of James VI from Scotland in 1603, and no doubt reinforced by the Union of Parliaments in 1707. It instances the fact that decentring does not necessarily lead to 'discontinuation' or 'disconnection' but can open up valid and arguably more individual new perspectives.

What may seem to represent a crisis in art and culture is thus turned into a creative affirmation of the same. The artistic control presumed by this particular reading of the ceiling is supported by Seton's position within international artistic and scientific discourses. Apart from a Chancellor with pronounced interests in architecture and neo-Stoic philosophy, Seton was also a Latin poet and a mathematician; his contemporary and fellow countryman John Napier, the discoverer of logarithms, dedicated to Seton the book in which he explained his calculating device.[5] Moreover, Mr Robert Pont, Lord of Session, father of the famous map-maker Timothy Pont, and charged with revising the new metrical translation of the psalms, dedicated his 'A Newe Treatise of the Right Reckoning of Yeares and Ages of the World' (1599) to Seton, calling him the foremost of the 'rare Maecenases of this Land'.[6] Seton's painted ceiling is based on a design, printed in Johannes Vredeman de Vries's *Perspectiva theoretica ac practica* (Antwerp, 1604–5),[7] that details the intricate mathematics involved in trying to depict correctly an eccentric as well as three-dimensional viewing angle. The painting thus visualizes the notion that an off-centre perspective can still function within a strictly organized superstructure. Order and idiosyncrasy, collective and individual, can co-habit in one vision. In the rest of the painted ceiling of Pinkie House, 'images deriving from Andrea Alciato's *Emblemata* jostled for attention with others taken from Otto van Veen's *Emblemata Horatiana*', key European names in emblem literature.[8] At the entrance to his gardens, Seton claims that 'for his own benefit, for the benefit of his descendants, and for the benefit of all good, humane and cultured men, [as] a devout lover of all culture and humanity, [he] founded, erected, and adorned his country-seat, gardens and these suburban buildings ... laid out ... for the honourable delight of body and of soul'.[9] The Pinkie House ceiling and gardens are thus clear examples at the heart of our period of investigation of the Scottish cultural ambition to maintain national social, cultural, and intellectual coherence on an international level.

The pleasure of the present volume is that it strives to recuperate aspects of this social and cultural coherence and its attendant pluralities, and to make our backward glance a contextualized one. Each essay demonstrates how particular texts respond to wider cultural contexts or social experiences, and seeks to recover some of the energy that this releases. Collectively, the essays thus outline how the texts and authors discussed illustrate the permeable as well as permeating nature of the literature and culture involved. This incremental effect makes it not only chronologically but also conceptually appropriate that the book opens with Keely Fisher's detailed analysis of how the 'native' genre of flyting was not only continued in the middle part of the sixteenth century but was also imaginatively adapted in the process, to suit new social realities as well as their attendant literary demands. In its wide range of coverage, this essay sets the tone for the other contributions in that it illustrates the willingness of early modern texts to continue established literary practices, to mix genres and registers, and to capitalize on elements of performance where a text is spoken as well as written. Fisher's paper also foregrounds the generic flexibility of early modern Scottish writers. Her subject, William Stewart, is more usually known for his lyrics or his lengthy verse translation of Boece's *Scotorum Historia*; his flyting, although less scholarly, is no less learned in the *mores* of writing.

The subsequent essays take us from the mid-sixteenth to the early eighteenth century and through many different cultural territories. Janet Hadley Williams analyzes in illuminating detail David Lyndsay's strikingly politicized version of the stock medieval genre of *de casibus* literature in his *Tragedie of the Cardinall*. Its 'translation' into English by Protestant activists in England, published very soon after the events that gave rise to the poem, involved a small but significant measure of textual interference to suit a Reformist ideology. This provides welcome information on the reception and circulation of Scottish texts abroad. The English version's subtle distortion of Lyndsay's commitment to the Protestant cause also points up Lyndsay's own much more nuanced and deliberately uncommitted political position in the Scots original.[10]

Marie Harker links Knox's attempt in *The First Blast of the Trumpet against the Monstrous Regiment of Women* to contain both male and female transgressions of natural order – i.e. (male acceptance of) female authority – to a number of issues. The *aporiai* that this analysis causes to appear in *The First Blast* reveal how Knox manipulates political and theological allegiances by appealing to a 'natural order': he turns the political sovereignty of the two female Catholic rulers in Britain in the mid-fifties, and courtiers' subservience to it (as well as the attendant class differences), into a gender issue. Harker's essay, in precise critical language, adds the important dimension of gender to our growing awareness of Knox's manipulations of a 'usable past'.[11]

Theories of government and gender are also in dialogue in Morna Fleming's essay on poems addressing James's accession to the English throne in 1603. This event forced English poets to reformulate their rhetoric of praise in order to suit a king rather than a queen. This problem had its source in the very arguments that had been presented to counteract Knox's formidable arsenal against the rule of women, and surely also in Elizabeth's dedication to her own virgin status, by means of which she ensured that she herself did not become subject to a legitimate male ruler in the form of a husband. To smoothen the transition to a male sovereign, the English poets after Elizabeth's death stress James's female English inheritance through his great-grandmother, Margaret Tudor, who thus passes to him, through only one highlighted generation, the mantle of Henry VII, the restorer of English unity after civil war. Like Knox and the 'Protestantizers' of David Lyndsay half a century earlier, Samuel Daniel and other English poets also seek to create a 'usable past' to determine the present. In contrast, the Scots have to come to terms with a king's *departure*, and therefore concern themselves primarily with elegiac complaints. Poets such as Craig and Ayton see the Union of the Crowns as foreshadowing the end of the Scottish pattern of intimate government, and as the loss of a central platform for the performance and circulation of certain kinds of early modern literature. The accession that united the two realms under one crown thus paradoxically foregrounds the different needs and expectations of the two countries.

The importance of the court and the rhetoric and literature attached to it can be seen in two other essays. The starting point of Theo van Heijnsbergen's inquiry is the authorship of a sonnet. Rather than pursue solely the identification of its author, the essay outlines how the assumption of ready-made rhetorical identities was a well-known feature of the 'writing game' apparent at James VI's Scottish court. This exploration of impersonation is another clear indication of the contemporary understanding of the role of literature in the construction and representation of identity. It provides indirect comment on Knox's fulminations against male courtiers taking up the rhetorical position of women, as noted in Harker's essay. It also opens up perspectives on the circulation at court of poetry that, although often limited to a relatively small group of men and women, uses a wide range of discourses to create a startling intimacy and intensity of tone. Studying the generic and rhetorical practices at play in the writing game exposes the eloquent layering of this Scottish rhetorical theatre and its interactive discourses of art, power, and public as well as private identity.

Intimacy of circulation does not imply narrowness of reference. Sixteenth-century Scottish courts generally welcomed texts and ideas from abroad. The European dimension of early modern Scottish literature and culture is made particularly manifest in Jamie Reid-Baxter's presentation of *Philotus* as a Renaissance comedy. The play instances the ability of the audience and the culture that produced it to absorb a wide range of influences, project these onto a European literary paradigm, and distil thereof a version uniquely its own. Moreover, the essay's reconsideration of the play's date re-integrates the text and the culture that produced it within contemporary European developments.

The removal of the court in 1603 signalled the departure of one particular audience, even though not all who were part of James's court entourage moved to England, and most who did kept ties with Scotland. In general, the court's move to England allowed other cultural intermediaries to provide an equally – though often differently – educated body of Scottish authors and readers, made up especially of merchants, lawyers, and other professional men and their families. An important part of this body is identified in Marie-Claude Tucker's survey of Scottish students who attended the University of Bourges in the sixteenth and seventeenth centuries. The survey clearly shows that, despite the Union of the Crowns with England and despite having several established universities in their own country, Scots in the seventeenth century continued to study at Continental universities, whence they brought learning and ideas back to Scotland. The resultant mixture of native and Continental influences bequeathed ways of pursuing and preserving knowledge to an eighteenth century that was consequently, in intellectual and cultural terms, European rather than insular.

The fact that the last student in Tucker's survey to go to Bourges has a Highland name neatly illustrates the point that an important feature of early modern cultural permeability in Scotland was the increasing engagement of Gaelic culture not just with Lowland but also with Continental writing and learning, a notion that underlies William Gillies's re-assessment of the historiographical practice of the Gaelic poet-historian Niall MacMhuirich. The latter combined popular Celtic beliefs and the traditional methods of historians, poets, and genealogists with an awareness of 'modern' kinds of historiography that were based on the critical assessment of sources. MacMhuirich was thus able to intertwine various traditions of historiography to create a 'usable past' for that audience, presenting historiography as a pragmatic and dynamic activity that at times overlaps with poetry, and in which multiple truths can co-exist. This open-ended, synthetic manner of composition suited the developing cultural practices and reading strategies of his audience very well.

David Parkinson's essay on *The Cherrie and the Slae* and the legacy bequeathed more generally by sixteenth-century Scottish literature to subsequent generations provides a fitting conclusion to the present collection in more than just chronological terms. Like Gillies's essay, it instances how traditional patterns of intertwining social, political, and cultural realities into forms of synthetic narrative were continued well into the eighteenth century, which questions current periodization and the distinctions between 'medieval' and 'Renaissance', at least in a Scottish context. We should therefore – adapting a term used by Parkinson – attempt to become 'strong readers' of the texts involved. That is, we should formulate appropriately contextualized questions by interpreting the way in which these texts within their own poetics teach their readers how to read and how to harmonize a variety of textual ideologies and meanings. This metafictional element foregrounds 'that conceivably educable, redeemable being, the Scottish reader', the latter a proposal from civic humanism in tandem with evaluations of late medieval, especially Chaucerian experiments with relations between author, narrator, and persona. Several of the essays unearth other Scots texts that similarly teach their readers to seek authority within themselves. This turns the texts involved into very writerly ones, and again counters attempts to locate the beginnings of a modern Scottish literary sensibility exclusively outside the pre-1707 period.

A poetics that takes the educability of the reader as its central concern requires an audience-based criticism, which is bound to produce different conclusions from an author-based one. Thus, William Gillies profiles a distinct Gaelic readership in order to be able to assess more accurately a text written *for* that audience. Like Janet Hadley Williams, Morna Fleming clearly distinguishes a Scottish and an English audience, which in 1603 nevertheless had to overlap and interact. Marie Harker suggests how political circumstances greatly affected the reception of Knox's *The First Blast* and that, therefore, attention should be paid to the ability of the *Blast*'s different audiences to decode the text's rhetoric and to infer its application to themselves, since the text is surely implying a course of action as well as a statement of belief. Theo van Heijnsbergen suggests how an inner and an outer circle of the court coterie formed two distinct audiences, while Marie-Claude Tucker sheds light on a culturally informed, academically and especially legally trained Scottish readership with a European background.

Another common theme that emerges in the essays, related to that of audiences, is that of circulation, in several different guises. It presumes the cultural permeability mentioned above and can be instanced through book-ownership or even book dedications. Moreover, by shifting critical emphasis from author to audience and culture, it pushes back the 'author-hopping' that has been forcefully diagnosed as one of the ills of modern Scottish literary criticism of the earlier period.[12]

The papers in the present volume provide much evidence of circulation, and an attendant mixture of social and cultural energy. Leakage from one audience or text into another indicates there is indeed a dynamic cultural continuum, at least in places. Keely Fisher's paper, for instance, demonstrates that canonically 'marginal' genres such as flyting and eldritch verse enjoyed a wide literary circulation, both written and spoken, and connecting folk and popular to court. It is one of many examples that show how the Scottish court was strikingly permeable[13] in terms of the cultural discourses and genres it practised, and was correspondingly diverse in its social make-up. The manuscript of 'The Pretended Conference', one of the ventriloquized texts mentioned by van Heijnsbergen, is reported to have travelled via, amongst others, the Abbot of Kilwinning and the Earls of Argyll and Mar to Knox.[14] The essays by Harker, Hadley Williams, and Tucker indicate that if Scots travelled abroad, so did their texts. The plentiful presence of Scots in France in fact led to publications of Scottish authors there, in both Latin and the vernacular; Lyndsay, a notable example of this, was also translated into Danish, in 1591.[15] The complaint by Erskine, reported by Tucker, that he could not learn French in Bourges because there were too many Scots around is indeed credible.

The year 1549, usually seen as a landmark year for vernacular literature because of Du Bellay's *Deffense et Illustration de la langue françoyse*, sees the dedication of the French translation of Alciato's *Emblemata* to James Hamilton, the young heir of the second Earl of Arran. This was a crucial edition in the bibliography of Alciato as it was the first attempt to classify the emblems according to subject matter, blending teaching and entertainment with the deliberate purpose of enriching the vernacular with classical imagery and epigrammatic wit.[16] The years 1549–51 saw a series of deliberate redactions of Alciato's emblems in various European vernaculars, part of a concerted attempt to absorb and categorize the legacy of humanist, Latin material. The dedication of the first of these translations to young Arran is a sign of Scottish prominence and circulation in the European cultural mind, and *vice versa*.

Similar traces of a Scottish cultural presence can be found in England. Just as David Lyndsay's work was quickly subsumed into English Protestant writing, so was George Buchanan's. His *De iure regni apud Scotos* was not only copied when it was still in manuscript by Edward Bulkeley, an English clergyman connected to the Sidney circle, but was circulating with great speed in Protestant circles in England soon after its publication in Edinburgh in 1579. Buchanan had firm links with these circles, and an English edition was immediately planned, its political theories finding its way into Sidney's own *Arcadia*.[17]

Likewise, poems by William Dunbar and Alexander Scott were recently located in an English manuscript.[18] Scott was no stranger to English poetry; his 'Lo quhat it is to lufe' is clearly inspired by, or even inspired, Thomas Wyatt's 'Lo what it is to love'. Scott's verse is almost uniquely preserved in the Bannatyne Manuscript, in which John Bellenden's poetry also features prominently. It is therefore intriguing to see the opening line of another Scott poem together with an extract from a poem by Bellenden (both texts included in the Bannatyne Manuscript) appear side by side in a Lydgate manuscript owned by Duncan Campbell, seventh laird of Glenorchy, who owned copies of several other important texts. It shows that this Scots material – written into an English manuscript of an English poet, moreover – also circulated in Gaelic-speaking regions.[19] This supports the connections between Gaelic and Scots literature noted by Gillies, and suggests that contact between Scots and Gaelic lyrical poetry – as in the famous Book of the Dean of Lismore, compiled in an area that was under the jurisdiction of the Campbells of Glenorchy and containing verse written by their relatives – was continued in the later sixteenth century as well.[20] Following the circulation of such texts lays bare a conjunction of humanist thinking, intercultural literary anthologizing, and court-related circles as a focus of cultural energy.

With regard to book-ownership as evidence for the circulation of texts, even if we limit ourselves to the inventories of the royal libraries of Mary and James VI, the number of books being 'borrowit' or given away indicates that book circulation was common.[21] This also emerges from memos of books being lent and returned, again a practice especially noted among jurists, clerics, and merchants.[22] Furthermore, in the information on early book-owners gathered by Durkan and Ross, the frequent addition of the tag 'et amicorum' to ownership inscriptions in books proves there was a considerable degree of pre-

Reformation book circulation. A case in kind is John Steinston, precentor of Glasgow Cathedral, rector of Glasgow University, Senator of the College of Justice, and apostolic protonotary. In the latter function he appears regularly in person at the Vatican,[23] and on these travels he must have picked up some of the books he owned. At least nineteen of these have survived. They are mainly from Paris, with several from Lyons, Venice, Cologne, and Antwerp, and one from Basle, and range from Livy, Cicero, and Quintilian to Rabanus Maurus, Ptolemy, Suetonius, and (defences of) Melanchthon.[24] Most significantly, Steinston records twelve of these books as belonging to 'J[ohannis] Steinston et amicorum', the 'et amicorum' in evidence over an extensive period, from 1529 to 1560. Steinston was a conscious as well as conscientious book-circulator; in one of his books he wrote:

> So oft my bukis beris my name
> Becauss oft sundry fra me tane
> Be fraud or stoulth, god thaim haf the sayme
> That haldis my bukis and seis my name. J. Steinston.[25]

One can resurrect a coterie of readers by tracing names of other owners or borrowers written into the books Steinston owned, which reveals links to the world of letters, such as to Robert Danielstoun, a close intimate of the Bannatyne family. The books Danielstoun owned indicate his wide-ranging reading interests: classical and humanist literature (Erasmus's edition of Seneca's *Opera*); science (Ptolemy); legal and political texts (*Acts of Parliament*) and religion (St Augustine's *Enarrationes in psalmos*). In the latter, Danielstoun's own inscription of ownership is also followed by the phrase 'et amicorum'.[26]

Steinston died *c.* 1564, but such habits of book circulation did not die with the Reformation, nor did the court, or rather, the royal household, cease to provide a platform for such practices. Taking into account the extent of material destruction during and since the Reformation,[27] for every known reader and book owner we may surmise the existence of several more, and thus a significant readership of some sophistication and knowledge both of homegrown material and that imported. Such experience in reading would make Scots an appreciative audience for texts which deliberately bridge national divisions, such as *The Countesse of Marres Arcadia, or Sanctuarie, Containing Morning and Evening Meditations ... by M. Ia. Caldwell, Sometimes Preacher of Gods Word, at Fawkirke* (Edinburgh, 1625).[28] The intertextuality of the title shows an awareness of current literary and cultural discourses on both sides of the border, and of their crucially different intentions regarding literary discourse and its distribution of sacred and profane. Caldwell's work patrols the boundaries of sacred discourse, seeking to make it impermeable to the profane, a characteristic defensiveness of much contemporary writing that robbed poetry of its adaptability to cultural change and of a wider expressiveness. At the same time, reading the only extant household book (1638) of the Countess of Mar, one cannot but be struck by the number and range of books she purchased or had bound within that one year: from bibles and a preaching book *via* political tracts, a 'David Lyndesay', and 'the buik of the Martyres of England's lives' (presumably Foxe's, a book closely linked to Lyndsay's work in the essay by Hadley Williams), to Juvenal and a Greek grammar.[29] She also owned a copy of Alexander Hume's *Hymnes or Sacred Songs*.[30]

'The Pretended Conference', mentioned earlier, finally came into Knox's possession through a female agent, Alison Sandelandis, herself a book owner and part of a landed literary coterie (through her husband, Cockburn of Ormiston), while admission of its authorship was confessed to a very private female audience.[31] Knox was a very close friend of Anne Lock; one of the sonnets from the sequence based on psalm 51 attributed to her was already circulating in Scotland soon after its publication in London in 1560, and was in the mid-sixties set to music in four parts by Andro Kemp, Master of the St Andrews song school, copied by Thomas Wode in the Wode part books 'at the desyre of maister gudman'.[32] Goodman, former professor of theology at Oxford, was in Scotland from September 1559 to September 1565, during which time he was Moray's parish priest. He was also a personal friend of Anne Lock and an outspoken ally of Knox.[33] This conjunction of Moray, Goodman, Wode, Kemp, and the Lock sonnet shows that the coming together of Reformist zeal and cultural production could be a productive one.

Gathering such facts about the Countess of Mar or Alison Sandelandis also instances how Scottish women readers – quite apart from women writers – formed an important conduit for cultural energy from the sixteenth to the eighteenth century. An early indication of a growing female involvement with authoring texts is to be found in the striking use of authoritative female voices, as instanced in the texts discussed by Harker, Reid-Baxter, van Heijnsbergen, and – by implication, in evoking Elizabeth's voice – Fleming. Gender mobility is markedly patrolled in the texts involved, through such divergent means as castigation in Knox's *The First Blast*, subordination in marriage in *Philotus*, or impersonation as in the Christian Lyndsay sonnet. Even though these voices are ultimately returned to female categories construed by male discourse, they nevertheless clearly indicate that women are accessing voices of authority.

This issue over authority leads to another recurrent theme in several papers, that of sovereignty or kingship. It is a staple theme in many Scottish texts, both literary and non-literary. The fear that male, sovereign discourse could be somehow 'emasculated' by feminized language, as noted by Harker, is the complementary half of the perception of James (as noted by Fleming) as the embodiment of a return to natural, more powerful male kingship after Elizabeth, who had of necessity been limited, as a virgin queen, to raising support by eliciting Petrarchan language. To the European or British iconography of kingship (Fleming) and the image of the sun-king (Reid-Baxter and Parkinson) are added more particularly Scottish signature genres linked to courtly competition such as flyting (Fisher) or coterie images such as the 'Castalian' smithy (van Heijnsbergen). When sovereignty is at stake, the issue of reliable counsel is never far away: Hadley Williams in note 23 of her essay reminds us that Thomas Elyot had written *Pasquil the Playne* as an 'examination of good and defective royal counsellors' that takes up 'the issue of the moral and political dimensions of language styles and diction levels'. This may have influenced the presence of counsel and language in the shape of Pasquil as used by 'Rob Stene' (see Chapter 5).

A closer look at *Philotus* indicates how a better understanding of Scottish audiences, readers, and the circulation of literature between them allows us to revise interpretations of Scottish literary texts. Not only does Reid-Baxter's essay on *Philotus* remind us of the contemporary practice of joint authorship,[34] but it also tentatively links the names of George Buchanan, Robert Sempill, and the Earl of Moray (who is known to have attended one of Sempill's plays) to *Philotus*. Moray, the Protestant half-brother of Mary, Queen of Scots, has a reputation not normally associated with Renaissance comedy, but if one looks closer and discards prejudices about Reformers' cultural preferences, a different picture emerges. When he was Commendator of St Andrews, Moray not only gave Thomas Wode, vicar of St Andrews, the task to oversee the collection of a metrical psalter in 'plane and dulce' harmonizations (although warning that these should not contain any 'curiosity of musike' which offended Reformed sensibility),[35] he also had an extensive library that included a copy of Plautus's *Comœdiæ*,[36] identified by Reid-Baxter as a generic 'mother-text' of *Philotus*. Robert Reid, bishop of Orkney, also owned a copy, and Plautus's comedies were part of Mary's Erasmian schooling in France.[37] Such knowledge of textual circulation may tell us more about the primary text and the culture in which it circulated than more directly biographical facts, cultural teleology, or purely literary text-analysis. In this particular case, it increases the likelihood of somebody like Moray as a possible audience to the performance of *Philotus*.

Renaissance comedies will have been seen by travelling Scots on the Continent, creating a relatively small but knowledgeable audience back in Scotland that included many who had spent formative periods of their lives in European cities. An appropriate example, considering the constellation of essays in the present book, is William Drummond. One of the key sources for

Philotus is prose novella II.36 by Matteo Bandello, Duke of Tuscany (1554, translated by Belleforest in *Histoires Tragiques*, 1571), which is based on *Gl'Ingannati*.[38] When Drummond was in Bourges in 1607 (four years after *Philotus* was printed) to study civil law, he witnessed a performance there of another novella by Bandello, making extensive notes about the performance.[39] Previous Scottish visitors to the Continent had no doubt been subject to similar cultural exposure. Mary, Queen of Scots had Bandello (in French translation, 1559) and several Italian comedies and tragedies in her library, from which Moray 'borrowed' extensively.[40]

The most important outcome of all this is that what seemed an unthinkable proposition a generation ago (*Philotus* performed in the later 1560s with the involvement of Buchanan or Sempill and with the Regent Moray as a likely audience) now appears quite plausible – not through an analysis of the text *per se* or any insertion of authorial intention but through collating evidence about audience, textual circulation, and Reformist poetics. Such revision involves cross-disciplinary work, and research away from the canonical texts and methods of inquiry. The essays in the present volume undertake precisely such work, and point the way forward. In the case of *Philotus*, the relation between Bandello's stories and *Philotus* (already signalled as a problematic one by Reid-Baxter) would be the next step forward.

The growing disaffection of the kirk with profane literature combined with the absence of a sustained involvement of the aristocracy with literature on a national level, particularly after 1603, meant that institutions of education and jurisprudence increasingly formed the secular cultural nexus. It is here that morality, language, education, and history came together, shaping the way in which contemporaries viewed themselves as well as others and, accordingly, represented experience, in areas where the sacred and profane were allowed to interact. The intensity of seventeenth-century religious debate may have forced this cultural discourse into Stoic withdrawal at times, but the last three papers in particular illustrate how the continuation of pre-Reformation patterns of education and reading prepared the way (and provided the institutions and literary formats) for later generations. The genres used for that include the dream vision, allegory, flyting, sermon, (family) history, and the legal tract. Scottish examples of the latter kinds are infrequently found on reading lists in modern literature departments. If we opened up the canon to include these kinds, traditionally seen as belonging to the sphere of letters but not quite so readily to that of literature, we would be able to see how seventeenth-century Scottish culture was dominated not by the literary but by the scholarly writer, versed in the practicalities and controversies of philosophical, theological, forensic, and historical writing. These make up the world of letters that provides the fertile soil out of which grew many of the achievements of eighteenth-century Scottish literature. The latter have often been too self-evidently and exclusively attributed to the effects of Scotland's 'liberation from independence' in 1707. The above-mentioned 'author-hopping' is in this respect at times in danger of being complemented by 'myth-hopping'. The editors of a textbook such as *Scotland in the Age of Improvement*, for example, speak of the later eighteenth century as a period in which Scotland, 'almost overnight, was snatched from the relative cultural isolation in which she had passed the seventeenth century and placed in the centre of the thinking world'.[41] The word 'relative' in this quote fails to alleviate the suspicion that this statement is not based on an investigation of that 'seventeenth century' in its own right but on a pre-occupation with post-Union cultural paradigms. Moreover, as the Pinkie House ceiling illustrates, the very notion of a 'centre', let alone Scotland's relation to it, needs to be urgently revised.

The study of Scotland's culture and of its seventeenth century in particular along these new lines of inquiry has much to gain from recent critical debates that have emphasized we cannot equate 'literature' or even 'culture' with 'creative writing' alone, or indeed – mindful of oral texts – with 'writing'.[42] One of the most promising areas in this respect is that of legal discourse. Marie-Claude Tucker's essay anticipates the last two contributions in the collection by breaking down the notion that 1603 marks the end of literary achievement in Scotland. She samples a learned audience of readers and writers in Scotland that connects the sixteenth to the eighteenth century. It also links the Highlands to the breeding ground of legal humanism that played such a pivotal role in making civil law 'the principle vehicle of social and cultural thought', i.e. France in general and Bourges in particular, with its pivotal figures of Guillaume Budé and Andrea Alciato.[43] Especially Alciato, who taught in Bourges from 1529 to 1532, is credited with making the law faculty there 'the most exciting institution for legal study not only in France but in all Europe', its influence spreading in many directions (Calvin studied law under Alciato in Bourges in 1530–31).[44] Law was seen as ' "the knowledge of things divine and human", that is, as *sapientia*, as wisdom itself', and jurisconsults (as opposed to 'mere' lawyers) functioned as philosophers.[45]

Because law and literature both scrutinize the exact meaning of words, focusing on *de verborum significatione*, civil law came to share the same philological concerns as humanist literature.[46] It was Lorenzo Valla who in the fifteenth century decisively influenced the debate about the historicity of law in favour of an emphasis on the *comparative* definition of words and, thus, on the relative nature of meaning. This notion lay at the heart of sixteenth-century legal humanism in France, where jurists studied Roman law in its historical context rather than from within a timeless, universal perspective, which made the study of civil law a context-sensitive and analytical rather than universal and synthetic activity. This altered contemporary perspectives on permanence and change, and (thus) on 'the individual' as well as on the practice of historiography, and profoundly affected notions about the nature of knowledge, the self, and community as well as of authorial intention and the problematic relationship between things, thoughts, and words. This could not fail to filter through to literature, also in Scotland, where education and legal reform had been the two pillars of civic humanism in the late fifteenth and sixteenth centuries, both under strong French influence.[47] MacMhuirich's writing, as discussed by Gillies, shows this influnce as well. Civil law therefore played a significant role in developing an *ars hermeneutica* in early modern Scotland.

With the French legal tradition in this manner foregrounding civil law for 'its logical underpinnings and its philosophical superstructure', Scots studying civil law in France in the sixteenth and seventeenth centuries – like Seton[48] – received an education that stressed a comparative historical approach of law, text, and thought, emphasizing the value of an encyclopaedic knowledge of theology as well as the arts, music, history, and rhetoric.[49] This was strongly resisted in English legal education throughout the sixteenth and into the seventeenth century, where students from the Inns of Court – a breeding ground for literati – were taught in a more empirical tradition, learning to pattern their thoughts after arguably more personal insights. The latter provided extremely fertile soil for the powerfully individual and urbane lyrical wit of the English metaphysical poets. In contrast, the legal training of many Scots men of letters prioritized the illocutionary over the more directly cathartic function of words; consequently, in their writing, to move others took precedence over being moved oneself. A Scots poetics developed that was premised on an understanding of writing as self-scrutiny and self-regulation with a strongly pronounced social referentiality, rather than pushing texts into self-expression or public self-fashioning. This created readers who were expected, from within their own modernity, to approach texts morally and to think allegorically and metonymically rather than associatively and metaphorically.

Legal humanism thus helped create an audience of writers and a republic of letters in seventeenth-century Scotland that was well positioned to continue humanist – as distinct from 'Renaissance' – evaluations of writing and reading. The latter functioned as primarily moral activities within a Christian *Weltanschauung* and an aesthetics in which allegories and dream visions were still creatively viable rather than residual genres. Away from more aristocratic and directly self-referential modes of literature, and working from a profound knowledge of classical, especially Stoic literature, Scottish readers and authors developed secular modes of reading and writing that provided an alternative to both the all-consuming religious polemics at home as well as to the more metropolitan discourses of self that were developed in contemporary England. In the seventeenth century, the 'educable Scottish reader' thus becomes the alternative to the churchman, the (now largely absent) courtier, or the urban wit as the main conduit for secular writing, for a humanist education and the arts 'as the only possible route by which a person might acquire both moral self-control and a capacity for effective public action'.[50]

Lay jurists thus became the best-placed cultural intermediaries to explain an increasingly complicated society to itself, and to preserve its cultural past. They had the historical perspectives and long cultural lenses required to overcome the religious divides that progressively separated pre- from post-Reformation sensibilities during the seventeenth century.[51] In the context of Scottish seventeenth-century literary culture, adopting a cultural perspective that gravitates towards the scholarly rather than the creative writer allows a more accurate and coherent picture to emerge than the traditional one according to which only folk literature survived in the seventeenth century, and in which the achievement of a writer such as William Drummond is the exception that proves the rule. Drummond, the one Scottish poet occasionally allowed semi-canonical status in studies of seventeenth-century British poetry, may have written in neo-Stoic detachment, but that does not mean he wrote in a cultural vacuum, as is often assumed. A recontextualization of seventeenth-century letters along the above-mentioned lines situates not just Drummond's works more meaningfully but also other seventeenth-century texts as diverse as, for example, translations of Petrarch's *Trionfi*, the works of William Lithgow, or the sermons of Zachary Boyd.

The establishment in an age of civil unrest of the Advocates' Library (1689), out of which grew the National Library of Scotland, is an example of the cultural muscle of the legal establishment and reveals how its interest in rhetoric and textual criticism carried with it quite specifically literary interests. Originally meant to house legal and related material only,[52] the Advocates' Library very soon broadened out in many directions, suggesting not only an academic interest in literary productions but perhaps also a patriotic one, related to the fact that law, like literature, necessarily arises from a broad culture and shared values. This happened at a critical time. Libraries such as those of the Duke of Lauderdale, with an extensive range of manuscripts that included the Maitland Quarto and Folio MSS, were beginning to break up.[53] Sir George Mackenzie of Rosehaugh, the main driving force behind the Library's foundation and himself a poet, novelist, and essayist, embodies the coming together of legal training and antiquarian interest that preserved the texts we have today, quite apart from private book-collectors such as Robert Gordon of Gordonstoun ('who suffered from uncontrollable urges as a book-collector') and Henry Erskine, both civil law students at Bourges in the early seventeenth century, or David Drummond, Lord Madderty, founder of Innerpeffray Library (1680).[54]

The educable reader, the continued popularity of texts such as *The Cherrie and the Slae* or the works of David Lyndsay as well as the moral-philosophical nature of much secular seventeenth-century writing in Scotland are based on such continuities. They passed on traditions of moral thought that recent scholarship, noting how 'literati concentrated upon the capacity of individuals to … develop as moral beings', has found also underlie the 'civic humanism, communal cohesion and polite Stoicism in eighteenth-century Scottish culture'.[55] We should therefore stop calling the second half of the eighteenth century 'the age of improvement', a period label that implies the preceding era was characterized by a lack of achievement. It would be more accurate to identify that period with, for example, the 'pursuit of virtue', continuing investigations already under way in pre-Reformation works such as Gavin Douglas's *Palice of Honour* and a range of other textual, often allegorical pursuits of virtue from the age of the makars. The latter were frequently revisited in the later sixteenth, seventeenth, and eighteenth centuries by a post-Reformation ethics and poetics. Early modern Scots writing thus continued to reflect well beyond 1707 upon its own cultural experiences both past and present, exploring the conflicts between an outer, public world and an inner, private one within a primarily ethical poetics in which readers and writers indeed continued to seek moral authority within themselves.

This introduction has opened a number of avenues of inquiry that follow from distilling common themes from the individual papers in the collection: the nature of reading, linked to key issues such as circulation, cultural permeability, and the role of the audience; Reformist aesthetics; the importance of legal discourse; the prominence of female voices – all conceptual ideas that might change our perception of Scottish literature, letters and the canonical in early modern Scotland. The reliance on less frequently studied texts and writers (and readers) such as 'The Pretended Conference', Alciato, or Alexander Seton shows how these, in spite of their canonically less 'central' position, reveal patterns of culture in many different ways, representing the relationship between texts and culture in contemporary Scotland in a structural rather than incidental manner.

If we follow these lines of inquiry, what gradually emerges is an endo-normative – i.e. determined by its own parameters[56] – cultural language, and an attendant critical one, that has visual parallels as well. It reminds us of the fact that the preface to the edition of Alciato's emblems which was dedicated to young James Hamilton stresses 'la doulceur delectable des vers … la pincture non vaine des images … il aura en ce petit livre … tout ce qu'il pourra, et vouldra inscripre, ou pindre aux murailles de la maison'.[57] Seton's ceiling at Pinkie House is indeed one of many instances of such emblematic painting found in Scottish houses from the mid-sixteenth to the mid-seventeenth century. Its 'applied emblematics' is a verbal as well as visual instance of a Scottish 'Renaissance' inflection of the time-honoured imperative to seek the delectable kernel of truth within artistic representation. It also suggests an audience that in often consciously metafictional ways sought authority within, based on a humanist understanding of the relationship between reader, writer, and society.[58] It is time that we take account of, rather than just note, such conjunctions of cultural phenomena across time and disciplines in this period in Scottish history, and indeed become 'strong readers' of these. This will generate new perspectives on its literature that are unique to itself and therefore both appropriate and potentially productive. The essays in the present volume, individually as well as collectively, promise to be important stepping-stones towards such a better understanding of the world of letters in early modern Scotland.

Notes

1. Priscilla Bawcutt, in a paper also presented at the St Andrews conference, similarly suggested the use of the more comprehensive term 'men of letters' to refer more accurately to 'authors' in Scotland during the reign of James VI: 'James VI's Castalian Band: A Modern Myth', *SHR* 80 (2001), 251–9 (p. 258).
2. Sally Mapstone, 'Introduction', in *A Palace in the Wild. Essays on Vernacular Culture and Humanism in Late-Medieval and Renaissance Scotland*, ed. by L. A. J. R. Houwen, A. A. MacDonald, and S. L. Mapstone (Leuven, 2000), pp. vii–xviii (p. xviii).
3. On the Pinkie House ceiling, see Michael Bath, 'Alexander Seton's Painted Gallery', in *Albion's Classicism: The Visual Arts in Britain, 1550–1650* (New Haven, CT, and London, 1995), pp. 79–108. See also his article 'Applied Emblematics in Scotland: Painted Ceilings, 1550–1650', *Emblematica* 7 (1993), 259–305, and his – at the time of writing still forthcoming – book, *Renaissance Decorative Painting in Scotland* (Edinburgh, 2002), chapter 4. We are extremely grateful to Dr Bath for introducing us to the Pinkie cupola and helping us with related references.
4. The decentring effect can perhaps best be seen, albeit in small black and white pictures, in the Royal Commission on Ancient and Historical Monuments and Constructions of Scotland's *Tenth Report with Inventory of Monuments and Constructions in the Counties of Midlothian and West Lothian* (Edinburgh, 1929), facing p. 84.
5. George Seton, *Memoir of Alexander Seton, Earl of Dunfermline* (Edinburgh and London, 1882), pp. 184–6. John Napier, *Rabdologiae, seu numerationis per virgulas libri duo* (Edinburgh, 1617); the dedication to Seton is on sig. 2ʳ–4ʳ.
6. George Seton, *Memoir of Alexander Seton*, p. 39.
7. De Vries's 'pattern book' for architecture is most easily accessed in a facsimile reprint, *Perspective* (New York and London, 1968), with an introduction by Adolf K. Placzek; the relevant drawing is plate 20 in the second part.
8. David Allan, *Philosophy and Politics in Later Stuart Scotland: Neo-Stoicism, Culture and Ideology in an Age of Crisis 1540–1690* (East Linton, 2000), p. 115.

[9] Royal Commission, *Tenth Report*, p. 85.

[10] On the reception of Scottish texts in England, see Priscilla Bawcutt, 'Crossing the Border: Scottish Poetry and English Readers in the Sixteenth Century', in *The Rose and the Thistle. Essays on the Culture of Late Medieval and Renaissance Scotland*, ed. by Sally Mapstone and Juliette Wood (East Linton, 1998), pp. 59–76.

[11] On this concept, see Roger A. Mason, 'Usable Pasts: History and Identity in Reformation Scotland', *SHR* 76 (1997), 54–68, reprinted in Roger A. Mason, *Kingship and the Commonweal: Political Thought in Renaissance and Reformation Scotland* (East Linton, 1998), pp. 165–86.

[12] Roger A. Mason, *SHR* 69 (1990), 101–2, a review of *The History of Scottish Literature. Volume. I: Origins to 1660*, ed. by R. D. S. Jack (Aberdeen, 1988).

[13] It would be misleading to use the word 'democratic' here, as Fisher's essay demonstrates; using different social discourses is not necessarily a 'democratic' activity.

[14] David Calderwood, *The History of the Kirk of Scotland*, ed. by Thomas Thomson, 8 vols (Edinburgh 1842–49), II (1843), pp. 515–25 (p. 525).

[15] *The Works of Sir David Lindsay*, ed. by Douglas Hamer, 4 vols (Edinburgh and London, 1931–36), IV (1936), pp. 60–2. In 1558, *Ane Dialog, The Dreme, The Tragedie of the Cardinall*, and *The Testament of the Papyngo* were all printed in Paris: *Works*, ed. Hamer, IV, 26–32.

[16] *Emblemes d'Alciat de nouueau translatez en francois vers pour vers iouxte les Latins* (Lyons, 1549). Aneau, the translator, says this dedication to young Hamilton was on the advice of yet another travelling Scots scholar, Florence Wil - ᵇetter known as Volusenus, a graduate of Aberdeen who spent most of his time in Paris and Lyons. On Volusenus, see Dominic Baker-Smith, 'Florens Wilson: A Distant Prospect', in *Stewart Style 1513–1542: Essays on the Court of James V*, ed. by Janet Hadley Williams (East Linton, 1996), pp. 1–14.

[17] James E. Phillips, 'George Buchanan and the Sidney Circle', *Huntington Library Quarterly* 12 (1948–49), 23–55 (pp. 41–5). One of the conduits between Buchanan and this circle was Christopher Goodman, mentioned below in connection to the circulation of Anne Lock's verse in Scotland.

[18] Priscilla Bawcutt, 'New Texts of William Dunbar, Alexander Scott and Other Scottish Poets', *Scottish Studies Review* 1 (2000), 9–25.

[19] Priscilla Bawcutt, 'The Boston Public Library Manuscript of John Lydgate's *Siege of Thebes*: Its Scottish Owners and Inscriptions', *Medium Ævum* 70 (2001), 80–94 (pp. 86, 88, 84).

[20] Donald E. Meek, 'The Scots-Gaelic Scribes of Late Medieval Perthshire: An Overview of the Orthography and Contents of the Book of the Dean of Lismore', in *Stewart Style*, ed. Hadley Williams, pp. 254–72 (p. 271).

[21] Julian Sharman, *The Library of Mary, Queen of Scots* (1889); G. F. Warner, 'The Library of James VI, 1573–1583', *Miscellany Volume of the Scottish History Society, Volume I* (1893), pp. xi–lxxv and 586–95.

[22] For example, the notarial notebook of William Stewart, elder, NLS Advocates' MS 19312, fols 1 and 150–1; *The Compt Buik of David Wedderburne, Merchant of Dundee, 1587–1630*, SHS (Edinburgh, 1898), pp. xxii–xxxi, 2, 89, 105, 168–70. For the book-possession of clerics, see John Durkan and Anthony Ross, *Early Scottish Libraries* (Glasgow, 1961).

[23] Catalogues of the Vatican Archives deposited in the Department of Scottish History, Glasgow University.

[24] Durkan and Ross, *Libraries*, pp. 145–6, 184–5; John Durkan and Julian Russell, 'Additions to J. Durkan and A. Ross, *Early Scottish Libraries*, at the National Library of Scotland', *The Bibliotheck* 11 (1982–83), 29–37 (p. 36).

[25] Durkan and Ross, *Libraries*, p. 145.

[26] Theo van Heijnsbergen, 'The Interaction between Literature and History in Queen

Mary's Edinburgh: The Bannatyne Manuscript and Its Prosopographical Context', in *The Renaissance in Scotland*, ed. by A. A. MacDonald *et al.* (Leiden, 1994), pp. 183–225 (pp. 204–5); Durkan and Ross, *Libraries*, p. 88.

27   See especially David McRoberts, 'Material Destruction Caused by the Scottish Reformation', in *Essays on the Scottish Reformation 1513–1625*, ed. by David McRoberts (Glasgow, 1962), pp. 415–62.

28   *The Countess of Mar's Arcadia or Sanctuary Containing Morning and Evening Meditations for the Whole Week, by Mr James Caldwell, Sometime Preacher of God's Word at Falkirk*, ed. by James Young (Edinburgh, 1862), pp. 19–20. Patrick Simson dedicated all three parts of his *Short Compend of the Historie of the First Ten Persecvtions* (Edinburgh, 1613–16) to her, and two more treatises on nobility, virtue, and piety were dedicated to the Countess, who was clearly glorified as a champion of virtuous, Protestant femininity, overcoming her inauspicious French upbringing.

29   *Extracts from the Household Book of Lady Marie Stewart* (Edinburgh, [1815]), pp. 24, 30, 34, 38, 42–3, 47, 50. The Countess also showed an interest in science, spending '6d to bye a bladder for trying a mathematicall conclusione' (p. 54).

30   Priscilla Bawcutt, ' "My bright buke": Women and their Books in Medieval and Renaissance Scotland', in *Medieval Women: Texts and Contexts in Late Medieval Britain*, ed. by Jocelyn Wogan-Browne *et al.* (Turnhout, 2000), pp. 17–34 (p. 26).

31   Calderwood, *History of the Kirk of Scotland*, II, 525; 'An Account of a Pretended Conference', in *The Bannatyne Miscellany*, ed. by W. Scott, D. Laing, and T. Thomson, 3 vols (1827–55), I (1827), pp. 31–50 (pp. 35–6); Bawcutt, ' "My bright buke" ', p. 25; Sally Mapstone, *'The Thre Prestis of Peblis* in the Sixteenth Century', in *A Day Estivall. Essays on the Music, Poetry and History of Scotland and England*, ed. by A. Gardner-Medwin and J. Hadley Williams (Aberdeen, 1990), pp. 124–42 (pp. 124–5). Alison Sandelandis's son Alexander, tutored by Knox, was at Bourges when recalled to Scotland at the Reformation in 1560: Robert Cockburn and Harry A. Cockburn, *The Records of the Cockburn Family* (Edinburgh, 1913), p. 120

32   *The Collected Work of Anne Vaughan Lock*, ed. by Susan M. Felch (Tempe, AZ, 1999), pp. xv, xxiii–xxix. Lock's sonnet 1 ('Have mercy, God, for thy great mercies sake') is set to music in all three of Thomas Wode's part books (*c.* 1562–1592) that are preserved in Edinburgh University Library, MSS La.III.483.1–3 (beginning on pp. 132, 136, and 131, respectively) in a section of entries dated 1566–67 or later; Goodman left Scotland in the autumn of 1565, but may have sent the poem to Scotland after his departure. Wode's comparatively lengthy note at the end of Lock's poem in the tenor part book, explaining why her poem is included, suggests that this particular sonnet was of special significance to the Protestant congregation at St Andrews. The identification of this text as one of Anne Lock's sonnets was communicated by Jamie Reid-Baxter, who recorded it with the Edinburgh University Renaissance Singers, *Psalms for the Regents of Scotland (1567–1578)*, available from the Edinburgh University Music Department. On Goodman, see also note 17 above; on Wode and Goodman, see Jamie Reid Baxter, 'Thomas Wode, Christopher Goodman and the Curious Death of Scottish Music', *Scotlands* 4.2 (1997), 1–20.

33   On Goodman and Lock, see *Anne Lock*, ed. Felch, pp. xxxiv–xxxv, where some of the Protestant cross-border lines of communication are discussed.

34   Chapters 1 and 5 in the present collection also provide examples of multiple authorship. An example of a jointly produced play in Scotland is the 1558 'Triumphe and Play at the Marriage of the Quenis Grace' in 1558, for which see Sarah Carpenter, 'Walter Binning: Decorative and Theatrical Painter (fl. 1540–1594)', *Medieval English Theatre* 10 (1988), 17–25 (p. 20). In 1538, Adam

Otterburn, James Foulis (both Scottish neo-Latin poets), and David Lyndsay collaborated in writing a welcome in French for Mary of Guise: *Extracts from the Burgh Records of Edinburgh*, ed. by J. D. Marwick, 4 vols (Edinburgh, 1869–82), II (1871), p. 91.

[35] Reid Baxter, 'Wode, Goodman', p. 3.

[36] Robert Donaldson, 'Three More Regent Moray Books', *The Bibliotheck* 4 (1963–66), 39–40; *Catalogue of the Books in the Library at Kinfauns Castle*, ed. by George P. Johnston (Edinburgh, 1928), p. 89. Moray's library has been charted in Durkan and Ross, *Libraries*, and several articles by D. W. Doughty: 'Notes on the Provenance of Books Belonging to Lord James Stewart, Afterwards the Regent Moray, Other Than Those in the University Library, St Andrews', *The Bibliotheck* 3 (1961), 75–88; 'The Library of James Stewart, Earl of Moray, 1531–1570', *IR* 21 (1970), 17–29; 'Notes on the Regent Moray's Books and Their Bindings', *The Bibliotheck* 6 (1971–73), 65–75.

[37] Durkan and Russell, 'Additions', p. 31; John Durkan, 'The Library of Mary, Queen of Scots', in *Mary Stewart. Queen in Three Kingdoms*, ed. by Michael Lynch (Oxford, 1988), pp. 71–104 (p. 75).

[38] *Philotus*, ed. by A. J. Mill, in *Miscellany Volume*, STS (Edinburgh and London, 1933), pp. 81–158 (pp. 92–3).

[39] Robert H. MacDonald, 'Drummond of Hawthornden: The Season at Bourges, 1607', *Comparative Drama* 4 (1970), 89–109 (pp. 99–100). MacDonald reports that what Drummond saw in Bourges *was* in fact a performance of *novella* II.36, but that must refer to a different edition of Bandello. In *Le quattro parti de la Novelle del Bandello*, 4 vols, ed. by Gustavo Balsamo-Crivelli (Turin, 1924), the story Drummond saw performed is *novella* II.44, while the one which has points of agreement with *Philotus* is indeed II.36.

[40] John Durkan, 'The Library of Mary', pp. 73, 80, 102. Drummond himself owned the first part of Bandello's *Novelle*, as well as Ariosto's *I Suppositi*, another key source text of *Philotus*: Robert H. MacDonald, *The Library of Drummond of Hawthornden* (Edinburgh, 1971), p. 216. Adam Bothwell, bishop of Orkney (d.1593), had three volumes of Bandello's *novelle* in Italian, as well as a copy of Alciato's *Emblemata*: see *The Warrender Papers*, ed. by Annie I. Cameron, 2 vols, SHS (1931–32), I (1932), pp. 396–413 (pp. 404–9); and Duncan Shaw, 'Adam Bothwell: A Conserver of the Renaissance in Scotland', in *The Renaissance and Reformation in Scotland*, ed. by Ian B. Cowan and Duncan Shaw (Edinburgh, 1983), pp. 141–69 (p. 160). NLS Advocates' MS SU 8 (an interleaved copy of Durkan and Ross, *Libraries*) notes that the first volume of Bandello's *novelle* owned by William Drummond was in fact originally Bothwell's copy.

[41] *Scotland in the Age of Improvement. Essays in Scottish History in the Eighteenth Century*, ed. by N. T. Phillipson and Rosalind Mitchison (Edinburgh, 1970), p. 1.

[42] Thomas I. Rae, 'The Origins of the Advocates' Library', in *For the Encouragement of Learning*, ed. by Patrick Cadell and Ann Matheson (Edinburgh, 1989), pp. 1–22 (pp. 9, 15).

[43] Donald R. Kelley, *History, Law and the Human Sciences. Medieval and Renaissance Perspectives* (London, 1984), p. ix. See also Allan, *Philosophy and Politics*, p. 15; and John W. Cairns, T. David Fergus, and Hector L. MacQueen, 'Legal Humanism and the History of Scots Law: John Skene and Thomas Craig', in *Humanism in Renaissance Scotland*, ed. by John MacQueen (Edinburgh, 1990), pp. 48–74 (pp. 48–9).

[44] O. F. Robinson, T. D. Fergus, and W. M. Gordon, *European Legal History* (London, 1994), p. 172.

[45] Donald R. Kelley, 'Vera Philosophia: The Philosophical Significance of Renaissance

Jurisprudence', *The Journal of the History of Philosophy* 14 (1976), 267–79 (pp. 267–8), reprinted in ibid., *History, Law and the Human Sciences*.

46 Richard J. Schoeck, 'Humanism and Jurisprudence', in *Renaissance Humanism. Foundations, Forms, and Legacy*, ed. by Albert Rabil Jr. (Philadelphia, PA, 1988), pp. 310–26; Kelley, *History, Law and the Human Sciences, passim.*

47 Roger A. Mason, 'Laicisation and the Law. The Reception of Humanism in Early Renaissance Scotland', in *A Palace in the Wild*, ed. Houwen *et al.*, pp. 1–25; van Heijnsbergen, 'The Interaction', pp. 186, 214.

48 *DNB*, vol. 51, p. 263; George Seton, *Memoir of Alexander Seton*, p. 19.

49 Donald R. Kelley, 'History, English Law and the Renaissance', *Past and Present* 65 (1974), 24–51 (pp. 39, 42, 45). In seventeenth-century Scotland, the academic training of Advocates involved 'at least two years' study of the civil law at a Continental university, generally either in France or the Low Countries' (Rae, 'The Origins', p. 17), the latter another important influence on seventeenth-century Scottish culture and philosophy.

50 David Allan, 'Prudence and Patronage: The Politics of Culture in Seventeenth-Century Scotland', *History of European Ideas* 18 (1994), pp. 467–80 (p. 469).

51 As Schoeck, 'Humanism and Jurisprudence', says, 'the libraries of lawyers of the *mos gallicus* would have markedly greater representation of humanistic texts than those of the *mos italicus*' (p. 316).

52 Rae, 'The Origins', pp. 18–19.

53 'Catalogus librorum manuscriptorum, e bibliotheca D. Joannis ducis de Lauderdale M.DC.XCII.', in *Bannatyne Miscellany*, ed. Scott *et al.*, II (1836), 149–58. The library of John, Duke of Lauderdale, was sold in three tranches in 1690–92.

54 David Allan, ' "Ane Ornament to Yow and Your Famelie": Sir Robert Gordon of Gordonstoun and the *Genealogical History of the Earldom of Sutherland*', *SHR* 80 (2001), 24–44 (pp. 31, 27, 26).

55 John Dwyer, *Virtuous Discourse: Sensibility and Community in Late Eighteenth-Century Scotland* (Edinburgh, 1987), pp. 1, 6. For examples of how past criticism stereotyped the 'dark age' of the seventeenth century, see Frank T. Gatter, 'On the Literary Value of Some Scottish Presbyterian Writings in the Context of the Scottish Enlightenment', in *Scottish Language and Literature, Medieval and Renaissance*, ed. by Dietrich Strauss and Horst W. Drescher (Frankfurt am Main, 1986), pp. 175–92 (pp. 175–6); William Ferguson, *The Identity of the Scottish Nation. An Historic Quest* (Edinburgh, 1998), p. 173.

56 A. A. MacDonald, 'Early Modern Scottish Literature and the Parameters of Culture', in *The Rose and the Thistle*, ed. Mapstone and Wood, pp. 77–100, provides an inquiry into such parameters that parallels the present one.

57 'The delectable sweetness of the verses … the purposeful painting of images … there will be in this little book … all that one can, and would want to, write down, or paint on the walls of one's house': from the preface to the French edition of Alciato's book of emblems, 1549, as quoted in Alison Saunders, *The Sixteenth-Century French Emblem Book. A Decorative and Useful Genre* (Geneva, 1988), p. 107, n. 40.

58 The term 'applied emblematics' is borrowed from Daniel S. Russell, *Emblematic Structures in Renaissance French Culture* (Toronto, 1995), p. 191. The early modern period is seen as an *aetas emblematica*, an era that used emblems as a key epistemological means to capture, represent, and preserve human knowledge. Reading from such an 'emblematic perspective' (236) must have affected the practice of writing too, in Scotland as elsewhere. In fact, the opening stanzas of Henryson's prologue to his *Moral Fabillis* eloquently anticipate such an *aetas emblematica*.

1

The Contemporary Humour in William Stewart's *The Flytting betuix þe Sowtar and the Tailȝour*[1]

K EELY F ISHER

George Bannatyne's 'Ballat Buik' of *c.* 1565–68[2] contains the majority of extant comic flytings in Older Scots, all within the 'mirry ballettis' section of the manuscript: fols 139[v]–41[r], the unique copy of William Stewart's *The Flytting betuix þe Sowtar and the Tailȝour;* fols 141[v]–2[v], the unique copy of Robert Henryson's *Sum practysis of medecyne;*[3] fols 147[r]–54[r], *The Flyting of Dumbar and Kennedie;*[4] and two unique flytings which Bannatyne inserted post-1568: fol. 163[r], Alexander Montgomerie's *Ane anser to ane Helandmanis Invectiue;* and fol. 163[r–v], the anonymous *Ane anser to ane Inglis railar praysing his awin genalogy.* Other literary flytings are *The Answer quhilk Schir Dauid Lindesay maid to the Kingis Flyting,* written some time before 1537 but not in print until 1568;[5] and the famous *Flyting betwixt Montgomerie and Polwart* of *c.* 1584.[6] Of all the comic genres to be found in Older Scots verse, poetic flytings have received the greatest critical attention to date.[7]

The Dictionary of the Older Scottish Tongue lists the following meanings under the verb *flyte*: 'wrangle violently'; 'employ abusive language towards others'; 'scold'; 'quarrel'; 'wrangle, or contend in abuse'.[8] Priscilla Bawcutt remarks that, by the sixteenth century, a *flyter* in Scots is roughly synonymous with a *scold* in English.[9] Flyting thus bears the sense of a public performance, which ups the inherent impact of the slander and scandal of this particular form of verbal abuse. Further, Bawcutt has outlined what constitutes the literary genre known as flyting in Older Scots, and distinguished two types. The first type is satirical, not comical:

> Works of the first kind had a serious polemical purpose – moral, polit-
> ical, theological – and were often anonymous, pseudonymous, or
> associated with the mysterious figure of Robert Sempill. Their authors
> wished to damage their opponents; they wanted publicity for their
> cause, but often feared it for themselves.[10]

The second type of flytings is characterized by its essence of 'sportive warfare' – they are humorous, with a patterned repartee, which was a literary vogue in Scots at the beginning of the sixteenth century, perhaps due to the publication of *The Flyting of Dumbar and Kennedie* by Chepman and Myllar in 1508: 'These poets, far from shunning publicity, make sure that their names are repeatedly mentioned. Personal antagonisms are undoubtedly present, but they are ritualized and turned into a literary game, in which the competitors vie in verbal and metrical ingenuity'.[11] Bawcutt has noted that these poets ensure that their names are associated with their invectives – Dunbar, Kennedy, Stewart, Lyndsay, Montgomerie, Polwarth – yet these flytings are essentially fantastic, inventive in nature and, though undoubtedly provocative, playful rather than polemical in content. In fact, these flyting poets are united from the start: by the desire to show off their own verbal and metrical skills, and to take the art of insult to new extremities in their invective ripostes.

All of these literary flytings are stylized forms of abuse. It has already been shown that invectives in this tradition are far from erratic, tumbling tirades, but have in fact a discernible structure: 'this is a calculated spontaneity, a simulated disorder'.[12] Bawcutt has discerned specific features in the comic repartee of these flytings – the court as the flyting rink; calls for public punishments and acts of penance; attacks on literary ability;[13] claims of spurious and degenerate pedigree; and the deployment of humiliating 'biographical' anecdotes to amplify the shaming impact of one's flytings, as well as evoke a feeling of general revulsion against one's opponent. However, structural analysis of comic flytings in Scots has hitherto focused on the two most famous flytings of the extant corpus: Dunbar and Kennedy's, and Montgomerie and Polwarth's. In contrast, William Stewart's *Flytting betuix þe Sowtar and the Tailჳour* has been almost totally ignored.

Stewart's shorter poems, not to mention his verse translation of Boece's *Scotorum Historia* (begun on 18 April 1531, completed 29 September 1535), are an integral contribution to the sixteenth-century Scottish literary tradition; alongside the work of David Lyndsay, 'they form an essential link in the chain of literary tradition that continued into the reign of Mary, and beyond'.[14] Details of Stewart's life might remain obscure,[15] yet to sixteenth-century readers of Scottish poetry, William Stewart (*c.* 1476–1548) was an esteemed makar. In the 'Prologue' to John Rolland's *The Seuin Seages* (written 1560, though not printed until 1578), Rolland pays tribute to Stewart's reputation in the days of James V: 'To mak in Scottis, richt weill he knew that art' (25).[16] And in the 'Prologue' of Lyndsay's *Testament of the Papyngo* (completed December 1530), Stewart is singled out for his 'staitly style' and 'full ornate werkis', which he could compose – almost effortlessly, it would appear – on a daily basis (37–45).[17]

Eleven shorter poems by Stewart have survived (i.e. texts attributed to Stewart beyond his translation of Boece).[18] His *Flytting betuix þe Sowtar and the Tailȝour* has a tripartite structure with two distinct flyting voices.[19] It is at once clear that the two voices in Stewart's *Flyting* are adversarial because their abuse is articulated in different verse styles — the tailor's *aaabcccb* versus the sowtar's more impressive ballat royal *ababbcbc*. This distinction in verse forms between flyters is a technique of polarization which features in Dunbar and Kennedy's flyting, and was later employed in that of Montgomerie and Polwarth, too.

It has been noted that Stewart's *Flytting* belongs to the same comic genre as that in which Dunbar, Kennedy, *et al.* wrote. 'There are, however, differences, of which the most important is that Stewart places the dispute in the mouths of two artisans (in other specimens … the interlocutors are all courtiers, and socially well connected)'.[20] That Stewart's *Flytting* is allied to this tradition is immediately evident in the fact that the poet is still proudly associated with his literary creation, even though Stewart's *Flytting* is more innovative, but also more traditional, than has hitherto been recognized. The comic motifs and repartee of the tradition are easily identified, yet an analysis of lexical features and new jokes in Stewart's *Flytting* reveals just *how much* this text took part in, and contributed to, this tradition. Names that crop up in Dunbar and Kennedy's flytings are echoed in Stewart; and Montgomerie and Polwarth were evidently readers not only of Dunbar and Kennedy's but of Stewart's *Flytting*, too, for they respond to hyperbolic insults that appear for the first time in Stewart. For example, Stewart's sowtar cracks a new joke on the low value of the tailor and his degenerate status by claiming that he is worth the price of a haggis ('of ane pudding pryce', 22). Similar abuse informs Polwarth calling Montgomerie a 'puddin eiter' (734) and a 'pudding wright' (793). Moreover, such continuity between these comic flytings is demonstrated by the fact that the poets employ the same words to describe the deformities of their opponents. Dunbar calls Kennedy a 'mismaid monstour' (53), while Kennedy calls Dunbar a 'mandrag, mymmerkin' (29), a 'myten' (494), and a 'mymerken, monstir of all men' (514). Stewart's sowtar calls the tailor 'mandrag mym̃merkyn and mismaid mytting' (7), and his tailor considers all sowtars 'monstrows mandraggis' (*6). The same lexical features are found in Montgomerie, who thrice calls Polwarth 'mismade mytting' (9, 10, 12), as well as a 'mandrag' (71); Polwarth hurls back: 'They mused at the mandrake, vnmade like a man' (289).[21]

The sowtar flytes the tailor with accusations that he is a 'kukald knaif' (1) with a misshapen body like a 'fowll taid cairle' (36),[22] which the tailor's wife finds sexually repugnant. Here Stewart is responding to the comic tradition in Scots concerning tailors and sowtars, for both artisans had been affiliated with

the crippled and the malformed. Disabled and deformed people were social
outcasts throughout the Middle Ages, and their malignant company was to be
avoided at all costs. The fifteenth-century Scots *Buke of Phisnomy* articulates
the general repugnance felt towards them, and prioritizes the following piece
of advice:

> And oure all thing first counsale I þat þow
> Fra man mysmade of nature vmbechew,
> [M]ankit, dememberit fra nature of mankynd,
> For commonly þa[i] haue ane aukwart strynd. (10122–5)[23]

Dunbar's 'Betuix twell houris and ellevin' is an eldritch dream vision, in which
the poet learns that tailors and sowtars will be awarded the ultimate bliss in
heaven for all their charitable work on earth, concealing physical deformities:
'God mismakkis ȝe do amend' (10).[24] And indeed, in the late-medieval imagination, to associate one's flyting opponent with beggars and cripples is an
insult which suits flytings in particular, for it articulates emphatically that this
opponent is an outcast from all society, not to mention the high society of
court or holy orders. Hence Dunbar's humiliating vignette in his flyting, which
enrolls the hearsay of Quintin, Kennedy's kinsman, to prove that Kennedy
mingles with old cripples and beggars, and even these social rejects loathe his
company (133–6).

   In the same humorous vein of accusing one's flyting opponent of being a
pariah on account of physical malformities, Stewart's sowtar argues that the
tailor's wife finds her husband physically repulsive and thus implies that she has
cuckolded him. This is because the tailor is feebly built, with a horrible face and
crooked legs which make him look like a dog on its hind legs, snarling and
ready to attack a cat. Or he looks like a toad in its characteristic, squat position:

> Thy wyif wount ane man scho gatt
> of the Quhen þat thow wes weill brankit
> And scho gat bot ane cur knakcatt
> Ane fowll taid cairle all tailȝour schankit. (33–6)

> > *brankit*: dressed
> > *cur knakcatt*: mongrel dog that snaps at cats

The tailor's wife was tricked into marriage, for she believed her future husband
to be more brawny and sexually appealing than he really is, on account of his
fine clothes which had concealed his puny frame. In reality, she married a man
'all tailȝour schankit' (36) – a feeble little man who sits cross-legged with his
knees bent up and sticking out, as tailors do.[25] The ideal man in the Scots *Buke
of Phisnomy* is one with thick, powerful legs (10368–70) – the very opposite
of the tailor's crooked shanks. Moreover, a fine pair of legs on a man was an

important focus for the erotic female gaze. An anonymous English verse epistle in the female voice, datable from the mid to late fifteenth century, 'Unto you, most froward, this letter I write', emphasizes the appraisal of a man's sexual prowess that is involved when women consider a man's legs.[26] Yet even crafty tailoring cannot conceal this man's physique: 'Your garmentes upon you full gayly they hinge, / As it were an olde gose had a broke winge' (23–4). The most graphic and humiliating abuse, however, is that which details his misshapen legs:

> Your thighes misgrowen, youre shankes mich worse,
> Whoso beholde youre knees so croked,
> As ich of hem bad oder Christes curse,
> So go they outward; youre hammes ben hoked;
> Such a peire chaumbes I never on loked. (25–9)

> *As ich* …: As if each of them swore at the other
> *hoked*: bandy
> *peire chaumbes*: pair of legs, buttocks

And of course Chaucer's Wife of Bath claims that she fell for Jankyn, her fifth husband – one of the pallbearers at her fourth husband's funeral – because

> ... me thoughte he hadde a paire
> Of legges and of feet so clene and faire
> That al myn herte I yaf unto his hoold. (597–9)[27]

Sowtars were commonly depicted as archetypal knaves. By the late-medieval period in England and Scotland, *sowtar* (meaning 'cobbler') was used as a term of abuse, and right through to the modern period sowtars were considered the least skilled of craftsmen.[28] Their sheer ignorance was so commonplace as to be proverbial: in Chaucer's *Canterbury Tales*, the exasperated Host spurs on the Reeve to tell his story with: 'The devel made a reve for to preche, / Or of a soutere a shipman or a leche' (3903–4).[29] The proverb was current throughout the sixteenth century in Scotland, employed by John Knox in his *Historie of the Reformation in Scotland* with reference to bailies in 1559: 'some of them so meet for their office, in this troublesome time, as a souter is to sail a ship in a stormy day'.[30] A political broadside from 1571 has: 'The soutar is the grett precho^r: the gray freir moks þe shone' (13);[31] and the James Carmichaell collection of Scottish proverbs includes: 'The devill made sowters schipmen, could neither stei[r] nor row'.[32] In comic literature in English and Scots, sowtars were fall guys – the butts of humour – functioning as lewd, churlish types. In Scots, moreover, the dirty, ignorant sowtar is partnered with a botch tailor, who is equally low. Tailors in this tradition are characterized particularly by two traits: they are infested with lice, as are all their wares –

hence all the jokes about them stabbing fleas with their sewing needles; and
tailors steal cloth from all their clients.

Two earlier comic poems in Scots in particular are of importance in relation
to Stewart's *Flyting*: *The Cursing of Sir Iohine Rowlis / Vpoun the Steilaris
of his Fowlis* of *c.* 1495–1503,[33] and Dunbar's burlesque *Turnament* between
a tailor and sowtar of *c.* 1505–7.[34] Rowll's *Cursing* preaches that there are
manifold tailors to be found in hell, each one damned for eternity for all the
cloth they have stolen (218–27). Rowll disparagingly refers to a tailor as one
who 'beiris þe nedill gorrit the lows' (221). Dunbar in his *Turnament* calls his
tailor protagonist a 'pricklous' (125) who parades with a host of similar rascals,
all of whom, as tailors, are thieves and lice slayers by trade: 'seme byttaris and
beist knapparis / … stomok steillaris and clayth takkaris' (130–1).[35]

Moreover, Dunbar's *Turnament* is the earliest surviving instance in Scots of
this comic pairing of tailor with sowtar. Here they are depicted as members of
spoof craft guilds, burlesquing the knights and their impressive retinues, which
were a central focus of the vying for dazzling display in aristocratic tournaments. Dunbar's tailors parade a patchwork banner, made entirely out of stolen
scraps of cloth, in hundreds of different colours (133–8). Further, Dunbar's
Turnament is the earliest surviving text in Older Scots to associate sowtars
with a mock patron saint – St Garnega – whose earliest extant reference occurs
in a list of devils in Rowll's *Cursing*: 'Sym skyɴnar and *Schir* garnega' (95). It
appears therefore that it was Dunbar who assigned Sir Garnega the role of this
diabolical inversion of the craft patron saint. Dunbar's wretched 'hobbell
clowttar' (125) marches under a banner of tanned hide 'quhairin Sanct Girnega
did glyd, / Befoir that rebald rowt' (164–5).

Another comic trait that is first witnessed in Dunbar's *Turnament* is that of
sowtars constantly vomiting both their food ('His breist held neuer a bitt', 174)
and the oily blacking that is used in mending shoes ('ane quart of blek', 179).
Indeed, Dunbar's sowtar even has projectile blacking spurting out of his plates
of armour: 'ay betuix the harnes plaitis / The vly birstit out' (167–8). Of
course, this spewing dimension adds much humour to the notion of the
craftsmen's lowly bodies in this burlesque. The *Turnament* ends with a graphically scatological denouement, with excreta emitting from both tailor and
sowtar, who defecate and vomit for fear at the prospect of fighting each other.

In this light, there is a key facet to the court flyting tradition which Stewart
innovatively employs in his flyting between two lowly craftsmen – that of
focusing one's invective on 'biographical' truths about one's opponent. In the
Scots tradition of literary flytings, much of the humour in the lampooning
character portrayals would have been recognized by the intended audience –
Dunbar's shortness of stature, for example, or Kennedy's deathly pallor.
Bawcutt has noted that flyting caricatures worked rather like political cartoons

do nowadays.[36] Potted forms of such caricatures regarding craftsmen and vendors are to be found in Dunbar's nightmarish 'This nycht in my sleip I wes agast', where the oaths cried by the tailor and sowtar in the market-place underscore the notoriety both of tailors' dishonesty and sowtars' revolting filthiness.[37] Indeed, the sowtar is so dirty that even the devil wants him to clean up before he leads him straight to hell: ' "Fy!" quod the feynd, "thow sairis of blek. / Ga, clenge the clene and cum to me" ' (34–5, Bannatyne MS).[38] From the position of the generic expectations of a literary tradition, therefore, it appears that Stewart is, innovatively, taking flyting back to its most spontaneous street origins by composing a verse flyting between two lowly artisans rather than between proud, self-consciously literary poets. Stewart's tailor and sowtar construct their abuse by characterizing each other according to a pile-up of stock motifs that were associated with these two crafts in sixteenth-century Scotland – namely that tailors are lying thieves who are infested with lice and that sowtars are rather like devils, in that they are blackened-up and filthy, they stink, and they constantly vomit, too.

The arena for Stewart's slanging-match between a tailor and a sowtar is that of the market-place. Nonetheless, it is emphasized that the tailor's and sowtar's flytings, beyond being spontaneous performances of abuse in the street, are actually written down. Stewart's sowtar indicates that he is responding to a written flyting when he declares that the tirade against him is 'war nor ane warlo in thy [i.e. the tailor's] wrytting' (5). In all of the flytings by named poets, the written as well as the spoken nature of flytings is a significant motif. The impact of flyting, linked to its street origins, is thus increased in Stewart by the suggestion that the tailor and sowtar's flytings, as well as being shouted on the streets, are also being read there, just like scurrilous broadsheets. Furthermore, in situating the *Flytting* on the streets of a Scottish burgh, the device of the 'biographical' anecdote (which intends to prove that ill opinion of one's flyting opponent is universal) is likewise turned on its head. For, unlike a court poet, neither tailor nor sowtar can hide from the disrepute in which they were both traditionally held. Here, too, the force of flyting as a genre of the market-place is enhanced by Stewart's deployment of it in combination with the literary tradition. In this particular instance, the motif of the declaration of universal contempt is charged with a reality that becomes almost political, with the tailor's call for each man to condemn sowtars, just as he does, presented as an incitement to craft riot:

> Wald every ma*n* do as I
> quhan evir we saw thame we suld cry
> Fy on þame fy fy
> Out fowll garniga. (21–4)

The tailor's two flytings supply an account of the mysteries of the shoemakers' craft guild, referring to its religious observance and meetings in church, the altar dedicated to its patron saint, and its street processions through the burgh, of the kind that took place during Corpus Christi celebrations or on the feast days of a guild's patron saint. Yet the pride of the shoemakers' guild – their cherished patron saints and exclusive rituals – is here perverted by the scornful tailor into accusations that sowtars worship the disgusting excrement of a vomiting, snarling devil. In retaliation, the sowtar demonstrates how the tailor's craft status is one defined not by guild exclusivity but, on the contrary, by his miserable exclusion from the privileges that craft guilds afford. The sowtar underlines the claim that the tailor cannot join a guild anywhere in Scotland, because everyone knows him to be a thief already.

By the 1530s, when Stewart composed his *Flytting* (on the date, see below), the crafts of tailors and cordiners (shoemakers) had been clearly defined and developed, and their respective craft guilds were well established in the Scottish burghs.[39] The disparity of status and skill between cordiner and sowtar was confirmed in the establishment of these craft guilds: cordiners made and sold new shoes, whereas sowtars patched and mended (as well as sold) old boots and shoes. In Edinburgh, for example, the cordiners' craft had had guild status since the first decade of the sixteenth century. The first craft seal of cause granted to the Edinburgh cordiners by the burgh council dates from 4 February 1510, bestowing upon them a legal identity, with a craft deacon and officers to be appointed annually. An altar dedicated to Saints Crispin and Crispinian – the patron saints of shoemakers – was erected in St Giles', and fees for guild membership were set at four merks, excepting the sons of burgesses, who only paid two. Apprenticeship was for seven years, with each apprentice paying six and eightpence towards the altar on entering the craft. No member of the cordiner craft, including apprentices, was allowed to set up booths in the burgh until he had passed an assay by the craft masters and was subsequently made a burgess.[40] Another seal of cause was granted to the Edinburgh cordiners on 17 September 1533 in the light of the guild's request that they might charge all outsiders selling cordiners' wares on market days a penny a week, paid towards the upkeep of the altar of Saints Crispin and Crispinian.[41] The trade protection thus afforded to members of the Edinburgh cordiners' guild during the first half of the sixteenth century was significant, as were, ostensibly, the standards of workmanship to be maintained henceforth by its members. Moreover, it is apparent that much of the cordiners' guild's pride was both invested in, and devoted to, the altar of their patron saints in their parish church. Indeed, craft-guild business was conducted in church, too.[42]

Stewart's tailor mocks the pride of such guilds by presenting its members not as highly skilled cordiners but as lowly cobblers, working with greasy tallow and oily blacking. Their exclusive religious observance at the craft altar in church is transformed into an eldritch account of sowtars receiving vomit from a patron saint who was a well-known devil: 'S*chi*r garnyga' (18). This all takes place on Monday mornings – a reference to the traditional 'morning speech' which took place at guild meetings:[43]

> Ʒone are sowttaris þat thow seis
> Law kneland on thair kneis
> > Thair god*is* till adorne
> Be sanct garnega þat grym gaist
> To heir thair hairsnes in haist
> off moltin tauche thay tak a test
> > On Mono*n*dayis at morn. (2–8)
>
> *hairsnes*: hoarseness
> *off moltin* …: they taste molten tallow

In this diabolical eucharist, the sowtars kneel before St Garnega, a spectre-like devil ('þat grym gaist'), to receive, in place of the body and blood of Christ, Garnega's projectile vomit of tallow and blacking, which he spews 'ane pynt at a pant' (19). Sir Girnega probably derived his name from his appearance, and so would have been readily identified as the devil who girned, and pulled ugly faces. *OED* notes that *girn* is a variant of *grin*, and defines it thus: 'To show the teeth in rage, pain, disappointment, etc.; to snarl as a dog'. It is plausible to suggest therefore that Sir Garnega / Girnega's most distinguishing feature was his girning countenance – a horrifically contorted face, with teeth and gums bared in a sinister grin. The joke here is, therefore, that dirt-black sowtars who vomit incessantly are well-suited to their mock patron saint, because they all look the same, and all of them belch forth copious amounts of black oil. Indeed, the tailor depicts spewing as so commonplace among sowtars that it is not only their chief recreational pursuit but also a bonding principle in their guild etiquette. Sowtars puke all over each other to strengthen a sense of guild camaraderie, much like the traditional 'kiss of love' which took place at guild initiation ceremonies, which embraced all members:[44]

> To hald thame helsum at hairt
> Sum of vlly spewis ane quairt
> Sum ane pynt to his pairt
> > Off fowll sowttar blek
> Sum sittis and su*m* sewis
> Vþir sum vly spewis

> Bot he keipis weill his kewis
>> Spowttis in his m*arr*owis nek. (9–16)
>
>> *kewis*: manners
>> *marrowis*: colleague's

The tailor's second flyting subverts the sowtars' craft ritual further. Here the tailor details how the sowtars parade their sacred host – Garnega's molten vomit – in a religious procession, proudly blazoning bags full of pabbling, oily spew, which spills out in bubbles:

> ʒone ar sowttaris be sicht
> W*ith* hiddous hoist vpoun hicht
>> Herkin and heir
> tha blaisit bla bubly baggis. (*2–5)
>
>> *hoist*: host
>> *tha blaisit* …: they blazon dark bluish-grey bubbling bags

This excremental craft worship is depicted as proceeding out of doors, in the freezing cold 'in to þe cra*n*ra [rime] and frost' (*11). The tailor thus mocks another major focus of guild pride: the cordiners' guild procession through the burgh which took place on the guild's patron Saint's Day, St Crispin's Day (25 October). Right up until the nineteenth century in the Canongate, the cordiners' guild celebrated St Crispin's Day with a pageant, which had been considered a time-honoured custom of the burgh since the seventeenth century at the least (earlier records have not survived). This procession was headed by a guild member who was elected 'King Crispin'; he was accompanied by a knight in armour called 'The Black Prince', along with the rest of the cordiners' guild, all dressed in costumes for the occasion.[45]

In addition, Stewart takes the spewing motif associated with sowtars to a new extreme. Literature in English and Scots attests to the fact that sowtars were renowned for having disgusting mouths, with rotten, worn-down teeth: the anonymous *Piers the Plowman's Crede* of *c.* 1393–1401 refers to a sowtar's teeth as being like a hand-saw, because they gnaw at leather in order to soften it up: 'a soutere y-suled in grees, / His teeth with toylinge of lether tatered as a sawe' (752–3).[46] And Dunbar's 'Schir, lat it never in toune be tald',[47] probably written in the winter of 1505–6,[48] refers to sowtars' characteristic champing on leather, too. Here the poet characterizes himself as a worn-out carthorse ('ane ald ʒald auer', 3), begging that, should he die while still in the king's possession, his hide will not be sold to the sowtars to be chewed for evermore 'with uglie gumes' (36). It seems a natural development to suggest that a sowtar, traditionally credited with a filthy mouth, is thus presented in the Scottish comic tradition – which is characterized by excess – not only with a rotten mouth, but with a mouth that is constantly spewing, too. Stewart contributes to this comic excess when his tailor claims that sowtars have blunt teeth because they gnaw on leather according to its bawdy sense in Scots. That is, the leather that sowtars chew on is that of female genitals – those of cows and old mares:

> Thair teith so bawchs and blunt*is*
> For cu*m*ring off cow cunt*is*
> And freting of ȝawd frunt*is*. (*21–3)

> > *bawchs*: blunt, poor, ineffectual
> > *freting*: rubbing, chafing

In his *Flyting* with Montgomerie, Polwarth recalls abuse hurled by Stewart's tailor when he calls Montgomerie a 'creishie soutter, shoe cloutter' (747), who should 'spew bleck' (765). Interestingly, in his final volley of abuse, Polwarth challenges Montgomerie, 'thrawin frunt, kisse the cunt, or the kow' (794).

In response to the tailor's first salvo, the sowtar scorns the tailor for being forced to live the life of a vagrant, (otherwise known as) a journeyman tailor, on account of his notorious thieving. Tailors' craft guilds had been established in Scotland at the beginning of the sixteenth century. They set trade standards, granted privileges, and provided some financial security for their members – in Edinburgh, the first seal of cause for the tailors' guild was granted on 26 August 1500.[49] Guild rules were strictly maintained: in April 1551, for example, an Englishman called Robert Pyndale, a non-guild member, was reprimanded before Edinburgh council. Pyndale confessed that he 'cuttit his veluitt and vther guidis in small peices and sawld the sam in Leyth', and had thus broken all the acts and freedoms pertaining to the burgh statutes on cloth trade. Pyndale was fined ten merks.[50] In direct contrast to the sowtar's freeman status (on account of his membership of a craft guild), Stewart's tailor thus represents the underprivileged and unskilled craftsman: he is an unfreeman, and a casually employed journeyman to boot.[51]

The sowtar's use of hostile vignettes in his flyting underlines the notion that the tailor is not at all eligible for guild status in any burgh because he is an outlaw. His vagabond lifestyle is mocked in the sowtar's charge that the tailor's bed is a makeshift sofa, constructed out of bundles of straw: 'Thy cowche is on ane sonk of stray' (21). This implies that the tailor is forced to sleep out of doors or in barns, being penniless and of no fixed abode. In opposition to the status and protection afforded to craft-guild members such as Stewart's sowtar, his tailor must needs wander from place to place, eking out a living with any work he can beg:

> Thow ʒeid w*ith* elwand scheir and thy*m*mill
> Full mony a day seikand thy craft
> For halfpe*n*nyis thy hand ʒeid ny*m*mill. (25–7)

> > *elwand* ...: ell-measure, shears and thimble (his tools of trade)
> > *nymmill*: nimbly

Stewart's sowtar aims to shame the tailor in public ('Ama*n*gis the wyffis it salbe wittin', 17) with details of his life on the margins of society. A string of biographical vignettes exemplifies the violent contempt already felt towards the tailor. He has been chased out of towns, with people crying out after him. When he is finally caught he will no doubt be hanged in public:

> Thay fallowit the w*it*h cry and schowt
> ha hald the theif þat stall the claith
> Thow wilbe hangit haif thou no dowt
> For mony presumptous forsworn aith. (13–16)

He has been beaten up so many times for his thieving and poor tailoring (the 'wrangus geir of vþir me*n*is', 32) that his dodgy reputation is common knowledge, and nobody will bother with him: 'quha delt w*ith* the thay wer fow daft' (29). It is added that the tailor's reputation is so bad that he dare not venture back to his home town. There can be no doubt that the tailor is compelled to live the life of a wretched outlaw, welcome nowhere: 'For clayis þat thow mismaid and ma*n*kit / Thow dar no*ch*t dwell quhair thow wes born' (37–8).

Sowtars might well engage their mouths with 'cow cunt*is*', but tailors have a gross occupation concerning their mouths, too. Stewart here cracks another joke in his *Flyting*, and in the process takes a stock insult in the tradition to new excess. One of the boast motifs of comic flyting is the poet-flyters' assertion that they speak with the golden mouth of rhetoric, so none stands a chance of victory.[52] To resolve this, Dunbar in *his* flyting inverts Kennedy's boast that he has 'goldin lippis' to suggest that the only gilded orifice Kennedy has is in fact his backside, his 'giltin hippis' encrusted through his perpetually loose bowels (97–100). Stewart's comic contribution involves an elaboration on the gibe at the tailor as 'priclous' (22). The sowtar claims that the tailor has a golden mouth, but not due to any flyting fluency; instead, 'for lowsy semis that thow hes bittin / Thy gwmis ar giltin quhair evir thow gay' (19–20). Tailors bit seams to flatten down the cloth. Like Dunbar's scatological subversion of the boast motif, Stewart's joke has converted the image of golden rhetoric into a charge of repellant degeneracy.

However, the climax of the new gags in Stewart's *Flyting* is the scatological attack towards the end of the tailor's final salvo, where it is claimed that the sowtar's continual diarrhoea, and the stench of it, is so rank that its effect reaches as far away as Flanders:

> Thay haif the hurle ay behind
> The stynk þat thay mak in the wind
>   will flanderis infeck
>
> Infeck flander*is* and fyle
> And abowt mony a myle
> Kulros Karrik and Kyle
>   Linlyt*h*qw and Lude. (*38–44)

The faeces perpetually supplied by sowtars manage to infect an area that extends from the reaches of Carrick and Kyle on the west coast of Scotland right across Fife and overseas to Flanders on mainland Europe. Yet to suggest that stinking excrement was capable of infecting such a wide area of western Europe is not a statement belonging to the realms of outrageous comedy alone. Such a notion is thoroughly in line with the contemporary belief that human ordure and waste infected the air and thus spread disease – a belief that persisted throughout the Middle Ages and well into the modern period. In this light, the tailor's accusations about the loose bowels of sowtars have resonances beyond the scatological denouement found in other comic flytings in the tradition – notably in salvos by Kennedy and Polwarth – to suggest the reality of the contemporary peril of the pest.[53]

The earliest printing of a medical tract in Scots is Gilbert Skeyne's *Ane Breve Descriptiovn of the Pest*, printed in 1568 by Lekprevik in Edinburgh.[54] Skeyne defined pestilence as follows: 'Ane pest is the corruptioun or infectioun of ye Air, or ane venemous qualytie & maist hurtfull Wapor thairof, quhilk hes strenthe and wikitnes abone al natural putrifactioun' (Sig. A ii). Skeyne attributed the chief causes behind outbreaks of plague in the burghs to filth that is left to fester: stagnant water, excrement and sewage on the streets, putrid vegetables, the stench of tanneries, and unburied human corpses. Steps were taken as late as October 1566 in Edinburgh to prevent human corpses being eaten by scavenging animals: the town council ordered that the Boroughmuir gallows were to be made secure with a door, so that dogs would no longer be able to drag off the bodies.[55] This was only two years prior to Lekprevik's printing of Skeyne.

Moreover, the way in which Stewart's tailor emphasizes the sowtars' collective grief, stressing the awful noise and mess they make while on parade, in fact characterizes the sowtars' guild as riddled with the pest, their wanton vomiting bespattering and infecting anything roundabout:

> Tha monstrows mandraggis
> Wall myre ane studfull of staggis
>   and fle thame throw beir ...
> Quhen thair ganting is gane
> Thay gaip thay glour Thay grane
> To heir the mvrnyng and the mane
>   Thay mak quhen thay meit ...
> Thay greit ay glewand in glitt
> Thay host thay spew thay spitt
> As thay war woid out of witt
>   Thay vary thair weird. (6–8, 17–20, 25–8)

> *staggis*: stags
> *beir*: din, outcry, shouting
> *ganting*: gaping, vomiting
> *glitt*: slimy filth
> *vary*: curse; *weird*: fate

The sowtars' ghastly noise is due to their incessant vomiting, and because they are wretched in spirit: 'in sorrow ay thay sitt / bowdin and bleird' (31–2). They are bleary-eyed, dejected, with black vomit jetting out of their filthy mouths and diseased excrement shooting from their anuses. The similarities between the tailor's description of sowtars and Skeyne's description of a victim of the pest are so striking as to suggest that Stewart is caricaturing sowtars as victims (not to mention perpetrators) of the plague. Skeyne notes the following symptoms: a state of wretched sadness ('Greit doloure of heid with heauynes, sollicitude & sadnes of mynd: greit disp[l]esour with sowning, quhairefter followis haistelie deth'); and 'frequent vomitting of diuers colouris' from a black, thirsty mouth ('Bitternes of mowth, and toung with blaiknit colour thairof, & greit drouth', Sig. A xi). Moreover, Skeyne's chapter on 'Signis of deth in pestilentiale personis' adds that victims' bodies balloon out. Looking like bad cases of dropsy, they spew black matter, and excrete noxious ordure: 'Vomitting, materis of diueris coloris, principallie inclyning to blak, w^t sic excrementis maist corrupt & teuch ... swolling of the bodie, as in hydropisie' (Sig. A xii). Stewart's tailor accuses sowtars of being 'bawch blobbis ... and bubillis full lyk' (33–6) – that is, they are useless blobs who are bloated like bubbles. The excremental climax of the comic flyting tradition is thus transfigured: from the realms of laughter at the fundamental humiliation of the scatological body, to a topical and political statement, where the bodily wastes of sowtars are identified with the dreaded pestilence, which a sixteenth-century audience knew promised swift, certain death.[56]

Indeed, both sowtar and tailor have been presented as essentially contagious. Trade in cloth and clothing was always restricted in times of pestilence, for it 'was common and reasonable to believe that the belongings of an infected person conveyed plague, especially his clothes'.[57] For Stewart's jokes to have functioned as sickeningly topical and inappropriate demands that his *Flytting* was composed in the light of a terrible plague, and especially one which hit Edinburgh and surrounding Fife. Such a plague threatened and then ravaged Edinburgh for most of 1530. On 11 February 1530, Edinburgh town council acted on the information that St Andrews had become infected with the pest.[58] It was decreed henceforth that no indweller of Edinburgh was to lodge anyone from St Andrews within the burgh, nor should anyone go to St Andrews or have any dealings with anyone from that burgh 'vnder the pane of deid'. The following week, on 18 February, one Margaret Cock was banished from Edinburgh for the rest of her life, and branded on both cheeks 'for the breking of the Kingis proclamatione and statutis of the tovne maid apon the contagius seiknes of pestilence'. Margaret had come into Edinburgh from St Andrews, carrying with her cloths that were infected with disease. In addition, she had stolen a kirtle from an Edinburgh house. All of Margaret Cock's contaminated cloth and clothing was burnt. On 20 February, Edinburgh town council issued a statement forbidding any Edinburgh inhabitant to go to the forthcoming fair at St Monans in Fife – situated, like St Andrews, across the Firth of Forth from Edinburgh – where 'infeckit personis is habill to repair with infeckit geir'.[59]

The pest had spread from Fife into Edinburgh by May. On 25 May, the town council imposed a *cordon sanitaire*, according to the current procedure in Scotland. Henceforth, any sickness had to be reported to the bailies as quickly as possible, and all sick people who did not go to the Boroughmuir had to incarcerate themselves within their homes and live under a strict quarantine. St Andrews remained off limits, and Edinburgh indwellers were forbidden to lodge any 'trumpouris or vagabundis'. Moreover, there were many stipulations concerning cloth and clothing. Under pain of death, no 'clething claith wou nor lynnyn' which hailed from St Andrews was to be received in Edinburgh, and inhabitants' dealings with second-hand clothes were forbidden 'vnder the pane of burning of thar chekis and bannasing of the toune for all the dayes of thar lyffis'. Steps were taken to keep the streets free of contagious waste. All the burgh's indwellers were ordered to clean the streets around their homes 'as thar is gret filth within this toune … quharthrow infectioune may spreid and ryse'.[60]

Contagion and new infection remained central issues in the Edinburgh statutes through to the autumn of 1530, so it is no surprise that the burgh's restrictions on all dealings with cloth and clothing were reiterated on 30 September 1530. Yet only a week later, on 6 October 1530, one Katherine Heriot was sentenced to be drowned immediately. Heriot was convicted on two very related counts: she was a common thief, who had stolen two sticks of cloth while in Edinburgh, and she had brought the pest with her from Leith into Edinburgh. Heriot, like Stewart's tailor, appears to be doing all she can to spread contagious disease. By December, the pest had spread back eastwards to Leith. Edinburgh council duly forbade any interaction with Leith indwellers, and restrictions on trade in cloth, both old and new, were reinforced.[61] In the light of these events throughout 1530 in Edinburgh and nearby Fife, and the concomitant burgh statutes, the artisan protagonists of Stewart's *Flytting* prove to be not only stock fools but also ghastly purveyors of epidemic disease: the guild sowtar with his multiple black excretions in church and all about the burgh streets while on parade; and the thieving journeyman tailor who roams and pilfers from one place to another and who is never without his bag of lousy, infectious weeds or his gilt gums. It is plausible to suggest therefore that Stewart's *Flytting* is datable to the early 1530s, when sensitivity to jokes on filthily contagious craftsmen would have been at a height, and while Stewart was well-situated at James V's court as a Scots makar, getting on with his grand translation of Boece into Scottish verse.

Clearly, William Stewart was sensitive to the matter of plague, as indeed was George Bannatyne, who preserved the unique copy of Stewart's 'Exortationis of Chryst to all Synnaris to repent thame of the Same' in the theological section of his manuscript, fols 35^v–7^r.[62] This poem appears to have been written during an actual time of plague in Scotland. The voice of Christ laments the deplorable state of mankind, which has turned against his teachings: 'My law w*ith* the is lychleit and laid by' (124). Nonetheless, heavenly mercy will remain ever possible for those who repent their sins. This is promised in the poem's refrain: 'Amend thy mys this plaig sall pas þe fra'. 'Exortationis of Chryst' ends in the voice of the contrite poet, who prays to Christ on behalf of everybody for deliverance from the pest:

> Haif me*r*cy lord our error we deploir
> We grant our gilt submittand ws to grace
> Latt no*ch*t this deid but pietie ws devoir
> Quhair we haif failit to the o lord allace
> We sall a*mm*end and thow will grant ws pece
> Haif me*r*cy lord Haif me*r*cy we the pray
> Thow fruct vnfyld Thow farest floure of face
> Beseik Oure god this plaig to put ws fray. (154–61)

Moreover, Stewart's 'Exortationis of Chryst' recalls the tone of Henryson's 'Ane Prayer for the Pest', also unique to the Bannatyne Manuscript.[63] The presence of these unique texts in the Bannatyne Manuscript indicates the attention given to the pest in the manuscript as a whole, and contextualizes as well as underlines the identification of the protagonists in Stewart's *Flytting* with plague-carriers.

George Bannatyne would have appreciated the black humour of Stewart's *Flytting*, compiling his compendious 'Ballat Buik' when he escaped the plague that raged in Edinburgh in 1568, a fact he explicitly mentions in one of his more prominent colophons.[64] None of the comic ritual associated with sowtars in Stewart's text would have been lost on a post-Reformation audience either, for the craft-guilds clung to their traditions for many years after the Reformation.[65] Stewart's infectious tailor and plague-ridden sowtar would have been recognized straightaway by any burgh indweller who had lived through a bout of pestilence or two and had been forced to adapt to the regimes of the *cordon sanitaire* that were necessarily imposed: the restrictions of Edinburgh town council in 1568 concerning plague and how to contain it are even more elaborate than those imposed when the plague hit Edinburgh in 1530.[66]

Stewart's *Flytting* thus responds in a complex, topical, and innovative way to the comic flyting tradition. Generic motifs and imagery are reworked, yet Stewart also raises political and social issues in his portrayal of antagonisms between crafts, between freemen and unfreemen, and in allusions to pestilence and infection. The origins of the incitements to craft riot instigated by Stewart's tailor, along with his disgust at the pomp and noise of guild processions, can be located in issues of tension and unrest in burgh politics that had only escalated in Scotland by the time that George Bannatyne copied down Stewart's *Flytting* in 1568. Stewart's *Flytting* was as blackly comic in the late 1560s as it had been in the 1530s: perhaps even more so.

Notes

1   A fuller discussion of comic flytings in Older Scots, and Stewart's *Flytting* in particular, is to be found in K. Fisher, 'Comic Verse in Older Scots', unpublished D. Phil. Thesis, University of Oxford, 1999.

2   Edinburgh, National Library of Scotland, Advocates' MS 1.1.6: the Bannatyne Manuscript. There is a facsimile: D. Fox and W. A. Ringler (eds), *The Bannatyne Manuscript: National Library of Scotland Adv. MS 1.1.6* (London, 1980); and a transcription: W. Tod Ritchie (ed.), *The Bannatyne Manuscript*, 4 vols, STS (Edinburgh and London, 1928–34).

3   *IMEV*, 1021.

4   *SIMEV*, 3117.8. The earliest witness to *The Flyting of Dumbar and Kennedie* is a fragment in a printing of *c.* 1508: Chepman and Myllar no. vii. See *STC* 7348; and Aldis, no. 9. Further witnesses are that of Cambridge, Magdalene College, Pepys Library, MS 2553: the Maitland Folio Manuscript, pp. 53–4, 69–72, 77–80, and 59–63; and Cambridge, Cambridge University Library, MS Ll.v.10: the Reidpeth Manuscript, fols 58ᵛ–64ᵛ. The Asloan Manuscript: NLS, MS 16500, contained a version of the flyting too, which is now lost. Quotations are from *The Poems of William Dunbar*, ed. by Priscilla Bawcutt, 2 vols, ASLS (Glasgow, 1998), I, no. 65, pp. 200–18.

5   Lyndsay's *Answer* was included in John Scot's printing for Henry Charteris of Lyndsay's *Warkis* in 1568. *STC* 15658, Aldis no. 70.

6 An excerpted stanza from one of Montgomerie's flytings in James VI's *Reulis and Cautelis* of 1584 is the earliest witness. There are two manuscript versions, datable from the late sixteenth to early seventeenth centuries: BL, MS Harley 7578; and Huntington Library, San Marino, California, MS HM 105: the so-called 'Tullibardine' Manuscript. Quotations are taken from the earliest extant printing of the *Flyting* by Andrew Hart in Edinburgh, 1621: *STC* 13954.3, Aldis no. 575. See further S. Mapstone, 'Invective as Poetic: The Cultural Contexts of Polwarth and Montgomerie's *Flyting*', *SLJ* 26 (1999), 18–40.

7 See P. Bawcutt, 'The Art of Flyting', *SLJ* 10 (1983), 5–24; D. Gray, 'Rough Music: Some Early Invectives and Flytings', *Year's Work in English Studies* 14 (1984), 21–43; R. Lyall, 'Complaint, Satire and Invective in Middle Scots Literature', in N. Macdougall (ed.), *Church, Politics and Society: Scotland 1408–1929* (Edinburgh, 1983), pp. 44–64; D. Parkinson, 'Flyting and Abuse in Scots Verse, 1450–1580', unpublished Ph.D. Thesis, University of Toronto, 1984; D. W. Riach, 'Walter Kennedy's Part in *The Flyting of Dunbar and Kennedie*', in D. Strauss and H. W. Drescher (eds), *Scottish Language and Literature, Medieval and Renaissance: Proceedings of the Fourth International Conference 1984* (Frankfurt am Main, Berne and New York, 1986), pp. 369–79; P. Bawcutt, *Dunbar the Makar* (Oxford, 1992), pp. 220–56; K. Simpson, 'The Legacy of Flyting', *SSL* 26 (1991), 503–14; D. Parkinson, 'Prescriptions for Laughter in Some Middle Scots Poems', in S. R. McKenna (ed.), *Selected Essays on Scottish Language and Literature. A Festschrift in Honor of Allan H. MacLaine* (Lewiston, Queenston, and Lampeter, 1992), pp. 27–39; D. Parkinson, 'Alexander Montgomerie, James VI, and "Tumbling Verse" ', in L. A. J. R. Houwen and A. A. MacDonald (eds), *Loyal Letters: Studies on Mediaeval Alliterative Poetry and Prose* (Groningen, 1994), pp. 281–95; P. Robichaud, ' "To heir quhat I sould wryt": "The Flyting of Dunbar and Kennedy" and Scots Oral Culture', *SLJ* 25 (1998), 9–16; and Mapstone, 'Invective as Poetic'.

8 See further *DOST*, II, 503–4, 'flyte' *v*; *MED* 'fliten' *v*; and *OED* 'flyte' *v*.

9 Bawcutt, 'Art of Flyting', 7.

10 Ibid., 10.

11 Ibid., 10.

12 Ibid., 18.

13 For attitudes, see ibid., 12; and Mapstone, 29–34.

14 A. A. MacDonald, 'William Stewart and the Court Poetry of the Reign of James V', in J. Hadley Williams (ed.), *Stewart Style 1513–1542: Essays on the Court of James V* (East Linton, 1996), pp. 179–200 (198). The unique manuscript copy of Stewart's verse translation is now in Cambridge: CUL, MS Kk.ii.16.

15 See J. M. Sanderson, 'Two Stewarts of the Sixteenth Century: Mr William Stewart, Poet and William Stewart, Elder, Depute Clerk of Edinburgh', *The Stewarts* 17 (1984), 25–46.

16 *STC* 21254; Aldis no. 152. Line numbers and quotations refer to G. F. Black (ed.), *The Seuin Seages*, STS (Edinburgh and London, 1932), in this case p. 2.

17 So claims the colophon of the 1538 printing of Lyndsay's *Papyngo*: see D. Hamer (ed.), *The Works of Sir David Lindsay of the Mount 1490–1555*, 4 vols, STS (Edinburgh and London, 1931–36), III, p. 64 and I, p. 103; and J. Hadley Williams (ed.), *Sir David Lyndsay: Selected Poems*, ASLS (Glasgow, 2000), pp. 58–97, 239. See also C. Edington, *Court and Culture in Renaissance Scotland: Sir David Lindsay of the Mount 1486–1555* (Amherst, 1994), p. 215. However, J. Hadley Williams in 'Dunbar and His Immediate Heirs' in S. Mapstone (ed.), *William Dunbar: The Nobill Poyet* (East Linton, 2001), pp. 85–107, suggests that this appraisal of Stewart by Lyndsay might actually be ironic.

18 The shorter poems here considered as part of William Stewart's literary canon (as

opposed to texts which are claimed to be by Henry Stewart, Lord Darnley) are listed in an appendix to MacDonald, 'William Stewart', pp. 199–200.

[19] Quotations from Stewart's *Flytting* are my own transcriptions from Fox and Ringler. All scribal abbreviations and suspensions have been expanded in transcription, and are printed in italic. Long *s* has been lowered, and final '-s', as an abbreviation for '-*is*', has been expanded. The ligature 'ff' at the beginning of a line of verse is rendered 'F'. No system of punctuation is attempted here. Line numbering is that of Ritchie (ed.), *The Bannatyne Manuscript*, III, pp. 22–6; line references to the tailor's final reply (fols 140ᵛ–41ʳ) are preceded by an asterisk, to distinguish them from references to his opening speech.

[20] MacDonald, 'William Stewart', p. 194. Hadley Williams in 'Dunbar and his Immediate Heirs' does not rate the poem too highly as a response to Dunbar. See also S. R. McKenna, 'Drama and Invective: Traditions in Dunbar's "Fasternis Evin in Hell" ', *SSL* 24 (1989), 129–41.

[21] There are verbal echoes, too, in Dunbar's 'Complane I wald, wist I quhome till', especially in its tirade against social climbers (15–27). Bawcutt (ed.), I, no. 9, pp. 67–8.

[22] To compare one's flyting opponent to a toad is a frequent insult in comic flytings, and in Older Scots literature generally. See the many entries under TOAD in R. Scheibe, *A Catalogue of Amphibians and Reptiles in Older Scots Literature* (Frankfurt am Main, 1996), pp. 241–5.

[23] S. Mapstone, 'The Scots *Buke of Phisnomy* and Sir Gilbert Hay', in A. A. MacDonald, M. Lynch, and I. B. Cowan (eds), *The Renaissance in Scotland* (Leiden, New York, and Cologne, 1994), pp. 1–44 (25). All quotations from this text are taken from the version in *The Buik of King Alexander the Conquerour*, as quoted by Mapstone.

[24] *SIMEV* 515.5. Bawcutt (ed.), I, no. 48, pp. 157–8.

[25] *OED* glosses the compound 'tailor-legged' as an adjective with the sense: 'having the knees bent by sitting cross-legged'. However, the first citation for this compound is 1767.

[26] *IMEV* 3832. R. T. Davies (ed.), *Medieval English Lyrics* (London, 1963; repr. 1991), no. 140, pp. 244–5.

[27] *The Riverside Chaucer*, ed. L. D. Benson *et al.*, 3ʳᵈ edn (Boston, 1987), p. 113.

[28] *MED* under *soutar* cites the insult 'horsoned souter' from the Court Rolls of Maldon, Essex, in 1478. *OED* notes that 'souter' was frequently used 'with depreciatory force, esp. to denote a type of workman of little or no education' throughout the sixteenth and seventeenth centuries. *OED* then provides a secondary sense for 'souter' as solely 'a term of abuse'. *Tailȝour* might be used as a term of abuse, too, though it was evidently not as highly charged as *sowtar*. *OED* notes that in proverbs and allusions, tailors are a means to imply 'disparagement and ridicule'.

[29] *Riverside Chaucer*, p. 78.

[30] *John Knox's History of the Reformation in Scotland*, ed. by W. C. Dickinson, 2 vols (London, 1949), I, p. 242. See further B. J. Whiting, 'Proverbs and Proverbial Sayings From Scottish Writings Before 1600, Part One', *Mediaeval Studies* 11 (1949), 125–205; 'Part Two', *Mediaeval Studies* 13 (1951), 87–164 (128).

[31] J. Cranstoun (ed.), *Satirical Poems of the Reformation,* 2 vols, STS (Edinburgh and London, 1891–93), I, no. xxix, pp. 201–3 (202).

[32] M. L. Anderson (ed.), *The James Carmichaell Collection of Proverbs in Scots* (Edinburgh, 1957), p. 105, no. 1574; the proverb is also in the Fergusson manuscript collection (which antedates the 1641 first printing, dating from the second half of the sixteenth century), p. 103, no. 1410.

[33] Extant in the Bannatyne Manuscript, fols 104ᵛ–7ʳ; Maitland Folio, pp. 141–8; and

a fragment in Reidpeth MS. Rowll's *Cursing* can be dated by the information it imparts concerning the current pope in office, who was Alexander VI (1492–1503). Thus, from the Bannatyne witness: 'And now of rome .... Paip alexander þat we do fynd' (6–8). Yet the poem's reference to 'grit glengoir' (63), which refers to venereal syphilis, suggests that the text was not written before 1495, and the earliest records of the disease in Scotland occur in 1497. See Bawcutt (ed.), II, p. 357.

[34] *SIMEV* 2623.3 and 2289.8. Extant in Asloan, fols 210^r–11^v; Bannatyne, fols 111^r–12^v; and Maitland Folio, pp. 162–5. Bawcutt (ed.), I, no. 47, pp. 152–6. Further, Dunbar's 'I that in heill wes and gladnes', written soon after July 1505, shows that Dunbar was aware of the poet Sir John Rowll and had probably read his *Cursing*. There are two Rowlls mentioned in the text, but Sir John Rowll is most probably the noble, 'gentill' Rowll of Corstorphine. Ibid., I, no. 21, pp. 94–7 (77–80).

[35] For a discussion of these abusive compounds, see P. Bawcutt, 'Dunbar: New Light on Some Old Words', in C. Macafee and I. Macleod (eds), *The Nuttis Schell: Essays on the Scots Language* (Aberdeen, 1987), pp. 83–95 (92–3).

[36] Bawcutt, 'Art of Flyting', 21.

[37] *SIMEV* 3634.6. Extant in Bannatyne, fols 132^v–3^r; Maitland Folio, pp. 55–7; and Reidpeth, 18^v–19^r. Bawcutt (ed.), I, no. 78, pp. 250–7.

[38] The Bannatyne and Maitland Folio witnesses for this text differ significantly, and this is apparent in their respective copying of the poem's refrain. Bawcutt's complete edition prints the witnesses in parallel. The only variant to Bannatyne's refrain, 'Renunce thy God and cum to me', in one verse from the text's seventeen stanzas is that of the devil's response to the sowtar. Maitland Folio's refrain on the sowtar reads 'Ga, wysche the weill, syn cum to me' (20).

[39] See T. C. Smout, *A History of the Scottish People 1560–1830* (London, 1969; new edn, 1985), pp. 160–1; M. Lynch, 'Scottish Towns 1500–1700', in M. Lynch (ed.), *The Early Modern Town in Scotland* (London, 1982), pp. 1–35 (9); M. Lynch, 'The Social and Economic Structure of the Larger Towns, 1450–1600', in M. Lynch, M. Spearman, and G. Stell (eds), *The Scottish Medieval Town* (Edinburgh, 1988), pp. 261–86; and J. Cherry, 'Leather', in J. Blair and N. Ramsay (eds), *English Medieval Industries: Craftsmen, Techniques, Products* (London and Rio Grande, 1991), pp. 295–318.

[40] Sir J. D. Marwick (ed.), *Extracts from the Records of the Burgh of Edinburgh*, 4 vols, SBRS (Edinburgh, 1869–82), I, pp. 127–9. See further Sir J. D. Marwick, *Edinburgh Guilds and Crafts*, SBRS (Edinburgh, 1909), pp. 61–2, 71, and 73.

[41] *Edin. Recs.*, II, pp. 64–6.

[42] See C. A. Malcolm, 'Incorporation of Cordiners of the Canongate, 1538–1773', *Book of the Old Edinburgh Club* 18 (1932), 100–50 (101).

[43] L. T. Smith and L. Brentano (eds), *English Gilds*, EETS o.s. (1870; repr. 1963), p. xxxiii. For example, see the ordinances for the Guild of St Thomas of Canterbury, Lynn, pp. 47–8.

[44] See Smith and Brentano (eds), for examples of the 'kiss of love'. On entry to the Guild of Sts Fabian and Sebastian in Aldersgate, London, a new brother or sister 'in tokenyng of loue and charite and pees, atte resceyuynge schul kisse oþer of þo þat ben þer', p. 9.

[45] See Malcolm, 135–6.

[46] H. Barr (ed.), *The Piers Plowman Tradition* (London, 1993), p. 93.

[47] *SIMEV* 2349.5. See Bawcutt (ed.), I, pp. 219–21.

[48] Ibid., II, p. 447.

[49] See *Edin. Recs.*, I, pp. 82–3. See also Marwick, *Edinburgh Guilds and Crafts*, pp. 56–7, 69–70.

[50] *Edin. Recs.*, II, p. 155.

51 See Smout, *History of the Scottish People*, pp. 163–4.
52 The golden mouth image is used in earnest in Dunbar's *The Goldyn Targe*, where the poet lauds 'morall Gower and Ludgate laureate' who have 'fair ourgilt oure spech, that imperfyte / Stude or your goldyn pennis schupe to write' (262–8). See Bawcutt (ed.), I, no. 59, pp. 184–92.
53 See Smout, *History of the Scottish People*, p. 151.
54 *STC* 22626, Aldis no. 73. See further J. F. Kellas Johnstone and A. W. Robertson, *Bibliographica Aberdonensis 1472–1640*, 2 vols (Aberdeen, 1929–30), I, p. 59.
55 *Edin. Recs.*, III, p. 221.
56 See T. C. Smout, 'Coping with Plague in Sixteenth and Seventeenth-Century Scotland', *Scotia* 2 (1978), 19–33.
57 Ibid., 23.
58 See ibid., 21, where it is argued that the bubonic plague was 'a disease of the towns'.
59 *Edin. Recs.*, II, pp. 18–20.
60 See ibid., II, pp. 28–30, 35–6, and 42, for brandings and banishments meted out during the summer of 1530.
61 See ibid., II, pp. 40–5.
62 Quotations from Fox and Ringler, *The Bannatyne Manuscript*.
63 *IMEV* 2420. The poem is written down twice: an incomplete version in the Draft MS, pp. 20–1 (1–64 only), and a full version in the theology section of the Main MS, fols 24ʳ–5ᵛ. *The Poems of Robert Henryson,* ed. by D. Fox (Oxford, 1981), pp. 167–9.
64 Fol. 375ʳ. As the sixteenth century went on, the plague was restricted to the south-east of Scotland. Not all Scottish audiences would have been as finely attuned as George Bannatyne (an Edinburgh man) to Stewart's jokes in his *Flytting*. See Smout, *History of the Scottish People*, p. 152.
65 See Lynch, 'Introduction: Scottish Towns 1500–1700', pp. 14 and 27.
66 The first mention in the town council records of this outbreak is on 13 October 1568. See *Edin. Recs.*, III, p. 253.

2

The Earliest Surviving Text of Lyndsay's *Tragedie of the Cardinall*: An English Edition of a Scottish Poem

JANET HADLEY WILLIAMS

The events of David Beaton's life, culminating in his murder at St Andrews Castle in mid-1546, provide the raw materials for *The Tragedie of the Cardinall*, composed by Sir David Lyndsay in early 1547.[1] In his poem, Lyndsay quietly promotes the inherent rise-and-fall structure of the life story. He lists Beaton's honours, for example, in order of their importance rather than in the actual chronological order of their receipt. He also omits mention of the French naturalization granted to Beaton by Francis I, allowing the reference to his provision to the Mirepoix bishopric (70) to make the point that Beaton had his own as well as the church's interest in mind when he opposed Scotland's peaceful rapprochement with England.[2] The selective use of biographical details reinforces the link that Lyndsay makes explicitly, early in the poem (5, 27), to Giovanni Boccaccio's *De Casibus Virorum Illustrium*. This work probably was known to Lyndsay only indirectly, via John Lydgate's popular English adaptation, *The Fall of Princes*.[3]

Yet Lyndsay in turn adapts his Boccaccian-Lydgatean model, and with some subtlety. He plays, for instance, on the possible multiple meanings of morally weighted words, such as *wysedome* (82), *counsall* (174), and *prudens* (176), so that face value and contextual value are contradictory. He further adapts tradition by giving Beaton's story a deceptive directness. Lydgate had narrated many of his tragic 'fates' himself, but Lyndsay gives the narrator's role to the satiric persona of Beaton's wraith, and presents his own part as that of mere amanuensis. Lyndsay also uses Beaton's supposed authorship of the narrative to remove much of the customary *De Casibus* stress on the role of Fortune. The fictional Beaton admits his own culpability – 'I causit all that trybulatioun' (110) – and rebukes 'Prencis' with the words, 'Ye bene the cause of this transgressioun' (346). In Lyndsay's poem, human agency and corrupt contemporary practices join divinely ordained punishment (Fortune or God) as sources of destruction.

It is notable that these comparisons and comments draw upon the later, 1559, edition of the poem. Lyndsay's care to distance himself from Beaton's story had enabled him to avoid open conflict with an increasingly repressive church hierarchy, but the *Tragedie*'s printer, John Scot, perhaps had less to aid him. Within a few months of the poem's composition and its rapid publication,[4] a sharply worded entry appears in the Privy Council Register, recording the failure of the constable and provost of Dundee to find and arrest 'Johne Scott, prentar', in order that he be 'punesit for his demerits and faltis'.[5] On the basis of this entry, together with an equally unspecific claim by the historian, Robert Lindsay of Pitscottie, that, at a somewhat later time, 'Schir Dawid Lyndsayis buike' was condemned and burned by a Dominican Provincial Council,[6] it has been argued that Scot's trouble with the authorities was caused by his printing of Lyndsay's *Tragedie*.[7] Whether or not the evidence cited is sufficient to make this a plausible link, no copy of the first edition of the *Tragedie* is extant. Its reconstruction now depends upon two much later texts, which, on good bibliographical evidence, are likely to have been based on it.[8] The earlier of these later texts, probably printed on the Continent in 1558, is occasionally marred by the compositor's unfamiliarity with Scots.[9] The second, an overall more reliable text of 1559, is the work of the undaunted John Scot, printer, who appended it with other poems by Lyndsay to unsold copies of the same poet's *Ane Dialog betuix Experience and ane Courteour*.

Given the lateness of both texts of the *Tragedie*, the poem's survival in another earlier, if adapted, edition is, potentially, highly important. This text was brought out in London, under the imprint of John Day and William Seres, in about 1548, thus very soon after Lyndsay wrote the poem, and ten years before the appearance of either of the previously mentioned surviving texts.[10] Modified though the London text is, as a very early witness it is notable on several counts. First, it is rare among extant Lyndsay editions, most of which post-date the poet's death. Authorial sanction of its London appearance, if not also its adapted form, is a possibility. Secondly, for this particular poem, with its late Scottish exemplar, the London text helps to solve small orthographic puzzles. When, for instance, a line in Scot's 1559 edition of the *Tragedie* ends, 'my faitell hure' (230), the first impression is that this is a reference to Beaton's long-time mistress, Marion Ogilvy.[11] But the words of the London text, 'my fatal houre', reinstate the *De Casibus* stress on the workings of Fortune, and point to the 1559 *hure* as a variant spelling.[12] Thirdly, the variety of adaptations from the Scottish poem that are found in the London text of the *Tragedie* help to illuminate aspects of Lyndsay's poetic method, and reveal something of the nature and extent of his reformist ideology; similarly, they also highlight the southern editor's priorities. These London adaptations thus recapture some of the nuances of cultural, religious, and political differences between Scotland and England during the minorities of Mary and Edward.

Immediately noticeable are the London *Tragedie*'s Anglicizations. These offer evidence of the extent of English understanding of Scots in the late 1540s, as perceived, it should be added, by the printers or their compositors, or by the probable editor of the poem, the Englishman Robert Burrant (of whom more later). This replacement of native Scots forms by the equivalent southern usages appears even in the *Tragedie*'s long title, which begins, in the Scots 1559 edition: '*Heir follouis the Tragedie of the Umquhyle Maist Reuerend Father Dauid*'. The London text substitutes *late* for *Umquhyle*; *Moste* for the Scottish text's *Maist* and the Continental text's faulty *Maister*. In the title's continuing description of Beaton's honours, the English word *whole* replaces *haill*: '*And of the whole realme of Scotland primate*'. As can been seen already, most of these are simple orthographic changes. Within the poem-text are many more: *authoritie* replaces *auctoritie* (64), *dolfully* is substituted for *dulefulliye* (240);[13] words ending in *-ed* are substituted for those ending in *-it*, such as *deposed* and *deposit* (7); *wh* replaces Scots *quh*; and *i* is often preferred to *y* (as in *miracle* and *myrakle*, 262). The periphrastic Scottish use of *do* in the fictional Beaton's instruction: 'And failȝe nocht … to put in wryte / My Tragedie, as I haue done indyte' (433–4), becomes in the English text 'nowe endyte'. Similarly, the several instances of the Scots verb *gar* (to 'cause', 'make'), are replaced by some more and less ill-fitting substitutes. For the line 'I purposit to gar thame lose thare lyfe' (212), for example, the London text has: 'to tyd them out of thys lyfe'.[14] Less happily, Scots *syne* ('then'), in the expression 'Sen syne', gives way to the English 'Sence y[a]t time' (222). These adaptations from Scots are what might be expected of an editor alert to a new audience with differing language requirements.[15]

Others, by contrast, rephrase and translate words and whole lines, sometimes to the disadvantage of the metre, in a greater effort to accommodate southern listeners and readers. Whoever made these changes to Lyndsay's text did not think of himself as one 'dull forhed and vayn' who should not dare to 'contyrfate sa precyus wordys', as Douglas, for instance, saw his relationship to Virgil's.[16] The English editor's ambitiously onomatopoeic word *blentheryng* (C5ᵛ), for example, though probably related to the verbs *blend* and *blent*, 'to mingle', is unknown to the *Middle English Dictionary*.[17] Nevertheless, what perhaps is a coinage replaces the Scots *bulrand* (and in the process creates a hypermetric line, 338), when the wraith of Beaton, encouraging others towards reform, describes how he 'laye *blentheryng*, bathed in my blude (italics added). Another instance of noticeable change is the substitution for the Scots word *cowhubeis* (381). In Lyndsay's poem this word appears in an alliterative list of prelatial deceivers and charlatans that is reminiscent of those of Dunbar.[18] Early editors of *DOST* glossed *cowhubeis* tentatively as 'a person of weak or trifling character'. More recently the word has been glossed, again as supposition only, as 'booby'.[19] Interestingly, the English editor of the poem replaced the word with a compound, *lacke lattins* (C6ᵛ), possibly a wordplay for bogus churchmen (without Latin learning).[20] Whether this was a true 'translation' (thus a possible source of assistance in resolving the previously obscure sense of *cowhubeis*) is impossible to say, for the *Tragedie* contains other instances in which the Scots undoubtedly is misunderstood. In these, furthermore, it is difficult to decide whether the apparent misunderstanding is unintended or wilful. The English *doughtie* (C6ᵛ), for instance, is no substitute for the Scots *doytit* (384), the word for a foolish or a stupid person.[21] Yet the alliterative emphasis of the Scottish text's *doytit doctoris* is retained in *doughtie doctors*, and leads to a suspicion that the London editor could be referring deliberately to the strength of the opposition to reform among learned clerics. Similarly, in the south, the Scots word *seir*, with the sense 'various', as in the fictional Beaton's claim that 'in France [he] maid seir honest uoyagis' (85), was a puzzle – or else added the wrong emphasis to Beaton's narrative. The London editor changed it quite deftly to: 'In France, sir, I made honest voyages' (C1ᵛ).

Comparison of the early London text with the later Continental and Scottish texts would yield much more material of a similar kind, but there are many other interesting facets of difference. In the London text, for instance, the attitude towards the arts of poetry has subtly altered. The London editor removes some of Lyndsay's alliteratively made thematic links, for example, such as that created by *dant, deuysit* and *diuinitie* (136–7): 'My prydefull hart to dant as I suppose / Deuysit by the heych diuinitie'. The Scots *dant*, with the sense 'subdue', 'vanquish', is replaced by the stronger *breake* (C2ᵛ). (The God who might seek to break the proud heart of an unrepentant sinner, it is worth noting, differs from the God of the Scottish text, who would seek to reclaim the same heart by subduing and humbling it.) More revealing is the London text's replacement of the poetic work *freik*, chosen in the Scottish text for its alliterative affinities: 'Than euery freik thay tuke of me such feir' (218). The word is common in both English and Scottish poetry, yet the London editor recognizes the distancing effect its use produces – related, as the word is, to the old diction of the romances. He replaces it with: 'Then euery man toke of me suche feare' (C3ᵛ), the substitution of the prosaic synonym, *man*, suggesting that what is being said is of the present day, open and honest. These are not the only instances in which the London editor changes Lyndsay's more elaborate and polished style.[22] A reason for this is later suggested in the account of Wishart's examination that follows the poem in the London text. There, Robert Burrant notes that Wishart's inquisitors had cited, as a mark against him, his beguiling use of rhetorical 'colours' (D8ʳ).[23]

If this is an inter-textual link, it strengthens the case for Burrant as the adaptor of Lyndsay's poem, but before further study of his possible role, another group of changes deserves attention. In these alterations there is a distinctive political or reformist element. One example of a politically motivated change is found towards the end of the fictional Beaton's narrative, where he laments that if Scotland had kept its contracts with England, 'on ather syde all wrangis had bene redrest' (201). Lyndsay's moderating *ather*, with the sense 'either', 'each', is notably different from the London text's 'on *thother* syde, al wronges had ben redrest' [C3ᵛ, italics added], in which Beaton (and Scotland) become the sole guilty parties. By far the majority of the changes of stance in the London text, however, are associated with the sharpening of the reformist edge of the poem. These are not simple Anglicizing revisions of *kirk* to *churche* (382, C6ᵛ), but deliberate re-alignments. For instance, in the Scottish text the fictional Beaton berates his fellow prelates for their inability to carry out their office, 'as cannone law and scripture yow commandis' (298). The London editor, on the contrary, replaces *cannone law* (or ecclesiastical law) with *commune law* (C5ʳ), in the change revealing an opposition to the Catholic church *per se* that is in keeping with the current outlook of Edward VI's Protestant government under Somerset.²⁴ Similarly, the London editor shifts the sense towards a more reformist agenda in the replacement of Lyndsay's detailed description of the red garments worn by Beaton's wraith, 'Of vellot and saityng crammosie' (20–1), with the collocation, 'Wyth fyne veluet and satten richely' (B6ᵛ). This change seems at first to derive from the need to translate the chiefly Scottish word for 'crimson', *crammosie*. A more attentive reading supports the argument that the change deliberately introduces an emphasis on outward excess, as opposed to the original use of symbolic colour and cloth-type to identify the speaker as a cardinal. A more conspicuous example is the London text's substitution of *idolatrie* (C5ʳ) for the Scottish text's *hasarttrie* (306). The term *hasarttrie*, a synonym for gambling, had been in English use since the thirteenth century; in changing it to *idolatrie*, on which topic debate was just as keen during the earlier phases of reform as it was in the time of Knox and others following, the editor of the London text was consciously honing the poem for reformist purposes.²⁵

Another prominent reformist change to Lyndsay's text is the London editor's addition of an emotive quotation immediately after the *Tragedie*'s long title (B6ʳ). This epigraph reads: 'The wordes of Dauid Beaton the Cardinall aforesaied at his death. Alas alas, slaye me not, I am a Priest'. (These words of course are well known from their quotation by the reformer, John Foxe, but the London's text's use of them preceded his *Actes and Monuments* by about fifteen years.)²⁶ On the surface, the quoted appeal to the slayers seems logical in its supposed allusion to a long-prevailing attitude, expressed, for example, in the lines from Hay's translation, the *Buke of the Ordre of Knychthede*: 'Alssua be vertu of fayth and gude custumes / knychtis defendis the clerkis and kirk men fra wikkit tyrane men'.²⁷ Yet the implication behind these words, that such a holy office should protect the bearer, is mocked in the contexts in which the London editor places it – its immediate location near the poem-title, and its (and the poem's) position in the make-up of the London volume as a whole. Further attention to these aspects is revealing.

The London book printed by Day and Seres is in three parts, the adapted *Tragedie* being set between two substantial prose works in much larger type. The reduced blackletter font size used for the poem text seemingly greatly diminishes its importance, yet the information on the book's title-page shows that, thematically as well as structurally, the poem was central to the volume:

> *The Tragical death of Dauid Beaton Bishoppe of sainct Andrewes in Scotland: Wherunto is ioyned the martyrdom of maister George Wyseharte gentleman, for whose sake the aforesayed bishoppe was not longe after slayne. Wherein thou maist learne what a burnynge charitie they shewed, not only towardes him: but vnto al suche as come to their handes for the blessed Gospels sake.*[28]

These lines are not the title of either the poem or the prose pieces, but are closer to a summary of total contents, with a moralizing annotation appended. The title-page thus connects the book's three parts: the introductory 'sermon' on biblical precedents by Robert Burrant; the *Tragedie* in adapted form (and, significantly, without mention of Lyndsay's name as author); and Burrant's report of the examination of George Wishart.[29] It also links Beaton's fate explicitly to the trial and burning of Wishart, and draws attention to the reformer's name by Bunyanesque wordplay: 'Wishart' becomes *Wyseharte*, and is spelled so, with unusual consistency for those days of orthographic variation, throughout the volume.[30] This is at odds with the Scottish text of the poem, which makes no direct link between the two men. It could be argued that Lyndsay makes a veiled allusion to Wishart's burning in the fictional Beaton's lament that he was 'rycht dulefulliye doung down amang the asse' (240), but it is more likely that this refers to lines from scripture used in the Ash Wednesday service, and to their association with penitence.[31] An allusion to Wishart is also possible in the fictional Beaton's admission that he intended that those with a reformist interest in the Old and New Testaments, especially those in Fife, should be 'distroyit' (213), 'sum with the fyre, sum with the sword and knyfe' (214). Locality gives away a great deal; nonetheless these are generalizing words – no names are mentioned. (Indeed, in his poet-persona Lyndsay carefully does not even name Beaton, leaving the fictional Beaton to identify himself as 'Dauid, that cairfull cardinall' (38), and, at the beginning of 'his' narrative, as 'Dauid Betone' (43).)[32] The London title-page's appended annotation, on the other hand, emphasizes the link between Beaton and Wishart, and draws attention to its nature: Beaton's 'burnynge charitie' to Wishart and others, it is made plain, is not zealous benevolence, but cruel persecution for true faith.

It seems likely that these lines summarizing and annotating the total contents were written by Robert Burrant, author-reporter of the two prose works within the same covers.[33] Burrant's only other publication, a book of translations from Latin titled *Preceptes of Cato with annotations of D. Erasmus of Roterodame*, which appeared in 1545 and in several later editions, has in its layout points of general similarity with the volume containing the *Tragedie*.[34] The *Preceptes* also includes two other texts besides the title work. The first two are loosely connected by a letter from Burrant's friend, William Wright, requesting that Burrant add 'the sage saiyinges of the seuen wisemen' (L2^r) to those of Cato. For good aphoristic measure, Burrant added to those pieces 'The saiynges of Publius', these again accompanied by the translated annotations of Erasmus.[35]

The format of each of these texts of annotated precepts is similar: Burrant's translation of a saying, whether it is by Cato, a wiseman, or Publius, is printed in flowing italic, and is followed by an annotation in close blackletter. For the first text, Cato and his annotator, Erasmus, are the only names on the page; in the next section ('The saiynges of the … wisemen', L7^v) the names of Periander, Pittacus, Cleobulus, Thales, and others replace that of Cato, and Burrant's own annotations take the position previously allocated to those of Erasmus. In the third ('The saiynges of Publius') it would seem that Burrant could not resist again adding his own remarks, although this time he had access once more to those of Erasmus. Buried within the blackletter annotations attributed to Erasmus, there appears from time to time the word 'Burrant'. It is usually followed by more words than those of the translated Erasmus himself.

Burrant's general motivation for translating and adapting these pre-Christian texts is made clear in his epistle to the reader, where he includes the *Preceptes* among works of 'Godlie knowelege' (A5^v), useful to 'man[,] woman and child' (A5^r).[36] More specifically, Burrant's method is bound to his reformist interests. This may be illustrated by his reworking of Publius 154. The precept reads: 'The greuoust rule and kingdome / Is that whiche is confirmed by custome' (S3^v). The Englished Erasmus adds: 'Custome dooeth plainelie obteine a certaine tyrannie in the worlde, in so moche that the moste foolishe thinges if thei haue ones growen into a custome, thei cannot be plucked backe or called in again' (S4^r). The careful Erasmian generalities are particularized with openly reformist purpose in Burrant's own following annotation:

> As, how great a dooe is it to withdrawe the vsurped power of the Bishop of Rome and to redresse his naughtie lawes and tradicionis, whiche were onelie by custome confirmed. And the onely refuge and defence of his fautours is custome, saiyng. So haue our fathers vsed. So thei beleued. And (excepte the more mercie of God) so thei are damned.

Such reformist interpretations and extrapolations are evident also in the London volume at the centre of the present study. Its distinctive revisions to the text of the *Tragedie* have been noted already, but they also occur in Burrant's opening prose address to the reader (a work of twenty-four pages introducing the fifteen-page poem). The address re-interprets Old Testament biblical story in the light of Burrant's own views and those revealed in the following poem in its adapted form. Burrant casts Adam, for instance, as an 'obliuious minister', Eve as the receiver of a corrupt doctrine (A2^v), and Cain as his brother Abel's tyrannous persecutor and murderer (A3^v), whom God punished with a 'lyke death'. The story of Cain and Abel thus is able to hint at a parallel with that of Beaton and Wishart. It is not made explicit, however, until after the listing of further examples of tyranny and idolatry through the ages (A3^v–B4^r) – the latter subject, as has been mentioned earlier, deliberately introduced into the London text of the poem. Not until the end of the list of tyrants and idolators is Beaton presented as the last and most 'notable', at one with the 'bishop of Rome, Christes onelie deceyuer in earth' (B3^r). In this highly charged context, Burrant refers his reader for more detail of Beaton's 'abhominable factes and tragicall dedes' to Lyndsay's poem, which he calls 'thys litle treatise folowing' (B4^r). There, states Burrant, 'they be manifestly declared' (B4^r).

Nevertheless, Burrant is all too aware that Lyndsay's poem, even in its adapted form, does not mention Wishart's name or particular fate; in his continuing commentary, Burrant acknowledges that not all may know 'the cause of his [Beaton's] death' (B4^r). Burrant now expands the information supplied on his title-page. He explains that it was Beaton who 'moste cruelly put to death ... the man of god maister George Wysehart ... for that he truly and sincerely preached the word of god to the simple and ignoraunt people' (B4^r). He follows this with exhortations to the administrators of 'commune weales' and to 'Elders' in the 'congregation' to 'auoyed lyke daungers' (B4^v–B5^r), and ends with a brief prayer (B5^v). Thus, when the reader's eye moves to the adjacent page containing both the full title of Lyndsay's poem – this time with full note of its author's name and style[37] – and the previously discussed epigraph, 'Alas alas, slaye me not, I am a Priest', the latter can be interpreted only as a condemnation. The reminder of holy office is, by its location, recast as an admission of guilt.

Following the London text of the *Tragedie* is the prose piece entitled:

> *The accusation of maister George Wysehart gentleman, who suffered martyrdome for the faith of Christ Jesu, at S. Andrewes in Scotland the first day of March. In the yere of our Lorde, MD.xlvi. with the articles, which he was accused of, and his suete answeres to the same, wherunto are ioyned his godly orations and praiers.*

Once more, this is not without the annotation and reformist colouring of Burrant, who presents the Church hierarchy as 'the bloudie enemies of Christes fayeth' (C7ᵛ) – 'rauenyng wolues' (E7ʳ) hunting Wishart in the role of sacrificial lamb (D1ʳ). It is Burrant who narrates in full, and interprets for the reformist cause, the various events of Wishart's examination. He quotes the articled debate between Wishart and his accusers; describes Wishart's manner (as at D3ʳ: 'Maister George hearynge thys, sate downe vpon his knees in the pulpet'); reports the details of Wishart's last hours – his confession, forecast of the early deaths of his accusers, and prayerful public address. He turns the reformer into a type of Christ by quoting, as Wishart's assertion: 'For thys cause I was sente' (F4ᵛ). Wishart's reported exhortation 'not to feare them that slaye the bodye, and afterwarde haue no power to slaye the soule' (F4ᵛ), becomes a direct reprimand and answer to Beaton's earlier epigraph, 'slaye me not ...'. Burrant's shaping of the Wishart material in this third section of the London volume thus creates a ready contribution for a book of modern-day martyrs, as indeed John Foxe recognized, though he did not acknowledge his use of Burrant's report.

In the ordering of the texts forming the volume as a whole, moreover, the juxtaposition of the *Accusation* with the foregoing *Tragedie* serves a related and balancing purpose, for it transforms Lyndsay's poem into a potential contribution to an 'anti-martyrology'. The argument that this was the intention is strengthened by the greatly reduced size of the font in which the adapted *Tragedie* was set, relative to that of the two prose works on either side of it. By such a differencing bibliographic detail, the words purportedly spoken by (from the reformist viewpoint) a corrupt and tyrannous Catholic persecutor cannot equal the impact of the Protestant utterances of either the editor, Robert Burrant, or the Christ-like persecuted innocent, George Wishart.[38]

The London volume's overt focus on the role of the *Tragedie* as 'anti-martyr' *exemplum* is new. By comparison, Lyndsay, in adapting the *De Casibus* model, had been astutely moderate. He had introduced a similar idea simply by allowing the fictional Beaton to refer to his murder as 'my passioun' (26), for these words had quietly underlined the impossibility, even blasphemy, of any association between the cardinal's end and the events of the passion of Christ – or of a saint or martyr. The comparison of Lyndsay's text with the adapted English edition is therefore helpful in revealing plainly a difference in the degree to which the poet was prepared to commit himself directly to Protestant ideology: it was at this time, after all, that Lyndsay (as Lyon King of Arms) had been sent with some formality by the government to negotiate with those who, having assassinated the Cardinal, now held St Andrews castle.[39]

Yet the present examination of the changes made to Lyndsay's text of the *Tragedie* also highlights the poet's attention to stylistic matters – for instance, to a careful word choice, deceptively open but verbally ironic, as in the case of 'passioun' just noted, to imply (from Beaton's mouth) its opposite; or to the ways in which Lyndsay has used alliteration not simply because this was a literary enrichment still popular in Scotland, but because it could further thematic strands within the poem. These small observations suggest in turn that Lyndsay could not have been involved in, or have condoned, the London editor's changes to the text of the *Tragedie*. (Whether Lyndsay knew of and permitted the poem's passage across the Border, however, is not so evident.) All the same, Lyndsay's adaptation of his Boccaccian model had opened the way for further experimentation.[40] The London editor and his printers recognized and utilized the opportunity, adapting a work in which the poetic and politicizing elements were in fine balance into an open promotion of the English reformist cause.

Notes

[1]   See M. H. B Sanderson, *Cardinal of Scotland: David Beaton c. 1494–1546* (Edinburgh, 1986). For the most recent edition of the poem, see *Sir David Lyndsay: Selected Poems*, ed. by J. Hadley Williams, ASLS (Glasgow, 2000), pp. 112–27.

[2]   Nov. 1537: Archives Nationales, Reg., Chancellerie de Paris, JJ 250, No. 190, fol. 53^v. See also E. Bonner, 'French Naturalization of the Scots in the Fifteenth and Sixteenth Centuries', *Historical Journal* 40.4 (1997), 1085–1115.

[3]   See further A. S. G. Edwards, 'The Influence of Lydgate's *Fall of Princes c. 1440–1559: A Survey*', *Mediaeval Studies* 39 (1977), 424–39.

[4]   Beaton was assassinated 2 May 1546. The seven-month delay before he was buried is noted in the poem (*Tragedie*, 267), suggesting a composition date after December 1546, but before the London edition appeared, *c.* 1548, which year was the earliest known of the Day and Seres partnership. See further D. Hamer, 'The Bibliography of Sir David Lindsay (1490–1555)', *The Library* 10.1 (1929), 10–42 (pp. 11–12).

[5]   *RPC* I, pp. 69–70.

[6]   *The Historie and Cronicles of Scotland … by Robert Lindesay of Pitscottie*, ed. by Æ. J. G. Mackay, 2 vols, STS (Edinburgh and London, 1899), II, p. 141.

[7]   See Hamer, 'The Bibliography', pp. 17–20.

[8]   Hamer, 'The Bibliography', pp. 11–12, 20.

[9]   Both the quarto and octavo 1558 Continental editions have the imprint: 'And Imprentit at the command, and expenses of Maister Samuel [octavo: 'Sammuel'] Iascuy, In Paris', but the octavo edition contains the main part of the device of Jean Petit of Rouen, on whom see P. Rénouard, *Répertoire des Imprimeurs Parisiens … depuis l'introduction de L'Imprimerie à Paris (1470) jusqu'à la fin du seizième siècle* (Paris, 1965), p. 341.

[10] *STC* 15683. The copy held by the British Library (288.a.49) was consulted. This copy is not noted by the *STC*, but Douglas Hamer, the STS editor of Lyndsay, also knew of it. (*STC* notes the existence of other copies at London, Lambeth Palace Library (not seen) and Oxford, Bodleian Library (Wood 736 [5]), a cropped volume lacking the title page.) For the possible means of its passage across the Border, see M. H. Merriman, 'The Assured Scots: Scottish Collaborators with England during the Rough Wooing', *SHR* 46 (1968), 10–34 (pp. 21–5, 28–34); J. Durkan, 'Scottish

Reformers: the less than Golden Legend', *IR* 45 (1994), 1–28 (pp. 3–4); J. Kirk, 'The "Privy Kirks" and their Antecedents: the Hidden Face of Scottish Protestantism', in *Voluntary Religion*, ed. by E. J. Shiels and D. Wood (Oxford, 1986), pp. 155–70 (p. 166); S. Alford, 'Knox, Cecil and The British Dimension of the Scottish Reformation' in *John Knox and the British Reformations* ed. by R. A. Mason (Aldershot, 1998), pp. 201–19 (p. 204); C. Edington, 'John Knox and the Castilians: A Crucible of Reforming Opinion?', in ibid, pp. 29–50; T. S. Freeman, ' "The reik of Maister Patrik Hammyltoun": John Foxe, John Winram and the Martyrs of the Scottish Reformation', *Sixteenth Century Journal* 27.1 (1996), 43–60; and E. Bonner, 'The French Reactions to the Rough Wooings of Mary, Queen of Scots', *Journal of the Sydney Society for Scottish History* 6 (1998), 9–161 (p. 64, note 312). Another contemporary work smuggled in the Protestant cause was Anne Askew's *Examinations*, ed. John Bale, 2 vols (Marburg [Wesel], Nov 1546 and 16 Jan 1547), [*STC* 848 and 850]; see II, B3[r].

[11] M. H. B. Sanderson, *Mary Stewart's People* (Edinburgh, 1987), pp. 3–21.

[12] This is confirmed in the 1558 texts (octavo and quarto) thought to be printed by Jean Petit of Rouen. See *DOST*, *hour, howr*, n.

[13] Scot's text has, in error, *auctorie*.

[14] Cf. also 121 and 182, examples where *gart* becomes *gate*.

[15] Scottish poets had also used them from an early period, for the stylistic and metrical flexibility they permitted; see A. J. Aitken, 'The Language of Older Scots Poetry', in *Scotland and the Lowland Tongue*, ed. J. D. McClure (Aberdeen, 1983), pp. 18–49 (p. 27).

[16] *Virgil's 'Aeneid' Translated into Scottish Verse by Gavin Douglas*, ed. by D. F. C. Coldwell, 4 vols, STS (Edinburgh and London, 1957–64), II (1957), Prol. I, 19, 23.

[17] See *OED*, *blend* v. and *blent*, v; *MED* sense 4 (c): 'blent in blisse' (immersed or bathed in bliss).

[18] The word itself may have been derived from Dunbar's 'In secreit place this hynder nicht'. See *The Poems of William Dunbar* ed. by P. Bawcutt, 2 vols, ASLS (Glasgow, 1998), I, no. 25, pp. 106–08, line 58.

[19] See Bawcutt (ed.), *The Poems of William Dunbar* II, p. 535.

[20] *MED* does not include this compound. See *OED*, *latten* (where the many variant spellings include *lattin*) for an alternative sense.

[21] See *OED*, *dote* v[2], sense 1.

[22] Cf. the similar changes at 328, from the Scottish text's *wes oblyste* (328) – linked to the idea of a bishop's 'conuenent' (327) to London's less thematically perceptive *dyd forget* (C5[v]).

[23] Thomas Elyot had also taken up the issue of the moral and political dimensions of language styles and diction levels in 1533, in his examination of good and defective royal counsellors, *Pasquil the Playne* (*STC* 7672): see *Four Political Treatises … by Sir Thomas Elyot*, intro. L. Gottesman (Gainsville, FL, 1967), pp. 41–100.

[24] See J. N. King, *English Reformation Literature: The Tudor Origins of the Protestant Tradition* (Princeton, NJ, 1982), pp. 26–8, and, on the nature of Protestantism in mid-Tudor England, T. Betteridge, *Tudor Histories of the English Reformations, 1530–83* (Aldershot, 1999), pp. 17–28.

[25] See C. Bradshaw, 'David or Josiah? Old Testament Kings as Exemplars in Edwardian Religious Polemic', in *Protestant History and Identity in Sixteenth-Century Europe*, ed. by Bruce Gordon, 2 vols (Aldershot, 1996), II, pp. 75–90 (pp. 82–90), R. Mason, 'Knox on Rebellion', in *Kingship and the Commonweal*, ed. by R. Mason (East Linton, 1998), pp. 139–64 (pp. 143–5), and R. Kyle, 'John Knox and the Purification of Religion: The Intellectual Aspects of his Crusade against Idolatry', *Archiv für Reformationsgeschichte* 77 (1986), 265–80.

[26] Foxe used the London text as his source for the report of Wishart's examination,

which first appeared in the earliest of the English editions (*STC* 11222) of the *Actes and Monuments* (London, 1563), pp. 648–54; see D. Newcombe, 'Appendix: A Finding List of Extant Sixteenth- and Seventeenth-Century Editions of John Foxe's *Acts and Monuments*', in *John Foxe and the English Reformation*, ed. by David Loades (Aldershot, 1997), pp. 12–35 (pp. 12–14). Cf. *Acts and Monuments* V, ed. by S. R. Cattley (London, 1838) pp. 632–6 (but on this and following editions by Cattley and Pratt, see J. N. King, 'Fact and Fiction in Foxe's *Book of Martyrs*', in *John Foxe*, ed. Loades, pp. 306–29, and Thomas Freeman, 'Texts, Lies and Microfilms: Reading and Misreading Foxe's *Book of Martyrs*', *Sixteenth-Century Journal* 30.1 (1999), 23–46.)

27   *The Prose Works of Gilbert Haye*, III, ed. by J. A. Glenn, STS (Aberdeen, 1993), ch. vii, fol. 98^v–9^r, 33–4.

28   The contents summary appears alone on the title page. The imprint (without date) appears only as a colophon (F6^r): 'Imprinted at London, by Iohn Day, and William Seres, dwellynge in Sepulchres parish, at the signe of the Resurrection, a little aboue Holbourne conduite.'

29   In no sense could the volume be called a gathering of works of a merely semi-related or disparate character; contrast Oxford, Bodleian Library Wood 736, wherein the poem is bound with several other works, including *A Paradoxe, proving by reason and example, that Baldnesse is much better than bushie haire* ..., *Fancies Ague-fittes, Beauties Nettle-bed* ..., *A breif and plesant discours of the duties in Mariage* and *[A faythfull and true prognostication upon the yere 1548 ... translated newlye out of hye Almayne into Englysh by Myles Coverdale]*.

30   Contrast 'Wysshert' and 'Wishert', *Hamilton Papers*, II, ed. by J. Bain (Edinburgh, 1892), pp. 218, 223, and 'Wischart' and 'wischeart', Durkan, 'Scottish Reformers', pp. 2–3 (quoting, with permission, NLS Acc. 9769, F / 319 / 1 and 2).

31   See Genesis 3.19; cf. Dunbar, '*Memento, homo, quod cinis es*', in Bawcutt (ed.), I, no. 32, pp. 120–1.

32   Neither the 1558 Continental title nor the 1559 Scots title mentions the surname 'Beaton', but both promote his identification, especially the former, which is unshortened, by the descriptive list of Beaton's titles and honours.

33   Beyond the sparse note in *DNB*, very little information on Burrant is available. In his opening address to the reader, Burrant refers to the people of Scotland as 'they' (B3^v), but he implies that he has close contacts there among those who were Beaton's 'familiars' (B3^v–B4^r). The book's printers, John Day and William Seres, were consistent supporters of the reformist cause, Day in particular later well known as the publisher of John Foxe's *Acts and Monuments*, but neither are known to have been authors as well; see C.F. Oastler, *John Day: The Elizabethan Printer* (Oxford, 1975); and B. P. Davis, 'John Day' and 'William Seres,' *Dictionary of Literary Biography*, vol 170: *The British Literary Book Trade 1475–1700*, ed. by J. K. Bracken and J. Silver (Detroit, MI, 1996), pp. 78–93 and 231–8.

34   No copy of this edition, printed by Richard Grafton, is known to exist; the 1553 edition (*STC* 4854) is quoted.

35   Erasmus's Latin edition of Cato was edited by Richard Taverner for grammar school use in 1540: *Catonis disticha moralia ex castigatione D Erasmi cum annotationibus R Taverneri anglico idiomate conscriptis vsum Anglicæ iuuentutis* (*STC* 4843). Nicolas Udall translated Erasmus's *Apophthegmata* (1514) [proverbs taken from classical authors] as *Apophthegmes, that is to saie, prompte, quicke, wittie saiynges. First gathered by Erasmus*, 1542 (*STC* 10443). Richard Taverner translated a selection into Latin and English in his [*Apophthegmata.*] *Flores aliquot sententarium ex variis collecti scriptoribus*, 1540 (*STC* 10445).

36   See also King, *English Reformation Literature*, pp. 361–3.

[37] 'Sir Dauid Lyndsaye of the mounte knyghte. Alias Lione, kyng of armes'.

[38] Wishart's trial has been assessed in somewhat similar terms, as a 'personal duel' with Beaton: see J. Dawson, 'The Scottish Reformation and the Theatre of Martyrdom', in *Martyrs and Martyrologies*, ed. by D. Wood, Studies in Church History 30 (Oxford, 1993), pp. 259–70 (p. 267). Note also H. C. White, *Tudor Books of Saints and Martyrs* (Madison, WI, 1963), p. 157.

[39] *SP Henry VIII*, V, 581–2.

[40] Note, for example, George Cavendish's *Metrical Visions* (British Library, Egerton 2402), *c.* 1555–57; Robert Sempill's *The Bischoppis Lyfe and Testament*, of 1571, in *Satirical Poems of the Time of the Reformation*, ed. by J. Cranstoun, 2 vols, STS (Edinburgh and London, 1891–93), no. 28; and *The Mirror for Magistrates* ed. by L. B. Campbell (New York, 1938), 1555 (suppressed first edition) and 1559.

3

John Knox, *The First Blast*, and the Monstrous Regiment of Gender

C. MARIE HARKER

John Knox's 1558 *The First Blast of the Trumpet against the Monstrous Regiment of Women*, the notoriously misogynist tract concerning female monarchs in both England and Scotland, provides examples of the constructing and policing topoi of hegemonic gender. Intent on proving that female rulership in both countries was counter to God's law, hence 'monstriferous', in this first of three planned denunciations,[1] Knox calls upon standard patristic sources of misogynist discourse.[2] Further than simple anti-feminine peroration, *The First Blast* argues that excessive association with women – not simply civil acquiescence to female rule – threatened to feminize men, and that men thus de-gendered acquired specifically feminine traits. This discursive technology of containment was not simply occupied with the monstrous transgressions of divine order, represented by Mary Tudor and the Scottish Regent, Marie de Guise, but equally with the male participants in those reigns, the very aristocrats and courtiers whose situational allegiances had so often denied God's truth in response to the practical political exigencies of the moment. It is these men upon whom Knox also trains his prophetic eye.

By 1558, Knox had become the product of twelve years of alternating pastoral cure and political exile. The legacy of these years and situations on both sides of the Scottish border was a new Knox: Knox the prophet. His early association with George Wishart had involved him peripherally in a drama which left him a French prisoner. Wishart's incautious preaching led in 1546 to execution at the stake at the hands of Cardinal Beaton. This in turn led to Beaton's murder in the castle of St Andrews, where the Protestant rebels were soon besieged, with Knox serving as their preacher. Surrender in 1547 left Knox a galley prisoner, released in 1548 to enter the England of Edward VI.

Here Knox enjoyed a period of increasing personal influence, as his religious politics and reforming zeal led from positions at Berwick to Newcastle and thence to a royal chaplaincy in London in 1552. While Knox continued to oppose liturgical practices smacking of the papacy, this was a period of pastoral concern and conciliation in which concession and conformity marked his response to religious debate.[3] Edward VI's death in 1553 signalled an abrupt interruption of Knox's and England's reformist stability, as England, in the days following Wyatt's unsuccessful rebellion, endured the beginning of Mary Tudor's (rightfully) suspicious reign. Knox fled to reformist Geneva. Over the next five years, Knox was repeatedly called back to Edinburgh where he was encouraged by Scots nobles in his new role as proselytizer and controversialist, returned to Geneva, thence again in 1557, only to be held waiting at Dieppe for several months as his value to a politically resistant Scots nobility waned.

The political circumstances in Scotland and England at this point were strikingly similar: both nations were led by female monarchs, both were reduced to the European periphery as allies in the greater chess game of France and Spain.[4] Moreover, that such a reduction was occasioned by the marriages of two queens regnant to foreign princes was a particular topical concern.[5] However, in Scotland, an absent female monarch and an initially tolerant French Catholic queen dowager, Regent from 1554, in conjunction with a notoriously corrupt Catholic clergy and a 'factious' aristocracy, left a field if not open, then at least moderately encouraging, to reforming interests.[6] On the other hand, in England the brief halcyon period of religious tolerance and sanctuary for Continental Protestants was followed by Mary Tudor's increasingly heavy-handed reign and reintroduction of state Catholicism. In both countries, nevertheless, Knox had had increasing occasion to be disillusioned by Protestant nobility for whom religious reform was as often a matter of political expedience as spiritual conviction. These were the elements which, during Knox's stasis in Dieppe – attending the political whims, rather than religious convictions, of the Scottish noblemen who had called for him – led to *The First Blast*.

The text, structured as a formal sermon,[7] begins with an exordium in which Knox figures his oratory within a tradition of Old Testament prophecy, frames its proposition, continues with a refutation of key opposing arguments, and concludes with a thunderous peroration exhorting the godly to resist the monstrous rule of women.[8] Drawing upon the Bible for *exempla*, and citing both the historic evidence of 'natural law' and the testimony of patristic and classical authors in support of his argument from Scripture, Knox attributes to divine revelation his central contention:

> To promote a Woman to beare rule, superioritie, dominion, or empire above any Realme, Nation, or Citie is repugnant to Nature, contumelie to God, a thing most contrarious to his revealed will and approved ordinance, and finallie, it is the subversion of good Order, of all equitie and justice.[9]

This is a proposition which Knox reiterates several times throughout the text. From Aristotelian descriptions of weak female nature to St Paul's injunctions against feminine exercise of public authority, Knox draws upon the commonplaces of Western misogyny to give his tract *amplificatio*.

He goes on to a *refutatio* of three opposing arguments: that Biblical women of authority such as Deborah exerted no temporal and heritable dominion over men, but only such proxy authority as divine inspiration accorded them, and therefore do not serve as precedent; that the inheritance of property attested by Moses' dispensation for the daughters of Zelophehad applied only to goods as public office, while concomitant dominion over men was not heritable; and that the support of long-standing historic custom was no sanction but rather a habit of customary transgression. Knox concludes with a call to righteous rebellion, threatening that the supporters of monstrous female empire would soon suffer God's vengeance. Throughout, Knox's rhetoric is vehement, circling obsessively around stock expressions of feminine incapacity.

In the main, *The First Blast of the Trumpet against the Monstrous Regiment of Women* has been seen by Knox's scholarly supporters as an embarrassing aberration from the majority of his writings, polemic and historiographical, in which his doctrinal commitment to combat idolatry is subsumed beneath a railing and repetitive misogyny.[10] Several critical appraisals have voiced degrees of bafflement at the passionate and persistent anti-feminism of the work. Writing in 1980, Richard L. Greaves described *The First Blast* as a 'confused mixture of righteous indignation, personal bitterness, animosity and frustration'; similarly, citing Knox's otherwise fine control of rhetorical effects, R. D. S. Jack observed that *The First Blast* suffered from a 'passion of involvement [which] distort[ed] to some degree the governing neatness'.[11]

In contrast, considerable scholarly energy has been expended to recuperate Knox's reputation from the charges of unreasoning and highly conventional anti-feminism. For example, in one early effort to recuperate the reformer's modern reputation, Jasper Ridley suggests that *The First Blast* merely represents Knox's attempt to flatter a popular misogyny not his own.[12] Others have simply observed that Knox's misogyny was in no way unusual for the period.[13] This is certainly an oversimplified apologetic; there was considerably contemporary disagreement concerning, for example, the subject of female rulership, not least as attested by the long-running textual debates on the subject.[14]

Further, some scholars have revisited the work to uncover less a traditional voice of misogyny than a message consistent with Knox's reformist ideology. Robert M. Healey contends that Knox's commitment to uphold Scriptural stipulations for gender hierarchy never constituted anti-feminist attacks: the later criticisms of Mary Stuart, for example, criticized her idolatrous rulership, but 'never demeaned her as a woman'.[15] In particular, Knox's correspondence with several Protestant women has been enlisted to demonstrate his empathy toward women and willingness to accept a relationship of spiritual equality between the sexes. Knox enjoyed several spiritually intimate relationships with Protestant women, such as his mother-in-law, Elizabeth Bowes; these relationships have been preserved in collections of letters that seem to attest a lack of misogyny. Several critics have noted a striking 'lack of gendered rhetoric' in these texts and also Knox's refusal to dictate to his female interlocutors, rather leaving them to make spiritual decisions at the discretion of their own consciences.[16] Susan Felch, in particular, has persuasively argued for ideological coherence between the more private writings and the very public *First Blast* – namely a coherence in the castigation of idolatry and the valorizing of obedience to God: for example, Mary Tudor, an obedient wife but an idolater, comes under censure, while the Protestant Anne Lok, a (potentially) rebellious wife yet rejecting idolatry, enjoys Knox's approval.[17]

Pace such scholarly apologetics, I suggest that this work is pervasively about gender – not simply a misogynist appraisal of gynaecocracy, but a consideration of *both* halves of the relational binary, Woman: Man. I take as my starting position recent contentions that while *The First Blast* undeniably comprises a texture of misogynist discourse, it presents no simply programmatic misogyny. What is at issue in *The First Blast of the Trumpet against the Monstrous Regiment of Women* is not simply a frothing diatribe against womankind in general, but rather an expression in which the discourse of normative gender is employed to police both female *and male* transgressions, such transgressions standing as figurations of specific contemporary political circumstances. And these circumstances were not simply the theoretical consequences of female monarchy – queens regnant who were axiomatically incapable of effective rule by virtue of their sex. A further subject occupies Knox's attention, one little mentioned by scholarship: the implications of these reigns anent men, both those men subordinate to and abetting such reigns and those occupying the specific condition of husband in the context of female dominion, both regnal and domestic. Allusively, this text figures both the male supporters – the aristocrats of both realms whose acquiescence to female dominion constitutes a significant element in Knox's charges of the monstrous – as well as, paradoxically, the putative husbands of those queens regnant, whose transgressions are still worse for threatening an idolatrous gender normalcy in violation of Protestant regnal autonomy.

While occupying a small space of the text, Knox's treatment of masculinity draws equally upon stock topoi of violated natural order as does his more extensive discussion of feminine transgressions. The consistent *tekne* at work is that of gender; *The First Blast* is not simply concerned with monstrous female incapacity to rule but also with the monstrous results of gender inversion: ruling women are rendered manly, and men thus ruled womanly, even unto catamitism. And it is this dual violation of divinely given gendered order between the sexes that drives Knox's peroration and coordinates with the reformist polemics of his other works.

Knox's *First Blast of the Trumpet against the Monstrous Regiment of Women* employs the discursive logic of gender in order to decry both the monstrous violation of natural order which womanly authority over men represents, as well as the equally monstrous consequences of acceptance of that authority for men thus subordinated. By *gender*, I refer to the culturally constructed categorical positions or performances of *masculine* and *feminine*: that is, the outward signs by which essential difference – biological sex: *male* and *female* – is supposed to be unambiguously indicated, and, more specifically, the semiosis which correlates 'sex to cultural contents according to social values and hierarchies'.[18] Unlike biological sex, in whichever way that is construed within a specific cultural context, gender is not a stable sign of sex, but a discursive system unmoored from any essential difference. In particular, not only are female monarchs signs of violated gender norms in this text, but so, too, are the men so ruled. Such men are consequently 'feminized', that is, rendered 'women' discursively. This term *feminization* describes 'a dramatized state … wherein men occupy positions and / or perform functions already occupied and performed … by women or normatively assigned by orthodox discourses to Woman'.[19] *The First Blast* reconfigures the distinctive subservience of the courtier to a ruler in terms no longer of class but of gender. His long-standing frustrations with the inconstancy of the Protestant nobles on both sides of the border inform this treatment. Such men, sycophants to female monarchs, fractious and inconstant, were become 'women', feminized by their subordination to a woman.

However, the relationships between text and context are never simply a matter of the *real* and its discursive *reflection*: the varying ideological tensions of a given work's historical origin are manifested by that text in complex mechanisms of 'resolution', containments, and resistance. In this analysis, in addition to several recent treatments of gender as an interpretive category, I have drawn upon Fredric Jameson's discussion of the 'political unconscious' – the absent yet informing interaction of the material conditions of a text's production with the literary act, an occulted dialectic signalled by the ideological inconsistencies or *aporiai*, evinced by a text – as a means of describing the relationship between the immediate manifestation of the tract and its historical context.[20] The representation of the twin sites of the religious politics of the Scottish and English nobility and dynastic negotiations in both countries through the discourse of misogyny depends upon gender as what Jameson terms a 'master code' of rhetorical containment; it is at this point that the political unconscious of the work becomes detectable. My examination of the context – both literary-textual and material – foregrounds points at which the deployed master code enacts a violent disjunction with its own genealogy. The religious transgressions of a first estate willing to shift allegiance from one theology to another are displaced onto the discursive matrix of gender, their self-serving inconstancies contained by a gendered representation. Likewise, the historically-contingent anxiety both xenophobic and doctrinal anent the potential exogamy of a queen regnant is mystified in representation in the stock topoi of the *molestiae nuptiarum* tradition.[21] This attempt to resolve class and religious anxieties functions as an aesthetic anaesthesia – working through the silencing and displacing of the 'historical' circumstances of the Scottish and English Reformations onto the 'timeless' grid of gender.

In the main, *The First Blast* is undeniably concerned with female transgressions of normative gender. Knox's characterization of Woman is entirely in accord with the misogynist discursive tradition. Knox voices the openly oppositional character of the sex-gender ideologeme: Man is sighted, strong, and constant, therefore Woman must be, 'naturally', the negative relational term:

> It is repugneth [*sic*] to *nature*, that the blind shall be appointed to leade and conduct such as do see? That the weake, the sicke, and impotent persons shall norishe and kepe the hole and strong? … And such be al women compared unto man … *Nature*, I say, doth paynt then further to be weake, fraile, impacient, feble, and foolishe; and experience hath declared them to be unconstant, variable, cruell, and lacking the spirit of counsel and regiment.[22]

Knox repeatedly asserts that Woman is vain, ambitious, proud, and avaricious; she lacks virtue, temperance, modesty, equity, and justice. Throughout, Knox's criticism derives from the traditional anti-feminist topos of Woman's fallen nature, in which women are conventionally believed the particular subjects of the sin of pride.[23]

In particular, it is the vices of covetousness and pride which characterize Woman.[24] That this is a bodily pride is axiomatic: quoting Tertullian, Knox condemns the 'abominable and odiouse' feminine urge to self-adornment of the descendants of Eve, herself the 'gate of the devil'.[25] Woman's dress is not only the site and occasion of her vice, but the mark of her subordination. Quoting Ambrose, Knox includes a curious passage in which women's dress is the semiosis of her lack of authority: 'Woman oght not onlie to have simple arrayment, but all authoritie is to be denied unto her: for she must be in subjection to man … aswell in habit as in service'.[26] A woman reigning over men is guilty of a metaphoric transvestism, presuming monstrously to the symbolic 'habit of man': rulership.[27] Nor is this concern inconsistent with Knox's writings elsewhere: in Epistle 31 of 1556, 'To His Sisters in Edinburgh', Knox inveighs against the monstrosity of literal cross-gendered dressing:

> Wemen to be apparellit in the claithing of men, and men lykwyse to be
> apparellit in the garmentis of wemen, doith teache us, that the ordour
> whilk God hes set in nature aught not to be invertit ...; [should men]
> spoill thame selves, and put on the apparell of wemen, then ar they
> abominable befoir God.[28]

Further, Knox configures Woman's excessive embodiment – 'the imperfections
of women, of their naturall weaknes and inordinat appetites' – as particularly
associated with uncontrolled sexual desire.[29] This carnality acquires a peculiarly
echoic rhetorical quality, as Knox asserts repeatedly that Eve's originary transgression led to the subordination of her 'appetites, and will' to her husband,
her punishment the denial of dominion over her own 'appetites, [her] owne
will [and] desires', for her inability 'to moderate [her] affections', while
monstrous female empire enables women to enjoy 'their pleasure and
appetites'.[30] In such a claim, Knox was voicing a contemporary commonplace
concerning gender transgressions: the notion that the 'virago', or manly
woman, was also characterized by an active, hence *masculine*, sexuality. This
belief of some currency found expression even in treatments of otherwise
admirable, *vir*tuous figures of female rulership such as Semiramis, a legendary
queen whose martial and political success was accompanied by an equally
heroic lack of chastity.[31] As the salutary female virtue is chastity, the corre-
spondent monstrous vice must therefore be its absence.[32]

However, much as *The First Blast* is undeniably a text concerned with the
supposedly transhistoric and immutable nature of Woman – as well as the
transgressive potential of that nature – it is also and necessarily a text about
Man and his nature: the binary logic of gender demands a differentiating term.
As David Lyndsay warned in his *Ane Dialog betuix Experience and ane
Courteour* (1554), female dominion presents the dual condition, 'Wemen for
tyll be to manlye / [And] men for tyll be womanlye' (3235–6).[33] If Knox's is a
text about monstrous female dominion, it must also figure an equally
monstrous male lack of dominion: 'women in power transformed the signification of men: instead of signifying masculine authority, men become
effeminate'.[34]

In so doing, Knox drew upon a discourse of particular timeliness. That the
early modern period was one particularly marked by gender anxiety is well
known. Such factors as economic changes, courtly politics, and medical
theories inherited from the classical world contributed to 'a crisis in gender
relations'.[35] Significantly, the social hierarchy of court culture already ritualized
the kind of feminization of which Knox warns: the reality of the Renaissance
courtier, 'politically subordinated, economically dependent, and legally

incapacitated', problematized his masculinity as positional, expressed variably in what Constance Jordan has termed 'a dialectical tension with authority'.[36] This was, moreover, a particular site of concern at the time. For example, Castiglione's influential description of the courtier (1528) notes that the art of courtliness, involving skills of social ritual, conversation, and dress, rendered a man 'soft and womanish'.[37] The semiosis of elaborate aristocratic costume and behaviour presented Knox with the unstable conjunction of gender and class, particularly significant in retrospect against the backdrop of the controversies raging later in England anent masculine apparel and the transvestite dangers of the theatre.[38] However, Knox mystifies that feminizing masculine reality, displacing its *class*-determined effects onto the axis of pure gender in posited monstrous female regiment.

Of still greater urgency than the gender-blurring occasioned by apparel, both literal and metaphoric, for Knox the discursive ground for such a transformation is allusively that of sexual practice. The expression of male sexual desire is both a sign of powerful, hence masculine, women and carnal, hence feminine, men. Nor was Knox alone in this discursive balancing act; for example, Semiramis's legendary unchastity was not without inverted effect: her virility was said to have occasioned the figurative emasculation of her son, become idle and pleasure-loving in response to his mother's masculinity.[39]

Knox considers concomitant transgressing masculinity through the condition of uxoriousness, or the debilitating male heterosexual attachment to a female desire object, long a commonplace of the policing discourse of gender. Sources for contentions that such male heterosexual interest leads paradoxically to an emasculated weakness span centuries. St Augustine, for example, attributes to such inordinate and unmanly affection at least partial responsibility for the Fall: Adam had 'refused to be separated from his only companion', putting 'his wife's will above God's commandment' in the first instantiation of monstrous female rule.[40] Both Calvin and Luther, in attributing the Fall to both Adam and Eve's transgressions, took up such an interpretation of Genesis 1, the latter reformer observing that '[Adam] preferred his wife's love to God'.[41] That the attachment of uxorious men to their wives was carnal rather than spiritual seems axiomatic; as Jean Bodin observed, arguing against female rulership in his *Six Livres de la Republic* (1576; translated into English in 1606), women already exerted considerable, if oblique, influence on men who 'shew themselves most obedient unto women's lusts'.[42] Here again, it is the transgressive and monstrous masculinity of dominating women, expressed in part in their active sexual appetite, which serves to feminize men. Similarly, in his *Historia Rerum Scoticarum* (1582), George Buchanan mocked the courtiers supporting Mary Stuart as uxorious weaklings apt to bring their wives to royal council for advice.[43] Hence, the suggestion of male subservience was ready occasion for intimations of shameful marital subservience, the scandalous inversion of the gender hierarchy of the household. Uxorious public policy, then, stands as a sign of private, domestic emasculation.

In this tautological discourse, women are made virile by virtue of dominion over men who are as much made subservient through their effeminate carnal desire for women as feminized in their domination by women. Such uxoriousness had long been associated with a luxurious embodiment, a becoming more embodied through the enthusiastic exercise of heterosexual congress. And this sensual wilfulness then invites the paradoxical charge of effeminacy: as Woman is the bodily – to be bodily, to desire carnally, is to become womanly.

Knox draws upon this circular discourse in which men become womanly through uxorious subordination to women and women become manly in response to masculine effeminacy. Citing Aristotle, Knox suggests that rule by magistrates obeying the 'empire of their wyves' would lead, as surely as the direct rule of women, to 'injustice, confusion, and disorder'. He goes on to warn that the polity of the Lacedaemonians was poorly esteemed, for their rulers 'were too muche geven to please and obey their wyves'.[44] Woman's fallen nature thus becomes particularly dangerous, Knox asserts, when *men* abrogate their natural marital ascendance – their domestic subservice robbing them of public masculinity: 'Some have thoght that men subject to the counsel or empire of their wyves were unworthie of all public office'.[45] Such men were thus rendered unfit for public authority, that is, rendered *women*. Though men in appearance, the men of England and Scotland thus *became* women under the influence of a female monarch as surely as if they had accepted the dominance of their own wives: 'Albeit the outwarde form of men remained, yet shuld [men such as Aristotle] judge that thair hartes were changed frome the wisdome, understanding, and courage of men, to the foolishe fondnes and cowardise of women'.[46] The influence of women, then, leads men to *be* women. On the other hand, as Chrysostom complained, the 'effeminate maners of men, who were so farre degenerate to the weaknes of woman' might well encourage women to exercise public authority in their place: the effeminacy of men might lead women to manliness.[47] Nevertheless, such masculine absence did not justify the rule of the thus-monstrously stronger member. As Knox hastens to assert, dominion is only meet for men: if degenerate (that is, *womanly*), men must therefore reform themselves to governance.

Moreover, interpreting Chrysostom's use of the bodily metaphor (head:feet, as man:woman), Knox goes on to assert that the 'monstruous' ascendancy of women in any arena was occasion 'that man was becomen … brutish'.[48] To descend the gender hierarchy thus also unmakes man's humanity – in subordination to Woman, Man is become beast.[49] Alluding to classical legend, Knox suggests that the spectacle of a nation ruled by a female monarch must surely argue for the transformation of its men 'as poetes do feyn was made of the companyons of Ulisses': that is, allusively, just as the sexual blandishments of Circe enabled the literal metamorphosis of men into swine, so would acceptance of female rule surely rob contemporary men of their humanity.[50] Knox returns to this legend, in vitriolic lament: 'Englishe men ... must have my Sovereine Lady and Maistresse; and Scotland hath dronken also the enchantment and venom of Circes'.[51] Indeed, the nobility of England and Scotland were worse than the beasts: as Knox complains, 'no man ever sawe the lion make obedience, and stoupe before the lionesse'.[52] Such men as support the 'monstruous empire' of female monarchy Knox characterizes as wilfully 'carnal', that is em*bodi*ed, tied to the flesh.[53] In the binary logic of gender, in inverting the man:woman hierarchy of dominion, such men likewise descend the conjoint spirit:flesh pair, losing their very humanity in the descent occasioned by the feminizing effect of female governance.

The First Blast draws upon this idea that enthusiastic heterosexual interest, especially of an uxorious nature, renders men weak, dependent, and passive, in a word: *Women* – long a staple of misogynist discourse.[54] Further, Knox's sermonic perorations gain momentum as he considers the gendered degeneracy of the men of England and Scotland, less manly than beasts in their acceptance of the rule of the respective Marys and the concomitant 'overthrowe of true religion'.[55] Moreover, with these passages, Knox's comments on the effeminacy of uxorious men in misusing their positions of power shift from allusions to polluting, un*man*ning heterosexuality to the still more monstrous gender transgressions of homosexuality. Set within a context of polluting female agency, it is the male courtier who occupies the rhetorical position of Woman. Hence, it is the male who is suggestively accessible as the recipient of male desire. The consequent association invokes the gender-destabilizing category of the homosexual: 'But just and rightuouse, terrible and fearfull, are thy judgementes, O Lorde! For as some times thou diddest so punishe men for unthankfulnes, that man ashamed not to commit villanie with man'.[56] This is an allusion to the first chapter of Paul's letter to the Romans:

> Therefore God gave them up in lusts of their hearts to impurity, to the dishonouring of their bodies among themselves. ... For this reason, God gave them up to dishonourable passions. Their women exchanged natural relations for unnatural, and the men likewise gave up natural relations with women and were consumed with passion for one another, men committing shameless acts with men. ... They were filled with all manner of wickedness, evil covetousness, malice. Full of envy, ... deceit, ... they are gossips, slanderers, ... insolent, haughty, ... disobedient of parents, foolish, faithless.[57]

The terms with which the Pauline text castigates those wilfully fallen from worship of the True God are not simply those of monstrous sexuality entirely loosed from the strictures of fertile nature, but cover the very catalogue of vices with which the nature of Woman had patristically been characterized: covetousness, envy, pride, unruly speech and action. In a society of idolaters, gender relations are entirely unmoored from sex, and all the transgressors are guilty of the sins of Woman: in such a state of misrule, the distinctions of gender collapse – all are gendered female in vice. Knox's Pauline intertext, then, is the cathexis of notions of feminine civil monstrosity, consequent masculine effeminacy, and – allusively – gross sexual transgression. Paradoxically, in Knox's text, as we have seen with Castiglione and others, the excessively heterosexual man risks emasculation in contact with and pleasure from women, and it is this effeminacy which associatively suggests the position of the *mollis*, the feminized homosexual.[58] The traditional western association of feminized male behaviour with the category of the male homosexual is well attested.[59] The male homosexual was categorically conceived as woman-like, effeminate – while inversely the heterosexual effeminate was discursively branded sexually deviant.[60]

Interestingly, Knox's use of Paul omits the degendered sexual transgression of women, implicitly made masculine in their 'unnatural' tribadism, to consider explicitly only men 'ashamed not to commit villanie' among themselves. Apparently, women in authority, monstrously taking upon themselves the authority of men, do not thus and co-ordinately become 'masculinized', but rather still more transgressively feminine and embodied, their natural defects all the more dangerous for the scope of their exercise. It is only the men who, in taking upon themselves a subordinate role, do violate their gender, allusively in sexual practices. Violations of ordered gender then serve to reduce all to the lowest term; all are become Woman: manly women and womanly men alike.

This concern with masculine collaboration demonstrates that it was not simply idolatrous female rulers who elicited Knox's scorn. However, it remains to contextualize such animus beyond a discursive calculus of gender in which, if women become manly, then men must describe a concomitant womanliness. Knox's experience, first as a successful and sanctioned preacher in Edwardian England, then later in his years of intermittent exile from both England and then Scotland, provides some insight. The years prior to his flight to the Continent were marked by an acute awareness of such English doctrinal compromises as kneeling at communion; still more distressing was Lord Cecil's politic submission to Roman Catholicism upon Mary's accession.[61]

His disappointment with powerful English Protestants must have been still greater with the inconsistently reformist Scots nobles whose situational Protestantism had directly affected Knox's career. Such Protestant nobles had supported his return to Scotland in 1555, when he enjoyed unexpected success preaching in Edinburgh, and it was to them that Knox appealed when the Catholic clergy, nervous with good reason, threatened him with excommunication in 1556.[62] Yet it was the same Protestant nobility who, recalling him in 1557, for political reasons halted his return, during which hiatus of a few months in Dieppe *The First Blast* was penned.[63] Upon his subsequent return to Scotland in 1559, he would find many of these same Protestant lords as much opportunists eager to acquire church lands as genuine believers.[64] Knox would later rail at such opportunism as a failure to honour a responsibility to uphold true religion.[65]

This kind of betrayal by powerful men remained a compelling theme for Knox. As viewed against this precedent, both Bullinger's and Calvin's subsequently equivocal responses to Knox's preliminary questions concerning obligations of obedience to an idolatrous ruler underscore his ideological isolation within the Reformist community.[66] Their later efforts to dissociate Protestantism from Knox and *The First Blast*, given the politically disastrous reception it enjoyed upon Elizabeth's accession, must have seemed like just so much more morally suspect politicking.[67] Later, in his *Historie of the Scottish Reformation*, he would attribute the failures of Scottish Reformers to 'compromising Protestants', in particular the 'Protestant courtiers who … desert[ed] God's word to become flatterers and compromisers with the Queen'.[68] It is such men, flattering and subservient to feminine dominion, who are figured allusively as the emasculates of *The First Blast*.

In this text, the discursive ground for such feminization was at its origin the condition of marriage, the state in which, as Knox, citing Genesis 3.16, insists, women must accept bondage to men. However, in contrast with the figuration of politic courtiers as emasculated in their subordination, *The First Blast*'s concern with the feminizing potential of marriage to dominating wives as an expression of monstrous female dominion seems at striking odds with the text's historic context. Undeniably, the question of marriage in conjunction with female rule was, in the middle years of the century, one of considerable urgency. But this was not an urgency born of fears of male subordination, but rather the contrary. The reality which *The First Blast* seeks to occlude in its fulminations on gender relations was the fear of subordination of a female monarch *as a woman* to a foreign prince *as her spouse*, a fear which its inverted representation of uxorious and emasculated men mystifies.

The concern that the marriage of a queen regnant would bring both her person and her nation under the domination of a foreign prince and nation was of particular practical immediacy in the later years of Edward's reign. Three claimants to the throne – all women, and the two closest yet unmarried – presented the issue forcefully. The question was whether a queen regnant would owe obedience to her consort as wife, or practise independence of him as monarch.[69] It was widely accepted that 'a wife, by definition, was subordinated to her husband's authority and her own authority subsumed in his'.[70] In the context of religious as well as territorial conflicts, the identity of Mary's future husband was of considerable political significance. Indeed, in response to this issue, as early as 1544, Henry VIII's Third Act of Succession stipulated that she was to marry only with 'consent of [her] councillors'.[71] Similarly, Edward's will voiced direct concern lest Mary Tudor marry a Catholic prince.[72] Accordingly, the 1554 *Act Concerning the Royal Power* was framed to ensure that Mary's independence as ruler would suffer no abrogation as a wife to Philip of Spain.[73] Nevertheless, she herself was apparently eager to accord dominion to Philip, complaining at her inability to permit him greater authority.[74]

For Knox, the issue was of greatest concern in the wake of Mary's marriage to the Catholic Philip; indeed, as originally planned, *The Second Blast* was to have expanded on this concern to consider explicitly the idolatry of the election of a stranger – a plan rendered unnecessary by Mary's death.[75] Moreover, this was no political abstraction but a pressing current issue in the 1550s: Philip's influence – in violation of the 1554 *Act* – seems to have led to war in 1557 and the resultant loss of Calais.[76] In part, the discursive containment of this anxiety may serve to explain Knox's excision of the Pauline reference to female sexual perversion noted above: in the context of Mary Tudor's gender *orthodoxy* – her oft-praised chastity and her desire to express wifely subordination to Philip – her gendered transgression was limited to her regnal status, her *virility* relational rather than absolute.

Both the situational religious politics of aristocrats of the mid-sixteenth century and the marriage controversy surrounding regnal queens, then, comprise the *matter* informed by Knox's representational technology of gender. *The First Blast* operates within a circulating discursive economy: the master code of gender – the expression of the powerful inherited topoi of misogyny – is used to construct the feminized – even sexually feminized – male aristocrats, the very persons whose support of Mary Tudor and Marie de Guise enabled their monstrous female rule. Furthermore, in a series of coordinate gestures, Knox draws upon the topos of the man feminized by his very heterosexuality, the uxorious male, in order to invert and thus contain the pressing fears of foreign regnal consorts who would in fact *fail* to be ruled by their royal wives and thus threaten the future of English and Scottish national autonomy and Protestant reform.

Notes

[1] *The Political Writings of John Knox*, ed. Marvin A. Breslow (Cranbury, NJ, 1985), p. 40. The other two projected denunciations of the violation of moral and civil government that the reigns of the two Marys represented were never written: upon the death of Mary Tudor in 1558, the succession of the Protestant Elizabeth — who felt considerable antipathy toward Knox as a result of this text — seems to have exerted sufficient pressure to have prevented Knox's sounding the remaining blasts.

[2] For example, Genesis, 1 Corinthians, Romans, and 1 Timothy, and various texts of Tertullian, Augustine, Ambrose, and Chrysostom; on the near-canonical status of these oft-cited expressions of anti-feminism, cf. note 23, below.

[3] Breslow, *The Political Writings*, p. 17.

[4] Ibid., p. 14.

[5] Melanie Hansen, 'The Word and the Throne: John Knox's "The First Blast of the Trumpet Against the Monstrous Regiment of Women"', in *Voicing Women: Gender and Sexuality in Early Modern Writing*, ed. by Kate Chedgzoy, Melanie Hansen and Suzanne Trill (Pittsburgh, PA 1997), pp. 11–24 (p. 17); Judith M. Richards, ' "To Promote a Queen to Bear Rule?": Talking of Queens in Mid-Tudor England', *Sixteenth-Century Journal* 28.1 (1997), 101–21 (pp. 104–5); Amanda Shephard, *Gender and Authority in Sixteenth-Century England: The Knox Debate* (Keele, 1994), p. 57.

[6] Breslow, *The Political Writings*, p. 11.

[7] Such formal quality is not surprising: Knox had been at St Andrews as a student of the Aristotelian and historiographer John Mair. See Kenneth D. Farrow, 'Humour, Logic, Imagery and Sources in the Prose of John Knox' *SSL* 25 (1990), 154–75, and on Knox's formal awareness of the *artes praedicandi*, see Pierre Janton, 'John Knox and Literature', in *Actes du 2e Colloque de Langue et de Littérature Ecossaises (Moyen Age et Renaissance)*, ed. by Jean-Jacques Blanchot and Claude Graf (Strasbourg, 1978), pp. 422–9 (pp. 427–8).

[8] Susan M. Felch, 'The Rhetoric of Biblical Authority: John Knox and the Question of Women', *Sixteenth-Century Journal* 26.4 (1995), 805–21 (p. 811), and Shephard, *Gender and Authority*, p. 16.

[9] *The Works of John Knox*, ed. by David Laing, 6 vols (Edinburgh, 1846–64, repr. New York, 1966), IV (1855), p. 373.

[10] Felch, 'The Rhetoric of Biblical Authority', p. 807, n. 9.

[11] Richard L. Greaves, *Theology and Revolution in the Scottish Reformation: Studies in the Thought of John Knox* (Grand Rapids, MI, 1980), p. 161; R. D. S. Jack, 'The Prose of John Knox: A Reassessment', *Prose Studies* 4.3 (1981), 239–51 (p. 244).

[12] Jasper Ridley, *John Knox* (Oxford, 1968), p. 267.

[13] A. Daniel Frankforter, 'Correspondence with Women: The Case of John Knox', *Journal of the Rocky Mountain Medieval and Renaissance Association* 6 (1985), 159–72 (p. 160); Greaves, *Theology and Revolution*, p. 157.

[14] See Dennis Moore, 'Recorder Fleetwood and the Tudor Queenship Controversy', in *Ambiguous Realities: Women in the Middle Ages and Renaissance*, ed. by Carole Levine and Jeanie Watson (Detroit, MI, 1987), pp. 235–51 (p. 236); and also Shephard, *Gender and Authority*, p. 9.

[15] Robert M. Healey, 'Waiting for Deborah: John Knox and Four Ruling Queens', *Sixteenth-Century Journal* 25.2 (1994), 371–86 (p. 385). The same claim has been made about several other notorious contemporary tracts: both John Ponet's 1556 *Shorte Treatise of Politike Power* and Christopher Goodman's 1558 *How Superior Powers ought to be Obeyed of their Subjects* criticize Mary Tudor as a tyrant, not as a woman. See Constance Jordan, 'Women's Rule in Sixteenth-Century British Political Thought', *Renaissance Quarterly* 40.3 (1987), 421–51 (p. 430, n. 17).

16 Felch, 'The Rhetoric of Biblical Authority', p. 811, and also ' "Deir Sister": The Letters of John Knox to Anne Vaughan Lok', *Renaissance and Reformation* 19.4 (1985), 47–68 (p. 51); Frankforter, 'Correspondence with Women', p. 168.

17 Felch, 'The Rhetoric of Biblical Authority', p. 807 n. 9, and p. 816: Shephard objects that the publication timing of *The First Blast*, at a time when Mary's illness and Elizabeth's accession could well have been predicted, demonstrates that it was any woman ruler, and not simply a Catholic one, which Knox had in mind (*Gender and Authority*, p. 23).

18 Theresa de Lauretis, *Technologies of Gender* (Bloomington, IN, 1987), p. 5. For a brief overview of the Western gender-sex-characteristics matrix, see Denise Riley, *'Am I That Name?': Feminism and the Category of 'Woman' in History* (Minneapolis, MN, 1988), pp. 19–25.

19 Elaine Tuttle Hansen, *Chaucer and the Fictions of Gender* (Berkeley, CA, 1992), p. 16.

20 Fredric Jameson, *The Political Unconscious: Narrative as a Socially Symbolic Act* (Ithaca, NY, 1981), pp. 7, 87.

21 This misogynist literary tradition, deriving from such seminal texts as Juvenal's *Sixth Satire*, had found fifteenth-century expression in the varied texts of the 'querelle des femmes', such as the anonymous *Quinze Joies de Marriage*. For a feminist consideration of this literary vogue, see Joan Kelly, 'Early Feminist Theory and the *Querelle des Femmes*', in Joan Kelly, *Women, History and Theory* (Chicago, 1984) pp. 65–109.

22 *Works*, IV, 373–4. The italics are mine.

23 See such seminal patristic texts, such as Jerome, and Matheolus, cited in Jill Mann, *Chaucer and Medieval Estates Satire* (Cambridge, 1973), p. 122, and p. 266 n. 78; and on the resultant associative nexus of Woman-artifice-seduction-the Fall, see R. Howard Bloch, 'Medieval Misogyny', in *Misogyny, Misandry and Misanthropy*, ed. by R. Howard Bloch and Frances Ferguson (Berkeley, CA, 1989), pp. 11–12.

24 *Works*, IV, p. 376.

25 *Works*, IV, pp. 381–2.

26 *Works*, IV, p. 385.

27 *Works*, IV, p. 416.

28 *Works*, IV, p. 228.

29 *Works*, IV, p. 376.

30 *Works*, IV, p. 378.

31 An emblem of female martial achievement, Semiramis was a figure of moral ambivalence: reputedly also the destroyer of her husband and seducer of her own son.

32 Richards, 'Talking of Queens', p. 114.

33 *The Works of Sir David Lindsay of the Mount*, ed. by D. Hamer, 4 vols, STS (Edinburgh, 1931–36), I (1931), p. 295.

34 Hansen, *Chaucer and the Fictions of Gender*, p. 20.

35 D. E. Underwood, 'The Taming of the Scold: The Enforcement of Patriarchal Authority in Early Modern England', in *Order and Disorder in Early Modern England*, ed. by Anthony Fletcher and John Stevenson (Cambridge, 1985), pp. 11–36 (p. 122).

36 Constance Jordan, *Renaissance Feminism: Literary Texts and Political Models* (Ithaca, NY, 1990), p. 20.

37 See Thomas Lacqueur, *Making Sex: Body and Gender from the Greeks to Freud* (Cambridge, MA, 1990), pp. 125–6.

38 For a discussion of the late sixteenth-century English pamphlet controversy concerning the feminizing influence of the theatre and concomitant / resultant masculine cross-dressing, see Lisa Jardine, *Still Harping on Daughters: Women*

and Drama in the Age of Shakespeare (Bury St Edmunds, 1983), and for discussion of the Elizabethan mystification of class-transgressing fantasies of transvestism, see Jonathan Dollimore, 'Subjectivity, Sexuality, and Transgression: The Jacobean Connection', in *Renaissance Drama and Cultural Change* ed. by Mary Beth Rose, *Renaissance Drama* n.s. 17 (1985), 53–81; Stephen Greenblatt, 'Fiction and Friction', in *Shakespearean Negotiations* (Berkeley, CA, 1988), pp. 66–93 (p. 76), Judith Lorber, *Paradoxes of Gender* (New Haven, CT, 1994), p. 87.

[39] Richards, 'Talking of Queens', p. 110.

[40] Augustine, *City of God*, trans. by Henry Bettenson (Harmondsworth, 1972), 14.11, 13.

[41] Shephard, *Gender and Authority*, p. 186.

[42] Jordan, 'Women's Rule', pp. 427 n. 7, 449.

[43] Quoted in Shephard, *Gender and Authority*, p. 157.

[44] *Works*, IV, p. 374.

[45] *Works*, IV, p. 374.

[46] *Works*, IV, p. 375.

[47] *Works*, IV, p. 388.

[48] *Works*, IV, pp. 386–7.

[49] See Aquinas on sexuality: 'In intercourse man becomes like unto the beast,' from *Summa Theologia*, quoted in Uta Ranke-Heinemann, *Eunuchs for Heaven: The Catholic Church and Sexuality*, trans. by John Brownjohn (London, 1990), p. 156.

[50] *Works*, IV, p. 375.

[51] *Works*, IV, p. 392.

[52] *Works*, IV, p. 393.

[53] *Works*, IV, p. 414.

[54] For example, Augustine's discussion of the Fall in which love for Eve resulted in Adam's willing sin (*City of God*, 14.11).

[55] *Works*, IV, p. 394.

[56] *Works*, IV, p. 394.

[57] Romans 1.24–31 (*Revised Standard Version*).

[58] For a discussion of Western perceptions of the *passive* or receptive – hence 'womanlike' – homosexual, see John Boswell, *Christianity, Social Tolerance and Homosexuality* (Chicago, 1980), p. 50 n. 20 *et passim*, and Lacqueur, *Making Sex*, pp. 44, 52–3.

[59] See Walter of Châtillon's remark that effeminates of his day had come to lead one another in a new kind of marriage: 'se mares effeminant … / virum viro turpiter iungit nouus hymen', cited in Mann, *Chaucer and Medieval Estates Satire*, p. 146.

[60] Monica E. McAlpine, 'The Pardoner's Homosexuality and How It Matters', *PMLA* 95.1 (1980), 8–22 (p. 20).

[61] See Shephard, *Gender and Authority*, p. 22; W. Stanford Reid, 'John Knox and his Interpreters', *Renaissance and Reformation* 10.1 (1974), 5–25, (p. 20); and Felch, 'The Rhetoric of Biblical Authority', p. 810. Later, after the publication of *The First Blast*, Knox would criticize Elizabeth for a similarly politic acquiescence to Catholic practice during Mary's reign.

[62] W. Stanford Reid, 'John Knox's Theology of Government', *Sixteenth-Century Journal* 19.4 (1988), 529–40 (p. 534).

[63] Breslow, *The Political Writings*, pp. 22–3.

[64] Reid, 'John Knox and his Interpreters', p. 22.

[65] Breslow, *The Political Writings*, p. 22.

[66] Reid, 'John Knox's Theology', p. 532.

[67] Felch, 'The Rhetoric of Authority', p. 806, n.6.

[68] Quoted in Melvin Cherno, 'John Knox as an Innovator in Historiographic Narration', *Clio* 8.3 (1979), 389–403 (p. 397).

69 Healey, 'Waiting for Deborah', p. 376, and Jordan, 'Women's Rule', p. 425.
70 Richards, 'Talking of Queens', p. 106, n. 15.
71 Jordan, 'Women's Rule' p. 425, n. 5.
72 Richards, 'Talking of Queens', p. 106, n. 15.
73 For a discussion of the oppositional rhetoric of the 1554 *Act* and Knox's *The First Blast*, see Hansen 'The Word and the Throne', p. 13 *et passim*.
74 Shephard, *Gender and Authority*, pp. 57–8; Jordan, 'Women's Rule', pp. 427–8.
75 Felch, 'The Rhetoric of Authority', p. 814.
76 Jordan, 'Women's Rule', p. 429.

4

Philotus: The Transmission of a Delectable Treatise

JAMIE REID-BAXTER

Philotus, 'Scotland's only Renaissance comedy', is a sparkling gem. Nevertheless, it has merited curiously little critical attention, and even less encomium. Damned by Anna J. Mill in her 1933 edition as 'a crudely constructed play' for which she 'cannot claim much intrinsic literary value', its inglorious status in the canon is not the result of physical inaccessibility: there are now three reliable modern prints of the text.[1] The root of the problem is that, ever since the 1835 Bannatyne Club edition, the critical consensus has been that the Scottish play is nothing more than a dramatization of an unimpressive piece of Elizabethan prose, Barnaby Riche's *novella* 'Of Phylotus and Emelia', the eighth of the optimistically titled collection *Riche his Farewell to Militarie Profession* (1581).[2] Ronald Jack, one of the play's few admirers, wrote thirty years ago that its author could not possibly have learned his mastery of the rules of Renaissance comedy from Riche, whom he nonetheless accepted as the playwright's source.[3] The present essay sets out an alternative transmission of the matter of *Philotus* as an international and eminently theatrical process, requiring no reference to the world of Elizabethan prose fiction. Released from the wan embrace of Barnaby Riche, our play can be redated and placed in a very different light. The final stages of the process whereby the material was shaped into the Scottish play require some detailed historical contextualization, and suggest an answer to the vexed question of the authorship of this little jewel of European Renaissance theatre.

Modern comedy grew out of the late-fifteenth-century Italian rediscovery of the plays of Plautus and Terence in performance. With their strong characterization and use of psychology, these plays were found to mirror the new humanist vision of man's dynamic role as the protagonist of a changeful reality, an anthropocentric world-view which was gradually replacing the theocentricity of the Middle Ages. Across a gap of 1500 years, the beginnings of modern comedy are as closely bound up with the Roman dramatists as the latter were with the Greek New Comedy from which they translated and adapted. In Greek New Comedy, human interaction leads to increasingly complex situations, the disentanglement or denouement of which produces a satisfying final resolution – frequently achieved, as in *Philotus*, thanks to a climactic 'recognition scene' in which long-lost siblings are reunited not only with each other but also with their fathers. The first great modern comedy, Ariosto's *I Suppositi* of 1509, was inspired by the *Captivi* of Plautus, which culminates in recognition and reunion, and also features a servant and a master changing identities.[4] In *I Suppositi*, this device is combined with another standard New Comedy situation, the young hero's need to outwit an older suitor.

These are devices also found in *Philotus*, of course, a textbook example of the new type of drama born with Ariosto and his contemporaries, *commedia erudita*. The 'learned comedy' was aimed at sophisticated, Latinate audiences who would pick up the quotations and allusions as well as admire the novel features and ingenious recombination of standard elements. Once launched, this cumulative process of combining, inventing, and recombining became self-generating: each new development became part of the repertory of resources available for the next play. The pedigree of the identical siblings who provide the complication in *Philotus* illustrates this perfectly. In Plautus's *Menaechmi*, based on a lost Greek comedy by Poseidippos, the comic confusion is caused by male twins and a woman's dress carried – not worn – by one of them. Confusion of identities was the mainspring of *I Suppositi*, and by the time we reach the major direct source of *Philotus*, the influential Siennese comedy *Gl'Ingannati* of 1532, we find that the *Menaechmi* brothers have long since become brother and sister.[5] That innovation had been effected in 1513 by Cardinal Bibbiena in his epoch-making *La Calandra*, and a comparison of *The Comedy of Errors*, directly inspired by *Menaechmi*, with the Italian-inspired *Twelfth Night* reveals just how much richer are the dramatic possibilities offered by siblings of both sexes.[6] Yet, while absorbing and developing new tricks, Renaissance playwrights constantly returned to the Roman originals, recombining elements old and new. An extreme example is the anonymous English *Buggbears* (c. 1565), a translation of Grazzini's *La Spiritata* of 1561 but adapted to include not only important scenes and elements from the already classic *Gl'Ingannati*, but whole scenes from Terence's *Andria* as well.[7] As we shall see, *Philotus* draws heavily on *Gl'Ingannati*, while also incorporating elements lifted straight from Plautus (and possibly from Terence) as well as from Charles Estienne's *Les Abusez* (1543), an adaptation in French of *Gl'Ingannati*, and from Jacques Grévin's *Les Esbahis* (1560).[8]

The plot of 'Philotus'

The absence of any act divisions in the printed texts has led to *Philotus* being treated as a mere 'interlude'. Yet it is a fully developed, if concise, neo-classical comedy. Roman commentators identified a five-act structure in the plays of

Terence that embodied an organic and satisfying process of exposition (*protasis*) in two acts, followed by complication (*epitasis* and *summa epitasis*) in two acts, leading to climax (*catastrophe*) and resolution in the fifth act thanks to a happy revelation. Ronald Jack noted the Scottish play's Roman elements in 1972, pointing out that it embodies the classical structure to perfection, although he did not mark the act divisions when he edited the text in 1997.[9] My own unpublished edition of *Philotus* shows the five acts:[10]

> *Act I* (1–432): Philotus, a rich old man, protests his love for young Emily. Rejected, he hires a bawd to seduce Emily into marrying him for his money. Emily indignantly rejects the bawd's attempts to persuade her, and Philotus makes a third attempt, buying her father's consent to the proposed marriage by making him an offer he cannot resist. Emily's refusal to accede to her irate father's wishes ensures that she is locked up.

> *Act II* (433–624): A young man, Flavius, sees Emily, falls in love with her, and passionately woos her. Her scepticism as to his real motives is removed by his immediately accepted offer of marriage. When he fails to devise a 'convoy' to allow her to escape the house, Emily tells him to get boys' clothes for her.

> *Act III* (625–792): Emily duly escapes and goes to live with Flavius, but a voyeuristic servant has seen her disguising herself. He tells the two old men Emily has fled in drag. Apoplectic with rage (Alberto) and distraught with grief (Philotus), they search for her, and run into Philerno, Alberto's long-lost son. Taking him for his sister, they force Philerno to agree to marry Philotus in a month's time, and meanwhile to go and live chastely with Philotus, 'her' fiancé, in the company (and even bed) of the latter's daughter Brisilla.

> *Act IV*, the *summa epitasis* (793–1121): Philerno, as 'Emily', convinces Brisilla that, like him, she is to suffer the unnatural cruelty of being married to an old man, and that it would be much better for them both if he could be turned into a man. To Brisilla's delight, fervent prayer to Venus does the trick. When Philotus takes his bride off to kirk, the marriage of Philotus and 'Emily' is witnessed by Flavius, who concludes that the girl in his house is a demon in Emily's shape. He rushes home, exorcizes her and throws her out, despite her attempts to make him see reason. Meanwhile, in Philotus's house, Philerno has to defend himself against Philotus's wish to bed his new wife. After giving him a good beating, he hires a whore to make Philotus think he has consummated his marriage.

Act V (1122–1340): Emily, weeping, returns to her father, who is furious with her husband for ejecting her. Philotus complains to Alberto that Emily is a harridan; the real Emily says she was never married to Philotus, but to Flavius. Baffled, they send for Flavius, who tells them that he married a devil. Philotus says *he* was the one married to a devil. At this point of total perplexity, Philerno and Brisilla arrive to 'red the stryfe' (1225). Philotus has to accept the *fait accompli* of Philerno's marriage with Brisilla. Alberto gets his son back (plus Brisilla's dowry!) and the two young couples celebrate a double wedding. The play ends with a self-righteous speech of repentance from a sadder and wiser old man, who claims to have learned his lesson.

Roman sources

The 'matter' from which *Philotus* is moulded owes more to Plautus than to Terence.[11] *Menaechmi* is the source *par excellence* of the *commedia erudita*'s fondness for long-lost siblings, and hence of *Gl'Ingannati* and *Philotus*. But Plautus's outrageous *Casina* provides one of *Philotus*'s major departures from *Gl'Ingannati*, namely a mock wedding leading to the beating up of an old voluptuary in the proximity of the nuptial couch. *Casina* shows a foolish old man going to inordinate lengths to secure his place in a young girl's marriage bed under cover of darkness. Unfortunately, the darkness actually covers the substitute put there by the old man's rival (his own son), a healthy young male slave who batters the aged suitor black and blue, which all too visible state of affairs leads to his well-deserved come-uppance. In *Philotus,* this device is considerably refined, in an impressive piece of Renaissance mirror-imaging: the old man is beaten up before he goes to bed to cuckold himself with a whore, while simultaneously being cuckolded by his own daughter who is sleeping with the boy he thinks is his shrewish bride.

Other specific elements lifted straight from Roman sources include Emily's choleric father, Alberto, a classic *senex iratus* or angry old man (and a very greedy one, too), and the use of disguise to gain access to a girl's bed under false pretences, as Philerno finds himself doing (in Terence's *Eunuchus*, a young man poses as a eunuch for that purpose, and, like Philerno, marries the girl in the end). But the influence of Terence is felt more in the sparkling verse and carefully wrought structure of *Philotus*. A far finer craftsman than Plautus, Terence took great care over both language and plot, and is, indeed, generally credited with inventing the 'double plot' featuring two pairs of lovers. The Scottish play has no loose ends, and its elegant structure features something of a double plot, namely the parallel stories of Emily / Flavius and Philerno / Brisilla. They form a neat chiasmus (Emily dressed as a boy escapes her father's house to live with Flavius, Philerno dressed as a girl invades Brisilla in her father's house), with the crux being Philotus himself (and not the cross-dressed heroine, as in *Gl'Ingannati* and *Twelfth Night*). The two stories are also linked by the other old man, Alberto, the father of the cross-dressed siblings, in a further instance of the Renaissance fondness for symmetry and parallelism which pervades the entire play.

Italian sources

Gl'Ingannati supplies the following elements: the ill-suited marriage arranged by two old men; the daughter who escapes dressed as a boy, is rejected by her true love and ultimately reunited with him; and the long-lost brother forced into the bedroom of the aged suitor's daughter by the deluded old men. It also supplies the strong female focus which is such a striking feature of *Philotus*. Richard Andrews has pointed out that, in 1532, *Gl'Ingannati* was a positively pioneering text 'and most of the important innovations revolve in the end around Lelia, and the whole notion of an active sympathetic heroine'. Roman comedy (and hence its early Italian imitations) had been 'short on sympathetic woman characters and on the female point of view'; in modern comedy it was *Gl'Ingannati* which 'opened the way to a more sympathetic investigation of the character and predicament of a young heroine', such as we find in *Twelfth Night* and, indeed, in 'the mainstream of European comedy over subsequent centuries'. Andrews further observes that 'in this story, astute women gain the upper hand over male characters who are either obtuse or confused'.[12]

This female focus is as central to *Philotus* as it is absent from Barnaby Riche's tale. In the play, Emily is the decisive mover: she rejects Philotus and resists her father, imposes conditions on Flavius, devises her own escape, and tries (thrice) to make Flavius see sense. She is also the innocent girl importuned by Philotus and his hired bawd, maltreated by Alberto, and wrongously rejected by her husband. Where Flavius is indeed obtuse, confused, and rather passive, the much-wronged Emily is active, sympathetic, and astute; this is part of the chiastic play whereby Flavius and Emily mirror the naïve, passive Brisilla and the active, astute Philerno. Other probable Italian sources of *Philotus* include Bibbiena's *La Calandra* for the fake sex-change involving siblings as well as the whore put in the suitor's bed and that character's consequent self-cuckoldry. It is possible that the Scottish poet was sent back to Plautus by Niccolò Machiavelli's reworking of *Casina* as *Clizia* (1525; published 1537).[13] Another famous comedy, Aretino's *Il Marescalco* (1527; published 1533) culminates in the mock wedding of the eponymous protagonist to a page boy in drag.[14]

French sources

Scotland and French Renaissance drama are directly linked in the person of George Buchanan. France was the first country to follow the Italian lead and attempt modern drama, and Buchanan played a seminal role in the development of tragedy there.[15] Although the Scottish humanist did not attempt comedy, modern comic theory greatly interested his friend and physician, the polymath Charles Estienne. Not only did he publish a French translation of Terence's *Andria* in 1542, but he brought out a fine adaptation of *Gl'Ingannati* in the early 1540s (*Les Abusez*), with an important preface that lauded it to the skies and which claimed that, had Terence himself written in Italian, he could not have done better, and no modern had done the like.[16] Estienne made some cuts in the rather prolix original, excising the slapstick sub-plot with the Spanish soldier, Giglio. He also wrote an entirely new final scene, which seems to be reflected in *Philotus*. The Italian play, as Richard Andrews has shown, is designed so that one actor (or actress) can play both the heroine and her brother; it 'avoids any meeting between them, and produces some rather disconnected closing scenes as a result, rather than the full family reunion which one would normally expect'.[17] The close is also marred by the fact that the old suitor, Gherardo, vanishes into his house several scenes before the end, so that the audience is deprived of the full closure of seeing him receive the information that he cannot marry Lelia. *Philotus*, of course, culminates in family reunion and the old man's discomfiture.

Estienne reverses the order of the last two scenes of *Gl'Ingannati*, and his new final scene, though eschewing a full reunion, does feature Gerard, the aged lover; Virginio, the father of the twins; and the twins' old nurse. Her reminder to Gerard that making love to a young wife would have killed him ('Croyez quelle vous eust envoyé bien tost en Paradis en poste')[18] finds a striking textual echo in *Philotus*, where Brisilla complains that the old men who wish to marry her and Emily / Philerno are subject to 'vane fantasies', and she asks: 'Is it not doittrie hes yow drevin / Haiknayis to seik for haist to Heavin?' (819, 821–2). Estienne's final scene, unlike the ending of *Gl'Ingannati*, is similar to the way *Philotus* ends, with the old lover's realization of the truth, Alberto's prompt suggestion – to 'pacifie' Philotus's indignation (1249) – that Philerno and Brisilla should marry, and the attribution of the happy outcome to God's personal intervention. In Estienne, the nurse observes of the healthy young couple: 'Dieu leur doit grace qu'ilz puissent faire de beaux enfants', to which the father replies:

> voylà que ie pense, puys que Dieu l'a ainsi permis, son nom en soit loué: Ie croy, que ça esté par son vouloir que le cas est avenu: car on dit que les mariages se font au Ciel. Parquoy Gerard, ne nous en faschons plus: il nous fault faire deux noces en un iour.[19]

The old man concurs, accepting the will of God. There are no such religious allusions in *Gl'Ingannati*.

There are also parallels to be drawn with a later and original French play, Jacques Grévin's *Les Esbahis*.[20] As the very first 'modern' (i.e. Italianizing) French comedy, its premiere in Paris in February 1561 caused a sensation. It was published that year as part of Grévin's *Théâtre*, along with the earlier non-Italian comedy *La Tresorière* and the tragedy *Jules César*. The volume, reprinted in 1562, contains encomiastic verses on *Jules César* by none other than George Buchanan, who had very probably taught Grévin at the Collège de Boncourt.[21] Like Ronsard, he saw the youthful poet as one of the white hopes of French culture.[22] Grévin, a doctor like Charles Estienne, was a very young man with little theatrical experience, and *Les Esbahis* is a clumsier, if more original work than *Philotus*, let alone *Les Abusez*. There are no twins in Grévin's play, and it draws on quite a range of sources, Roman and Italian.[23] Yet Grévin, who in 1559 fell in love with Charles Estienne's daughter, took over a number of elements from the Italian play and Estienne's new final scene. There is an old man, engaged to a most unwilling young woman who loves someone her own age. There is the use of disguise in order to enjoy sexual congress, leading to an entertaining argument between the old men, owing to their confusion as to the identity of the lover seen *in flagrante* by the father. As in Estienne's *Les Abusez*, we again find the old lover, Josse, on stage at the close, being browbeaten by the father of his former fiancée. These elements are all present in *Philotus*. More importantly, we find Josse soliloquizing at the beginning of the play about his passionate love for young Madalene, which brings us a step nearer the dynamic opening confrontation of the old man with the object of his lust in *Philotus*.

The young Frenchman's boldly original and selective approach to his material may well have inspired the Scottish playwright to feel free to recast *Les Abusez*, while the presence of the *macquerelle* Claude in Grévin's cast could have prompted the idea of the protatic macrell of the Scottish play, who has no antecedents in the *Ingannati* material.[24] The Scottish Alberto's greed and heartlessness might also have been inspired by Grévin's depiction of Gerard's relationship with Madalene. Money is not an issue in *Gl'Ingannati*, but it certainly is in *Les Esbahis* and *Philotus*. It could be the Scottish play Madeleine Lazard is describing when she writes in a discussion of the representation of France in the *comédies humanistes* of the sixteenth century that

> the relationship between father and child draws attention most sharply to the question of money. This traditional conflict between the generations ... is triggered at the time of a marriage. ... [The father often] seeks to marry his own daughter at as little cost as possible by promising

her to a rich old man, whose lust outstrips his greed. Marriage is treated as a business contract between families, in which the opinion of the interested parties counts for nothing.

Paternal greed provides the necessary dramatic impetus; legacies, dowry, sums and wedding costs are bitterly and minutely negotiated:

> The sole means employed by the lovers to counter their parents' notions of respectability, indeed their honour, is to '[faire] Pasques avant les Rameaux' [jump the gun]. ... Presented with this *fait accompli*, the family has no means of avoiding the ensuing scandal other than to endorse the marriage plans.[25]

Lope de Rueda and playing to an audience

Critics of *Philotus*, who regularly write that it is 'not certainly intended for performance',[26] would do well to recall a point made by an editor of Lope de Rueda's *Los Engañados* (*c.* 1545), namely that any estimate of this Spanish reworking of *Gl'Ingannati* must take account of the visual dynamism and even violence of live performance quite as much as of the words on the page.[27] Rueda cut the play so heavily that the printed text, like *Philotus*, calls for a real effort of theatrical imagination to fill in apparent gaps.[28] While Rueda's cuts go far beyond Charles Estienne's, it is interesting to note that he shared the Frenchman's dissatisfaction with the rather disjointed original ending. Rueda's final scene has the old suitor, Gerardo, on stage, and sounds a religious note.[29] But where the Spanish actor-manager is writing to amuse the general public with a farce, *Philotus* is aimed at a courtly élite, like the *commedia erudita* it so faithfully echoes. Its concentrated, elegant verse is the vehicle for a sharply focussed, superbly structured treatment of Philotus's folly and Emily's ultimate vindication, and the material has been pared down still further than in *Los Engañados;* gone are the inn-keepers, the pedagogue, and the various clownish servants (barring the crucial, tiny role of Stephano). But where Rueda, purely for the sake of laughter, inserts whole self-contained scenes, unconnected with the plot, the Scottish poet employs a device that baffled nineteenth-century commentators, namely Plesant, a figure on stage who is not part of the plot but comments on the action.[30] Plesant heightens both the comedy and the drama of the action with his brief, strategically placed interjections, jeering at everyone, including the spectators – except Emily and Brisilla, it should be noted, thus further underlining the play's sympathetic female focus. The idea of Plesant, who describes himself as a fool (1011–12), may well be inspired by the on-stage presence of Folly itself in *Gl'Ingannati* / *Les Abusez*, in the shape of the inn called 'The Fool' (*Il Matto* / *Le Sot*). With regard to the verbal wit in the proliferating 'arbitrary invention' of further inn-signs, Richard

Andrews actually observes that 'in a certain sense it is a game played across the footlights, appealing directly to the audience and almost involving them', which is certainly what Plesant does.[31]

A court comedy for Mary, Queen of Scots?

That *Philotus* is a court comedy seems certain; the text itself says as much.[32] It has always been assigned to the court of James VI, after 1581, because of the publication date of *Riche his Farewell*.[33] But 'maskings' and 'farces' seem to have been much more frequent at the court of James's mother – a court which can be shown to have been aware of Italian *commedia erudita* and of the work of Charles Estienne and Jacques Grévin. Queen Mary's future father-in-law, Henri II, had been the dedicatee of Charles Estienne's *Les Abusez* while still dauphin; as king, his triumphal entry into Lyons in 1548 had featured a performance of Bibbiena's *La Calandra*, while his Italian queen Catherine de Medicis patronized Italian troupes. It is hence unsurprising that Mary's library at Holyrood contained volumes of French and Italian comedies.[34] Nor will the work of Jacques Grévin have been unknown to the Scottish court: the young poet composed and published an *Hymne a Monseigneur le Dauphin, sur le mariage dudict Seigneur et de Madame Marie d'Estevart, Royne d'Escosse* in 1558, which must have made an impression, for Henri II commissioned him to write his first comedy, *La Tresorière*, for the wedding of Princess Claude to Mary's cousin the Duke of Lorraine in February 1559. Grévin also published a *Pastorale sur les mariages de tres excellentes Princesses Madame Elizabet, fille ainée de France, et Madame Marguerite, soeur unique du Roi* – Mary's sister-in-law and aunt by marriage, respectively – in 1559. There was, moreover, a personal link with Charles Estienne, Jacques Grévin, and dramatic performance physically present in the Queen's personal circle in the shape of George Buchanan, who functioned as a kind of poet laureate.[35] The great humanist supplied various Latin texts for performance at court festivities – such as Mary's wedding to Lord Darnley, and, most notably, the spectacular Renaissance 'triumph' at Stirling Castle in December 1566 that marked the baptism of Mary's heir, Charles James.[36]

Buchanan was imbued with deep kin-loyalty to Darnley's family, the Lennox Stewarts, who had been rivals to the Hamiltons as next in line to the throne after Mary's birth in 1542. The Hamilton claim prevailed, and Darnley's father had spent twenty years in English exile, until restored to his estates by Queen Mary in 1564. The Lennox fortunes took an even more spectacular turn with the Queen's marriage to Darnley in July 1565 and the promise of the Crown Matrimonial. Buchanan's kin-loyalty underpins his quatrain 'Ad Henricum Scotorum Regem', probably a *strena* or New Year poem, comparing the king to the sun on which the marigold's opening and closing depends, and saying:

'nos quoque pendemus de te, sol noster, ad omnes / expositi rerum te subeunte vices'.[37] Buchanan celebrated Darnley's regal status in the *strena* 'Ad Henricum Scotiae regem', addressing him as 'optime Rex' and claiming that the poet's only wish was that 'sit tibi certa salus … te sospite nobis / succedent regno prospera cuncta tuo'.[38] By December 1566, the estrangement between king and queen meant that the Lennox fortunes were at a low ebb, to the extent that Darnley, although in Stirling, was absent from the baptismal celebrations. Buchanan, like any other Lennox partisan, would have been anxious to see Darnley and Mary reconciled.

This provides a suggestive background to the curious imagery of the *Sang of the foure Lufearis* in *Philotus* (1281–1308) which marks the triumphant resolution of the star-crossed love of Emily and Flavius. This song is one of the original features of *Philotus*, as are the macrell and the exorcism. A closing song celebrating the resolution of all the complexities and bidding the audience farewell with a *captatio benevolentiae* is, of course, a regular feature of Renaissance comedy. *The Buggbears*, for example, concludes with this cheerful ditty:

> Syth all our greff is turned to blyss
> We all with ioy reioyce at this
> The old foolkes care hath end at last
> The young foolkes must needes ioyfull bee
> We boyes ar glad, our payne is past
> & you We trust take all in gree.[39]

But the *Sang* is a culmination, not a closing ditty; Philotus will point the moral, and only then will the Messinger crave the spectators' indulgence. We are meant to heed the *Sang*; the verse form changes to Chaucerian rhyme royal in solemn, joyous thanksgiving, lent greater weight by the use of unexpected Old Testament and classical imagery. The image of the Israelites 'glaid in hairt to be / Fred from all feir, befoir in bondage bound' (1283–4) under Pharaoh and Artaxerxes, was adumbrated by Flavius in the preceding stanza, when he cried: 'Give gloir to God … that hes fra thraldome set us frie' (1275–7) – and continues, significantly: 'And hes us placit in sik degrie, / Ilk ane as hee wald wisch to be' (1278–9). There is more to *Philotus* than meets the eye.

Louise George Clubb has made the point that in Italian Renaissance comedy

> a denouement may work in two ways: to conceal and to reveal. The plots lifted from novellas about cuckolds and dissatisfied young wives accommodate adultery and the deceits accompanying it, potentially anti-social actions that are kept secret …. On the other hand, plots from New Comedy, with its inheritance from romance, are resolved by marriages and new beginnings, correction of old errors, forgiveness of

> past deceits, recognitions and reidentifications of kin. … Comedy of
> concealment, if hardy, lost some ground as the century unfolded. The
> spirit of carnival gave way to the celebration of social order. … The
> reintegration achieved at the end is one that continues the old order, but
> that by shifting power to those who are next in line to become parents
> makes the society new.[40]

Philotus, descended from New Comedy, fits this mould perfectly. But the *Sang*
'makes the society new' on a cosmic scale — for it begins with the Red Sea
crossing of the Children of Israel, a type both of the burial and rebirth of the
individual in baptism, and of the Crucifixion and Resurrection, which renewed
fallen creation itself. The *Book of Esther* is also drawn on, where the entire
Hebrew nation is saved from the extermination decreed by King Artaxerxes of
Persia when the wrongfully denigrated Mordocheus, the uncle of godly Queen
Esther, foils his rival, the evil Haman.[41] These are odd images for a simple neo-
Plautine love intrigue. The second stanza's evocation of the story of Jason is
also odd; not only is Jason himself an ambiguous figure, who betrayed his wife
Medea, but the stanza's focal point is his father, Aeson, who had been wrongfully dispossessed of the throne by his wicked brother Pelias. It is against this
background that the third and fourth stanza praise 'leill and mutuall lufe'
between man and woman as incomparably the greatest of all earthly joys and
celebrate the end of 'our former pane / And miserie' (1303, 1307–8). *Philotus,*
with its marked feminine focus, may well be designed to carry a carefully coded
plea to Mary, Queen of Scots, for a reconciliation with her errant husband.[42]

Authorship

We have seen that Buchanan is a possible channel through which an interested
party could have had access to *Les Abusez* and *Les Esbahis* and indeed to
the Queen's library, with its volumes of Italian comedies. With his doubtless
encyclopaedic knowledge, as a pedagogue, of the works of Terence and
Plautus, Buchanan could have collaborated with a vernacular poet to create
Philotus; after all, *Gl'Ingannati* itself was the product of a collective effort.[43]
The surviving verse of Robert Sempill, Buchanan's fellow Lennox kinsman and
propagandist, demonstrates complete mastery of metrical forms and the Scots
alliterative register, and effortlessly draws on Old Testament and classical
imagery to make its points.[44] Sempill is known, moreover, to have written two
dramatic entertainments performed for a courtly audience (the Regent Moray
and James VI, respectively) in 1568 and 1581.[45] We have no reference to
vernacular works amongst the entertainments at the baptism of James VI, but
a fortnight later, on Twelfth Night, a smaller event took place at court in
Stirling, which provides a very plausible setting for *Philotus*. Indeed, the
Messinger who concludes the play, speaking in the character of the playwright,

seems to allude to Latin entertainments as what the court would expect (and had recently enjoyed), when he apologizes for his 'ferse … unformallie set out in vulgar verse' (1341–3). Twelfth Night 1567 saw the marriage of the queen's beautiful lady-in-waiting, Mary Fleming, to the much older William Maitland of Lethington, the powerful royal secretary. Lethington's long wooing had caused some amusement even in international circles, but the Scottish courtiers would have laughed more at the parallels they would have seen with the crusty English ambassador Thomas Randolph and his infatuated pursuit of Mary Beaton, another of the Queen's Maries, only eighteen months earlier.[46] There was also the recent marriage of the elderly John Knox to a girl of seventeen, which had scandalized the court. *Philotus,* with all its stress on the divine institution of marriage and its joys, would strike several chords. The witty Lethington, whose support the Lennox cause needed to secure, would doubtless have been highly amused. After all, Maitland, unlike Philotus, did get his girl.

Philotus is the story of an old fool and how he is taught a lesson. But he is paralleled by a young fool, Flavius – Emily actually compares him to James V's famous court fool, John of Lowis (1003), during the exorcism which exemplifies Flavius's foolish lack of faith in his wife.[47] Flavius, like Darnley, had used verse in courting his later wife; like Darnley over Mary's relations with David Riccio, Flavius had dreadfully misjudged and maltreated her. Flavius, like Philotus, repents his folly: 'To deme my dow, was I not vaine, / That thow had bene a spreit?' (1259–60), and when Mary went to Darnley in Glasgow on 20 January 1567, the king made an elaborate speech of repentance, asking 'maye not a man of mye aege .. falle twise or thrise, and yet repent and be chastised by experience?'[48] The Queen's visit resulted in her taking Darnley back to Edinburgh with her, and it seemed the Lennox Stewarts had achieved the reconciliation they sought. Darnley was to be restored to his rightful place 'as hee wald wisch to be' (1279), and could echo Flavius's joyous cry:

> Now sen I am fred fra that feir,
> And vaine illusioun did appeir,
> Welcum, my darling and my deir. (1261–3)

Vain illusion is, of course, the key to all the comedies we have been considering. Hilarious on stage, illusion in real life is another matter, and Darnley's belief in his illusory reconciliation led to his being strangled in the garden of Kirk o'Field on the night of 10 February 1567. In the uproar of rebellion, deposition, civil war, and long-drawn-out political and religious strife which ensued, Scotland's brief engagement with European Renaissance drama was forgotten. When Charteris printed *Philotus* in 1603, it was not as a stage play, but as a 'delectabill Treatise'. Four hundred years later, this masterly little *commedia erudita* still awaits general recognition of its exemplary theatricality.

Notes

1   A. J. Mill (ed.), *Philotus*, in *Miscellany Volume*, STS (Edinburgh, 1933), pp. 89,
    83. The other two editions are: David Irving (ed.), *Philotus*, Bannatyne Club
    (Edinburgh, 1835, which also includes the text of Riche's tale 'Of Phylotus and
    Emelia'); and R. D. S. Jack and P. A. T. Rozendaal (eds), *The Mercat Anthology of
    Scottish Verse 1375–1707* (Edinburgh, 1997), pp. 390–432. References in the
    present article are to the latter edition.
2   Facsimile edition by T. M. Cranfill (Austin, Tex., 1959); modernized edition for the
    Barnaby Riche Society by Donald Beecher (New York, 1992). I have made a
    detailed comparison of the Scottish play and Riche's *novella* in: 'Rich and rollicking
    or flat and unfocussed? Barnaby Riche's *Phylotus* contrasted with the Scottish
    Philotus', in Neil McMillan and Kirsten Stirling (eds), *Odd Alliances: Scottish
    Studies in European Contexts* (Glasgow, 1999), pp. 11–24.
3   R. D. S. Jack, *The Italian Influence in Scottish Literature* (Edinburgh, 1972), pp.
    42–53 (48). There is a real problem with trying to derive Riche's tale 'Of Phylotus
    and Emilia' from earlier prose fiction, pointed out by A. J. Mill (*op. cit.* pp. 92–3),
    namely that his supposed source, the *novella* by Bandello (1554, translated by
    Belleforest in *Histoires Tragiques*, 1571) based on *Gl'Ingannati*, does not contain
    several crucial elements common to the Italian and Scottish plays and to Riche.
4   In *Ludovico Arioste: Commedie*, ed. by Cesare Segre (Turin, 1976). Translated into
    English as *Supposes* by George Gascoigne in 1566, available in F. S. Boas (ed.), *Five
    Pre-Shakespearean Comedies* (London, 1934), pp. 273–341; also *Ariosto: The
    Supposes*, ed. by D. Beecher and J. Butler (Ottawa, 1999). The play underlies the
    subplot of *The Taming of the Shrew*. Modern English translations are included in
    The Comedies of Ariosto, ed. by Edmond M. Beame and Leonard G. Sbrocchi
    (Chicago, Ill., 1975) and in *Ariosto's 'The Supposes', Machiavelli's 'The
    Mandrake', Intronati's 'The Deceived'. Three Italian Renaissance Comedies*, ed.
    by Christopher Cairns (Lampeter, 1996).
5   Nerida Newbigin (ed.), *Gl'Ingannati* (Bologna, 1984) provides a 'diplomatic'
    reproduction of the 1537 printing. The edition by Florindo Cerreta (Florence,
    1980) takes account of all printings. Available as *The Deceived* in Bruce Penman
    (ed.), *Five Italian Renaissance Comedies* (London, 1978), pp. 195–277.
6   *La Calandra*, ed. by Giorgio Padoan (Padova, 1985) is the recommended edition.
    An English version is provided in *The Genius of the Italian Theater*, ed. by Eric
    Bentley (New York, 1964), pp. 31–99.
7   The dating is entirely speculative. *The Buggbears* was reprinted from the
    manuscript by Carl Grabau in *Archiv für das Studium der neueren Sprachen*,
    1897, and, with copious notes, by R. W. Bond in *Early Plays from the Italian*
    (Oxford, 1911). Matthew Macdiarmid, in his stimulating '*Philotus*: A Play of the
    Scottish Renaissance', *Forum for Modern Language Studies* 3 (1967), 223–35,
    finds possible textual links with *Philotus*.
8   There is no modern edition of *Les Abusez*, the text used is the 1549 Paris print by
    Estienne Groulleau. *Les Esbahis* is available, with detailed source notes, in Jacques
    Grévin, *La Tresorière. Les Esbahis. Comédies,* ed. by Élisabeth Lapeyre, Société
    des textes français modernes (Paris, 1980).
9   *The Italian Influence in Scottish Literature*, pp. 49 and 51.
10 For Jack's edition, see n.2 above. My own edition, with detailed notes, is available
    from the Department of Scottish Literature, Glasgow University.
11 For parallel texts in Latin and English of the complete works, see *Terence*, transl.
    and ed. by John Sargeant, 2 vols, Loeb (London, 1912), and *Plautus*, transl. and ed.
    by Paul Nixon, 5 vols, Loeb (London, 1926–38); for modern English performing
    versions, see Terence, *The Comedies*, transl. and ed. by Betty Radice

(Harmondsworth, 1976) and Plautus, *The Pot of Gold and Other Plays*, transl. and ed. by E. F. Watling (Harmondsworth, 1965).

12 'Background Notes' to his unpublished translation, pp. iii–iv, available from the author c/o the Department of Italian, University of Leeds. I am extremely grateful to Richard Andrews for providing me with copies of his work on *Gl'Ingannati*.

13 Niccolò Machiavelli, *Mandragola, Clizia*, ed. by Gian Mario Anselmi, with 'Presentazione' by Ezio Raimondi (Milan, 1984); English translation in J. R. Hale, *Literary Works of Machiavelli* (Oxford, 1965).

14 *Il Marescalco* in *Aretino: Teatro*, ed. by Giorgio Petrocchi (Milan, 1971); available as *The Stablemaster* in Penman (ed.), *Five Italian Renaissance Comedies*.

15 See I. D. MacFarlane, *A Literary History of France: Renaissance France 1470–1589* (London and Tonbridge, 1974), pp. 424–5; P. J. Ford, *George Buchanan, Prince of Poets* (Aberdeen, 1982), pp. 7, 70, 74–5; Raymond Lebègue, *La Tragédie réligieuse en France: les débuts (1514–1573)* (Paris, 1929), pp. 195–254. In the introduction (p. 7) to his own outstanding Scots language *George Buchanan's Jephthah and The Baptist* (Edinburgh, 1959), Robert Garioch gives details of other translations.

16 'Si Terence mesmes l'eust composée en Italien, à peine mieux l'eust il sceu diter, inventer, ou deduyre. ... Nul des poëtes modernes, soient Italiens, ou Françoys, jusques à present en ayent faite la pareille': *Les Abusez*, Paris, 1549, sig. A, [v]–[vi]; this preface has been reprinted in Bernard Weinberg, *Critical Prefaces of the French Renaissance* (Evanston, Ill., 1950), pp. 135–8 (138).

17 Andrews, 'Background Notes', p. iv.

18 'Believe me, she'd have sent you posting off to heaven soon enough'. Another striking parallel with *Philotus* in Grévin's work is to be found in his sonnet sequence 'L'Olimpe': 'Olimpe ... c'est mon seul Hélicon, Parnasse à double front / C'est de là dont j'ay pris tout le style fécond / Dont ores je me plains du but auquel j'aspire' – cf. *Philotus*, 515–17 (Grévin, *Théâtre complet et poésies choisies*, ed. by Lucien Pinvert [Paris, 1922], p. 248): 'Olympia ... is my only Helicon, my double-browed Parnassus / It is from thence that I have drawn the fecund style / In which I weep over the goal to which I aspire.' All translations in the present paper are my own, except where indicated.

19 *Les Abusez*, sig. M, [v]–[vi]. 'God grant them grace to make bonny bairns'; 'Well, I think that since God allowed this to happen, His name be praised for it. I believe that it was by His will that this affair has fallen out this way; after all, they say marriages are made in heaven. And so, Gerard, let's not fash about it any more; we'll just have to celebrate two weddings on the same day'.

20 See n.8.

21 See P. J. Ford, *Prince of Poets*, p. 7, and Henri Chamard, 'Le Collège de Boncourt et les origines du théâtre classique', in *Mélanges offerts à Abel Lefranc* (Paris, 1936), pp. 246–60.

22 Never reprinted, these lines read in the 2nd edition of 1562 (BL: 240.f.15(2); I am grateful to Dr Lawrence Normand for his help in locating them):

GEORGIVS BVCHANANVS SCOTVS IN IACOBI Greuini Caesarem Tragoediam.

Ne nimium spoliis placeas Caesar tibi Gallis
    En habet vltorem Gallia victa suum.
De Latio ducens ad patria templa triumphum
    Bacchi hedera, lauro clarus Apollinea,
Greuinus statuit Phoebo Musisque trophaeum,
    Quod nulla euersum posteritate ruat.
Vtque magis constet victoria clara trophaeum,
    Indutus spoliis Caesar es ipse tuis.

Lest thou be o'er content, O Caesar, with thy Gaulish spoils,
  Behold defeated Gaul, who now has her avenger.
From Latium leading the triumphal procession
  To the temples of his native land, Grevin, wreathed in Bacchus' ivy
And Apollo's laurels, has set up a trophy to honour Apollo and the Muses,
  Which shall never be oerthrown through all posterity:
And so that a shining victory confirm this trophy all the more,
  Caesar, thou thyself now speakst the tongue of them thou conquerdst.

[23] For a list of 'Sources et ressemblances', see Élisabeth Lapeyre's edition, pp. 223–8; she resolutely downplays Grévin's debt to *Les Abusez*.

[24] The Scottish macrell is, however, an entirely different character from Grévin's Claude; she is based on Ovid's alcoholic old Dipsas, who, as her name indicates, never looked with sober eye upon the rosy dawn: *Amores*, I, viii, 3–4, in *Ovid. The Erotic Poems*, ed. by Peter Green (Harmondsworth, 1982); see *Philotus*, 71. See also *Philotus*, 109–12, lifted straight from *Amores*, I, viii, 105–9.

[25] *Renaissance Studies* 9 (1995), 349–63 (360). See *Les Esbahis*, 674–5, 988–1001, and 1487–90 for strong parallels with the father-daughter relationship in *Philotus*, especially the use of threats and the daughter's appeal to freedom of choice. Compare, especially, Grévin's 992–6 and 1487–90 with *Philotus*, 381–4 and 395–400, respectively. On our increasing understanding of the intertextuality of the whole genre, see *The Italian World of English Renaissance Drama: Cultural Exchange and Intertextuality*, ed. by Michele Marrapodi (Newark, Del., and London, 1998), *passim*. Publication of this book came too late for its findings to be taken into account in the present paper.

[26] The phrase is Alasdair MacDonald's, in footnote 2 to his '*Dixit insipiens*: Sir David Lindsay and Renaissance Folly', in *Media Latinitas, A collection of essays to mark the occasion of the retirement of L. J. Engels*, ed. by R. I. A. Nip *et al.* (Turnhout, 1996), pp. 263–8; the same attitude is evinced by, *inter alia*, Sarah Carpenter, 'Early Scottish Drama', in R. D. S. Jack (ed.), *The History of Scottish Literature Volume 1: Origins to 1660* (Edinburgh, 1988), pp. 199–211 (p. 208).

[27] He highlights 'el movimiento de los personajes sobre las tablas, sus acciones escénicas, que llegan hasta lo circense en los momentos cómicos'[the movement of the characters on the stage, their stage actions, which become pure circus at moments of comedy]; the play is dominated by 'un marcado dinamismo, incluso por un signo de violencia'[a striking amount of energetic action, even a hint of violence]. Rueda wanted to create situations 'en que gestos, actitudes, movimientos, etc., encierran toda su importancia, tanta, por lo menos, como la palabra' [in which gestures, poses, movements, etc., are fully charged with significance, and are at least as important as the words spoken]: Fernando González Ollé (ed.), *Los Engañados, Medora*, Clásicos Castellanos (Madrid, 1973), p. xxxiii.

[28] Othón Arróniz comments in his *Influencia italiana en la comedia española* (Madrid, 1969): 'elimina lo innecesario, poda toda la hojarasca verbal y deja el argumento en tan sustanciales huesos que muchas veces quedan cabos sin unir, inexplicables sin el contexto italiano' [he eliminates what is unnecessary; he prunes all the florid verbiage, and leaves the plot reduced to such bare bones that frequently there are loose ends which are inexplicable unless we know the original Italian context]. Arróniz notes that in Lope de Rueda, the sudden appearance of the male twin is totally unprepared and hence confusing (as in *Philotus*, in fact), but he comments that 'tal confusión debía disiparse fácilmente ante los espectadores mediante el hábil juego escénico de un actor tan experimentado como Lope de Rueda' [any confusion would easily have been cleared up for the spectators by the skilful stagecraft of an actor as experienced as Lope] (pp. 85–6).

[29] Gerardo tells the heroine's father that '¡Las cosas que son encaminadas por Dios,

cómo siempre vienen a parar en buen sucesso!' ['What God puts in hand always ends well!'] and then, 'pues no ha servido Dios que Lelia fuesse mi muger' ['since it was not God's will that Lelia should become my wife'], he welcomes Fabricio as his son-in-law.

30 David Irving's preface to his 1835 edition, for example, complains that 'the probability of the incidents is sometimes impaired by the introduction of a certain character denominated the Pleasant, who, without any apparent concern in the business of the drama, intrudes himself into the most private conferences for the mere purpose of aiming at a joke' (pp. vii–viii).

31 Richard Andrews, '*Gli Ingannati* as a Text for Performance', *Italian Studies* 37 (1982), 26–48 (pp. 29–34).

32 Stanza 172 indicates that at least part of his intended audience consists of those whose 'courtesies' (1348) are on the level of 'courteours that princes hallis do hant' (1345).

33 The closing stanza's reference to praying for 'the persoun of our King … Ane prudent Prince above vs for to ring' (1358, 1360) – a line reminiscent of Robert Sempill's 'our fair young tender King, / Quho[me God] hes set above vs for to Ring' in his *Exhortatioun derect to my Lord Regent* of August 1567 (*Satirical Poems of the Reformation*, ed. by James Cranstoun, 2 vols, STS (Edinburgh, 1891–93), p. 52, 4–5) – is susceptible of two explanations. Either a preceding stanza in honour of the Queen has been deleted by Charteris for his 1603 printing, or else he has added the stanza himself.

34 John Durkan, 'The Library of Mary, Queen of Scots', in *Mary Stewart, Queen in Three Kingdoms*, ed. by Michael Lynch (Oxford, 1988), pp. 71–104, item 7 in Appendix 1 (and pp. 73 and 80).

35 P. J. Ford, *Prince of Poets*, p. 108.

36 Peter Davidson has made these available in parallel text: 'Three Entertainments for the Wedding of Mary, Queen of Scots', *Scotlands* 2.2 (1995), 1–10, and 'The Entry of Mary Stewart into Edinburgh, 1561, and Other Ambiguities', in *Renaissance Studies* 9 (1995), 426–9. For a detailed account of the 1566 baptismal festivities at Stirling, see Michael Lynch, 'Queen Mary's Triumph', *SHR* 69 (1990), 1–21.

37 George Buchanan, *Poemata omnia quae extant* (Amsterdam, 1641), 'Miscellaneorum liber', p. 424; available in parallel text in P. J. Ford, *Prince of Poets*, pp. 274–5. 'We too depend on you, our sun, exposed as we are to all the changes you undergo.'

38 Ibid., 'Epigrammatum liber III', p. 392; available in parallel text in Arthur Williamson and Paul McGinnis (eds), *George Buchanan: The Political Poems*, SHS (Edinburgh, 1997), pp. 274–5. 'May you enjoy solid good health … With you well, all things will go well for us under your reign.' The reference to 'certa salus' may well concern Darnley's serious illness at the end of 1566.

39 R. W. Bond, *Early Plays from the Italian*, p. 153. Given with its music in Carl Grabau's edition, p. 314.

40 *Italian Drama in Shakespeare's Time* (New Haven, Conn., and London, 1989), p. 36.

41 In his *Treatise on Fasting* of 1565, inspired by the threat to the people of God represented by the Queen's successful defeat of the rebellion provoked by her marriage, John Knox recommended the story of Mordocheus and Artaxerxes as suitable matter for sermons; *Works*, ed. by David Laing, 6 vols (Edinburgh 1846–65), VI, 392–426, at 398–9 and 421.

42 This raises fascinating questions in connection with ' "A Lamentable Storie". Mary Queen of Scots and the Inescapable *Querelle des Femmes*', dealt with in David Parkinson's essay of that title in *A Palace in the Wild*, ed. by L. A. J. R. Houwen, A. A. MacDonald, and S. L. Mapstone (Leuven, 2000), pp. 141–60, and in Sarah

Dunnigan, 'The Creation and Self-Creation of Mary Queen of Scots: Literature, Politics and Female Controversies in Sixteenth-Century Scottish Poetry', *Scotlands* 5.2 (1998), 65–88.

[43] See Andrews, '*Gli Ingannati* as a Text for Performance', 26–8.

[44] For Sempill's extant verse, see Cranstoun (ed.), *Satirical Poems of the Reformation*, *passim*, and also John MacQueen, *Ballattis of Luve* (Edinburgh, 1970), pp. lxiii–lxv, 116–20. His commitment to the Lennox cause receives ferocious expression in his poems calling for Darnley's murder to be avenged on the Queen.

[45] Mill, *Philotus*, pp. 83–5.

[46] See Antonia Fraser, *Mary Queen of Scots* (London, 1969), pp. 215–16 and 250–1; see also pp. 210–11 for an account of the Queen's fondness for male attire, which would add another level of allusion to be enjoyed by the courtly audience of *Philotus*.

[47] See Macdiarmid, '*Philotus*', p. 226, for details of John of Lowis.

[48] *CSP Scot.*, II, 313–15.

5

Masks of Revelation and 'the "female" tongues of men': Montgomerie, Christian Lyndsay, and the Writing Game at the Scottish Renaissance Court

Theo van Heijnsbergen

Introduction

Helena Shire has outlined how poets at James VI's court in the early 1580s practised poetry as a writing game, a *lusus regius* ('kingly sport') in which writers used *noms de guerre*.[1] She discusses several examples of this, but does not consider the following sonnet an instance of such impersonation:[2]

> Oft haive I hard, bot ofter fund it treu,
> That Courteours kyndnes lasts bot for a vhyle;
> Fra once your turnes be sped, vhy then Adeu,
> Your promeist freindship passis in exyle.
> Bot (Robene) faith, ye did me not beguyll;
> I hopit ay of you as of the lave.
> If thou had wit, thou wald haif mony a wyle
> To mak thy self be knaune for a knaive.
> Montgomrie, that such hope did once conceave
> Of thy guidwill, nou finds all is forgotten;
> Thoght not bot kyndnes he did at the craiv,
> He finds thy freindship as it rypis is rotten.
> The smeikie smeithis cairs not his passit trauel,
> Bot leivis him lingring, deing of the gravell.

> *lave*: rest
> *smeikie smeithis*: smoky smiths
> *gravell*: kidney- or gall-stones

The unique copy of this sonnet appears in the Ker MS (*c.* 1600), a single-author manuscript exclusively devoted to 'Captain Allexander Montgommerie's Poëm[s]', though also including a few poems written *to* him, in an exchange of verse. The sonnet's title reads: 'Christen Lyndesay to Ro. Hudsone'. We have no other poems attributed to Christian Lyndsay, but other contemporary texts do bring her into the orbit of literary circles at James's Scottish court.

Rather than imposing an interpretation based on authorial 'intentions' on an isolated text, it is more appropriate to consider coterie verse such as this within its original, culture-specific context, as intertextual and 'continuous with other forms of communication'.[3] Such contextualization suggests that this particular sonnet (henceforth 'CL sonnet') could be an act of ventriloquism within a literary coterie, a possibility Shire perhaps side-stepped in order to keep the door open for a possible 'sister' in the 'Castalian' brotherhood.[4] Although it remains possible that a real Christian Lyndsay indeed wrote the sonnet, the present paper explores the possibility that her name was used as a rhetorical identity by another poet, as part of the writing game at James's court. In the latter case, 'Christian Lyndsay' may still refer to an actual poet of that name, or else to a historical individual who was not a poet but whose name had developed specific literary or coterie connotations. Recovering the CL sonnet in such a manner opens up perspectives on the nature of textual impersonation that provided James's court with a dynamic coterie mimetics, which in its turn allows for a more wide-ranging interpretation of the uses of poetry and the writing game at the Scottish Renaissance court in general, through a study of James's 'Ane Admonition to the Maister Poete'.

The Christian Lyndsay sonnet

Reservations about Lyndsay's authorship of the CL sonnet (*c.* 1583) are not new. Both Laing and Cranstoun, Montgomerie's earliest modern editors, thought Montgomerie used Lyndsay's name to plead with Hudson; Rait, editor of James VI's poetry, is more careful when he concludes the sonnet is 'put into the mouth of a third person addressing Hudsone'.[5] Sarah Dunnigan's necessarily brief section on Lyndsay in *A History of Scottish Women's Writing* delicately balances the impact of female presence in the poem with the likelihood of male ventriloquism.[6]

A closer look at the text increases suspicion about Lyndsay's authorship. The opening instantly reveals the sturdy yet intricate directness of Montgomerie at his best. There is no apology for writing the poem, nor any conventional epistolary opening formula. Instead, it opens *in medias res*, instantly grabbing our attention with the paradoxical 'Oft haive I hard, bot ofter fund it true.' On the syntactic surface, the word 'bot' identifies the two half-lines as oppositional, but on the level of meaning it makes them mutually reinforcing: the speaker has often heard about, and even more often experienced, 'courteours kyndnes'. Hearsay and truth, more conventionally thought of as opposites, are here made complementary. The word 'bot' registers the persona's painful awareness of courtly reality, as well as alerting the reader to the poem's layeredness of signification.

We are thus instantly placed in a world of shifting realities; hearsay and truth are both slippery slopes at court, where 'courteours kyndnes lasts bot for a vhyle'. The alliteration in the latter line offers another undermining paradox, this time one of semantic positives (courtesy and kindness) undercut by their own potentially caustic phonaesthetics, and by the poignant pun on kindness as 'of a kind', which addresses Hudson in his moral capacity as a fellow courtier. This play with conflicting realities at court is continued in line 3: 'turnes' evokes the eddying currents of court life, combining the notion of a nourishing flow with that of a deadly vortex. This is underlined by 'once' at the beginning of the line, its momentariness contrasting tellingly with the eternity of 'adeu' at the end. The latter is a word Montgomerie uses several times to great effect when turning his back on former allies or lovers.[7] It is the word of a proud individual who leaves rather than compromises but who also uses other people's awareness of such a temper to apply emotional pressure. Making threats in order to avoid having to implement them is part of a literary game, posing with suspended thunderbolts as in the 'generically deferring genre' of flyting.[8]

Images of betrayal and its consequences are evoked to show Hudson what, given the open-ended nature of the final line, is still his to avert. The sonnet thus rhetorically appropriates the future, but immediately mortgages it in order to control loyalty in the present. The fact that these words to Hudson are allegedly spoken by Lyndsay inserts a third person between the two courtiers and the two time levels of past and future, which provides the author with a quasi-objective, fictional balance within the historical imbalance. Lyndsay thus becomes a mouth-piece (literally a *per-sona*, the mask used in classical performance) through which Montgomerie's relationship with Hudson and with the court in general can be comprehensively manipulated.

The diction, style, and tone of the poem is that of an author who can address Hudson (a professional musician and minor court-poet who became Treasurer of the Chapel Royal in 1587)[9] on equal terms, both socially and poetically, in a way that an obscure female poet, arguably and conventionally, might not. The interaction between the conventional, the startling, and the colloquial in a tight lyrical format; the rhetorical construction of both speaker and addressee through a wide range of voices; the assertive personal stance; the pithy, often proverbial lines; the poignant use of alliteration – all these features of the first eight lines characterize 'Castalian' writing in general but, especially in their striking quality, Montgomerie's in particular. This prepares the way for the opening word of the third quatrain, appearing in small capitals: 'MONTGOMRIE'. That personal name thus becomes a strikingly foregrounded word, both syntactically, thematically, formally, and even visually. Its occurrence at the very heart of the sonnet keeps a firm grip on the inscribed audience's desired response.

An experienced hand is also reflected in the sonnet's robust 4-4-4-2 arrangement and the internal structure of each of these parts, the three quatrains each moving from positive to extremely negative values. Moreover, it is an immaculately 'Castalian' sonnet: it has the rhyme scheme prescribed by James (*ababbcbccdcdee*) and responds eloquently to James's prescription to use sonnets only 'for compendious praysing of any bukes, or the authouris thairof, or ony argumentis of vther historeis, quhair sindrie sentences, and change of purposis are requirit'.[10] The image of the smoking smithy (13) underlines the link to James's courtly company: it is used by Montgomerie and Stewart as the domestic emblem of James's court as a place of sustenance and the work-place for forging poetry.[11] In poignant contrast, the final line contains a strikingly personal signature, with its direct reference to a medical condition that seems to have plagued Montgomerie throughout his adult life.[12] It provides a particularity of personal detail that characterizes Montgomerie's verse generally.

The CL sonnet's final lines turn it into an inverse eulogy (praise of authors was the recommended sonnet subject in the *Reulis and Cautelis*, as quoted above) in the shape of a premature epitaph (the epitaph was one of the modes of composition taught in grammar schools).[13] They manipulate time by rhetorically forcing anticipations of death to bring about a return to life (that is, court), or at least a suspension of dying. The last line provides the necessary dimensions of time and poetry for this paradoxical process to play itself out: the present continuous tenses of 'lingring' and 'deing' turn death into a process rather than a state, and thus create an opportunity for Hudson to provide the desired closure: the coterie 'smithy' can still raise Montgomerie from the dead. The moral profile of Hudson provided by the sonnet itself makes this an unlikely prospect, but keeping that possibility alive means that the poem continues to focus on Hudson's disloyalty rather than on Montgomerie's anger. The poem thus challenges Hudson on all kinds of levels: as a moral being; as a fellow courtier; and as a fellow poet within a coterie context.

The sonnet's author is clearly well acquainted with contemporary poetic conventions as well as with the ways of the court in general and the 'maister' poet's presence within it in particular, continuing Montgomerie's most personal themes and style. The poem highlights rather than camouflages the possibility that Montgomerie is its author. Its voice is that of experience, confidently imperative in expecting the audience to be able to pick up the sonnet's complex process of coded signification. It is unlikely to be its author's one-off literary performance; rather, its belief in its own literary art and the playfully assertive emphasis on wishing to belong to the courtly coterie are clearly reminiscent of Montgomerie's verse of the 1580s. Moreover, the empathetic and emotive tone reflects a partisan concern for a sidelined fellow poet that is remarkable within the competitive court culture that is sketched in an anonymous poem addressed, again, to Robert Hudson, which describes how poets in search of advancement at James's court turned their daggers into 'horns of ink'.[14] In such a context, Lyndsay's empathy, together with the distinct resemblance to Montgomerie's style, makes it plausible that Montgomerie himself was in some way associated with this sonnet's composition, and has a strong claim to being its author.

The above arguments do not imply that no case can be made for Lyndsay as author of the CL sonnet. After all, poems in the writing game are intertextual rather than authorial, so the fact that the CL sonnet is sophisticated or displays a 'sinewy' style, 'linked to the metaphorics of the male body in its prime', does not mean that it must have been written by a male poet.[15] Lyndsay may simply have used the discourse available to her, and her interest in Montgomerie may indeed be a 'decorous displacement of attention from the poet to her object of praise' by a female poet who is not in competition with others.[16] Moreover, if the CL sonnet is indeed a case of ventriloquism, that surely confirms the existence of a real Christian Lyndsay who had *some* form of literary or moral voice, otherwise there would have been no foreseeable effect of impersonating her. Either way, we are witnessing the beginnings of a female literary presence.

Impersonation and gender

Poetic impersonation took many shapes during James's Scottish reign. Firstly, there are examples of joint or even 'proxy' authorship. Robert Ayton, William Alexander, and (possibly) Alexander Craig co-wrote a sonnet sequence in the 1580s.[17] Alexander was also the author of many of *The Psalms of King David Translated by King James* (not published until 1631), while a contemporary colophon credits Sir Thomas Erskine of Gogar with part of James VI's 'Amatoria'.[18] Erskine was James's lifelong friend, here emerging from behind his king as a participant in court poetry; we cannot rule out the possibility of similar joint authorship for the CL sonnet. Furthermore, authors impersonate real-life characters. Thomas Maitland 'does' the Protestant leaders in five voices in 'The Pretended Conference', a compliment returned in George Buchanan's *De Iure Regni apud Scotos* (1579, but circulating in manuscript already in 1569), in which Maitland is cast as one of the debating scholars.[19] Such fictional impersonation indeed intruded upon the factual: Maitland felt compelled to write to Mary to say he had had no hand in Buchanan's politically sensitive fictional debate on her deposition.[20] Mary herself presents a fascinating case of suspected ventriloquism: it is still hotly debated whether or not the 'Casket Sonnets' are indeed the best-known example of cross-speaking in Scottish history.[21] James himself was ventriloquized, too: Nicolas Breton, who claimed to have been with James in Scotland, circulated a 'passionate Sonnet'

James had supposedly written to Anne, but contemporary readers realized that Breton had written it himself.[22]

Montgomerie, too, impersonated historical male individuals, twice stepping into the shoes of men writing to their future wives.[23] A particularly intriguing case – involving ambassadorial, competitive impersonation directed at a fellow poet, as in the Hudson sequence, discussed below – is the brief poetic exchange between Barclay of Ladyland and 'Ezekiel Montgomerie'. The latter was indeed a close relative of Alexander Montgomerie, but in his reply, Ladyland says he is 'nocht ignorant vhose [bag] that [bolt] came fro / Ye lent your name to feght against your frene', and he tells Montgomerie: 'Ye crak so crouse, I ken, becaus ye'r tuo'.[24] This poignantly applies to the CL sonnet as well, written in double persona. Moreover, in three sonnets in the Ker MS, just before the Ladyland exchange, Montgomerie rejects accusations of having written certain other poems. Impersonation was clearly a well-known phenomenon, with Montgomerie himself impersonated as well as impersonator.

Used to speaking *in persona*, Scots Renaissance poets often simply 'perform' the female. A case in point is Stewart of Baldynneis's work. His 'Ansuir of the Foirsaid Hostes' mockingly parodies social and literary conventions as well as stylistic decorum regarding female speech, illustrating very graphically how women entered poetry as part of the rhetorical conversion of woman into an object for the male gaze.[25] The relatively large number of answer poems Stewart addresses to women, in combination with poems written 'in name of' or 'at the desyre of' noble ladies, suggests that women were eager to partake in poetic exchanges but still frequently spoke, either literally or discursively, through male writers.[26] Ventriloquizing the female had already provided earlier Scots male poets with 'a challenging opportunity to exercise their *inuentioun*, to impersonate not only the feminine voice but through that impersonation to evoke, often ironically, other voices and texts';[27] with female potential authors entering into literary circulation in the 'Castalian' period in their own right, the CL sonnet is able to exploit that opportunity in even more ways.[28] In the ambiguity that results from such ventriloquism lies an author's power over the audience's response.

Montgomerie himself uses a woman's voice in a short sonnet sequence, 'A Ladyis Lamentatione', showing developed powers of empathy.[29] Robert Sempill, himself linked to both Montgomerie and Lyndsay in Montgomerie's short sequence of sonnets 'To Robert Hudson' (henceforth 'Hudson sequence'), used 'Maddie of the Cailmarket' as his polemical persona.[30] These examples suggest reasons for the use of a woman's voice in the CL sonnet. They indicate that a woman's voice was associated with literary lament and complaint but was simultaneously, as the figure of 'the abandoned', endowed with moral authority.[31] Elizabeth Harvey's study of male ventriloquism of female voices concludes that Renaissance poetry reveals 'a profound affinity between the representation of the abandoned woman and male constructions of the feminine voice'. With abandonment as woman's ontological condition ('When a man is abandoned, in fact, he feels like a woman'), the genre of the complaint 'is *the* paradigmatic ventriloquized text ... its querulous tone and exiled condition has [*sic*] come to define a version of woman'.[32] Harvey cites Ovid's *Heroides* as the archetype of many Renaissance female complaints, but in a Scottish context Henryson's *Testament of Cresseid* also immediately springs to mind, 'the most accomplished example of female-voiced complaint in Middle Scots poetry'.[33] That ventriloquizing female complaint, and Cresseid's in particular, was indeed an active practice in 'Castalian' days is shown by *The Laste Epistle of Creseyd to Troyalus*, attributed – doubtfully – to William Fowler.[34]

When writing the CL sonnet, Montgomerie (or, indeed, Lyndsay) was undoubtedly aware of this gendering of the lyrical voice. Manoeuvring that voice into a courtly context triggers the language of accusation inherent in the voice of complaint, activating the subordinate discourse of the victim of courtly persuasion who has become only too aware of the conditional nature of courtiers' 'kyndnes'. It is a discourse that shares its vocabulary with anti-court and anti-Petrarchan literature, and gives the CL sonnet the moral edge, and Montgomerie the role of victim, that the latter was looking for.[35] The sonnet, in a deliberate generic and stylistic shock effect, thus breaks the usual prescriptions for female reticence and docility, instead adopting the 'virile, masculine style' that was propagated by Sidney.[36] The female speaker's robust style and her sharply worded accusation of betrayal purposefully counter the expectations raised by courtly decorum, and they are all the more powerful and urgent because transgressive.

Montgomerie's motive for ventriloquism is not difficult to find. The CL sonnet is linked to a period in which Montgomerie was exiled from court, as an analysis of its content in combination with manuscript evidence shows: the Ker MS, which is very deliberately organized,[37] leads up to the CL sonnet with a set of five sonnets (the Hudson sequence) that explicitly deals with such a period of exile from court, when getting his voice heard there was a priority. Perhaps anticipating how his own voice would be received at court, these five sonnets dissipate that voice in a range of different tones and genres (epistle, fable, eulogy) in an attempt to speak through, and hide behind, a persona, a genre, or another text, thus turning political necessity into an opportunity to display literary skill. Lingering away in enforced rural exile, Montgomerie in this way tries to persuade Hudson to be his ambassador to the king. These sonnets thus provide instances of textual ventriloquism, speaking with the tongues of other texts in a serious game of courtly politics. The CL sonnet involves the same addressee, deliberately echoes words and images from the Hudson sequence, and immediately follows that sequence in a purposefully organized MS. Most importantly, its mixture of complaint and justified assertiveness is precisely the tone Montgomerie reserves for the poem to follow up the Hudson sequence (i.e. the CL sonnet), if Hudson does not respond positively to the sequence itself. The Hudson sequence and the CL sonnet are thus causally and formally linked in a manner that strongly suggests they constitute one makar's 'inventioun', one composite voice, with Lyndsay embodying the 'offer' of a final ultimatum.

Using a ventriloquized intermediary who can plead with moral authority and discuss Montgomerie's case objectively enables Montgomerie to be participant as well as observer, speaker as well as narrator, in a subtle but very powerful manipulation of deictic and forensic rhetoric. Speaking with these two tongues, 'Lyndsay' can express bitterness but at the same time make that bitterness remove its own causes. Moreover, transparently transferring the qualities of the verse to a third person forces the reader to articulate these in the act of re-establishing their 'makar'. The latter's poetic skill is thus effectively highlighted in the very act of being quasi-denied, the poem impressing the author's identity by erasing it. An understanding between audience and author regarding the illocutionary nature of such poetry is crucial in order for such artistic commu-nication to be appreciated, diverting tension towards more playful, less personal domains. If the audience lacks the means or ability to remove the mask and recognize the display of literary parody and skill that the imperson-ation involves, the poem risks having the opposite effect of that intended, unable to convey its artful representation of courtly reality, its deferral, through play, of finality. To minimize that risk, the CL sonnet provides its readers with the means to deconstruct it as a mask of revelation.

At court, with faction immanent or at least always imminent, such speaking *in persona* remained standard poetic practice, providing author and audience with room to manoeuvre in trying to connect mimesis to reality. In this context, the Hudson sequence and the CL sonnet are best read, in tandem, as a rhetorical play with the lyrical voice on the theme of courtly supplication, yet at the same time preserving an intensely personal quality resembling that of Thomas Wyatt, who also impersonated female speakers within a literary coterie.[38] The CL sonnet thus comes most into its own if read as an act of transparent impersonation.

'Ane Admonition to the Maister Poete'

The first poem Shire discusses in her analysis of 'the first phase of the writing game' (1579–82) is a poem that mentions Christian Lyndsay and, it would seem, Robert Hudson.[39] James VI's 'Admonition to the Maister Poete' makes affectionate fun of Montgomerie, who has lost a horse race after having boasted beyond measure about his horse. He has now slipped away from court with an 'ill … grace' (95). One 'Robert' has reported all this in rhyme and makes fun of him (13, 32), while 'elf gett Polluart helpis the smithy smuik' (14) in order to become the new royal favourite. The poem refers several times to flyting, 'crakking', and other potentially playful (quasi-)literary forms of expression, but the attendant convivial images, in fact, bring out the poem's serious message. James considered it a poem of some relevance, quoting from it in his *Reulis and Cautelis* as embodying 'heich & graue subiectis, specially drawin out of learnit authouris'.[40] The poem's camaraderie embeds repeated assertions of hierarchical relations that anchor positions of counsel and authority at court. This mixture of tones makes it difficult to see where jocularity turns into seriousness, but that ambiguity is exactly what constitutes James's authority in this poem. Moreover, it is a mixture of the light-hearted *because of* the grave: James needs to admonish Montgomerie without alienating him, to continue a system of literary exchange that serves a political one.

Interaction between gender and a form of ventriloquism again plays a role in this. To outline the roles he allocated to himself and Montgomerie, James refers to – what must be Henryson's – fable of the lion and the mouse (3), in which 'Henryson is most experimental with the female-voiced complaint': Henryson's mouse is female, her genre that of complaint, but, when required to adopt a role of leadership, she is represented as male.[41] In its turn, the lion, identified with the masculine qualities of royal power and physical strength, switches to female modes when captured; as Fox noted, his lament has striking similarities with Cresseid's.[42] In contemporary poetics, James's advisory role as mouse is thus gendered 'female', yet it is invested with socio-political authority through its interaction with 'advice to princes' literature, in a sophisticated inversion of master-servant reality. That gender roles are at play here is confirmed by the metafictional prologue that frames Henryson's fable. Its reference points and speaking parts are all explicitly identified as male: the narrator-persona discusses literature and authority with Aesop, who calls him 'sone' and whom the persona calls 'father' and 'maister', anchoring 'fatherheid' in the joint forces of law, morality, and fiction.[43] In the CL sonnet, a similar awareness of the interaction between morality and shifts in literary gender in the configuration of power and identity underlies the use of 'the "female" tongues of men', which appears to have been a well-known feature of sixteenth-century Scottish poetics.[44]

James's interest in poetry was due to its potential to invest a sovereign with epistemic power to determine meanings and structure the kingdom's hierarchies. That is why the 'Admonition' is sensitive to the fact that Montgomerie has caused poetry to be associated with vain 'crakking', as the poem's full title indicates: 'Ane admonition to the maister poete to leaue of greit crakking

quhi[lk he] / deid shau leist he not onely sklander him self bot alsua the haill
professours of the airt'. Montgomerie's 'crakking' undermines not only his own
but also James's position, disturbing the kind of political and cultural exchange
at court that James desired. At the heart of this metapoetic 'defence of poetry',
the name 'Christian Lyndsay' is suddenly sprung upon us, as the second of three
rhetorical identities which James conjures up at the end of the 'Admonition' to
allocate the roles of those partaking in his court's political poetics:

> Nor yit ye uald not call to memorie
> Quhat grund ye gaue to Cristiane Lindsay byit
> For nou sho sayis quhilk makes us all full sorie
> Youre craft to lye uith leaue nou haue I triit. (106–9)

Montgomerie has apparently given her 'grounde' for raising objections against
poetry, the language of the coterie, by his vainglorious arrogation, even abuse,
of the language of truth (poetry), in an act of boastful lying.[45] A note in
James's hand on the verso of the folio that contains this section of the
'Admonition' in MS Bodley 165 shows that this greatly concerned James:

> to admit my protestatioun quhilk I made in the beginning. fullis uill
> quhiles giue uise men ane counsal. felix quem faciunt aliena pericula
> cautum. that a the haill airt is sklanderit be him quhilk giues Christiane
> Lindsay a ground.[46]

The defensive tone of this note underlines James's anxiety. The embedded
Latin proverb ('Happy is the man who is made cautious by the perils experienced by others') is also the last quotation in James's *Basilikon Doron*,
emphasizing its final message to its very private audience,[47] and is echoed in
the 'Admonition' ('Greit hape hes he quhom uthers parrellis ganis', 101). It
communicates James's concern about Montgomerie's behaviour and at the
same time tells Montgomerie to read the poem as counsel. The note's reitera-
tion of the value of 'fullis counsall' is similarly expressed in a close verbal
parallel in the 'Admonition' (99) which links the poem's end to its beginning,
where the reference to 'The Lion and the Mouse' had introduced the subject
of counsel. The Ker MS quotes the first half of Proverbs 1.7, 'The fear of the
Lorde is the beginning of wisdom', as an epigraph in a very prominent place,
namely on its title page. The complementary half of that quote is: 'but fools
despise wisdom and instruction'. This sentiment was clearly charged with
special meaning at the time, reflecting a continuous dialogue between the
individual and authority.

The other two names that flank Lyndsay at the end of the 'Admonition' are
likewise linked into James's attempt to mix counsel with conciliation, using the
rhetorical figure of the fool as a catalyst. In the concluding stanza James gives

himself the pseudonym of 'William Mow' (112). A *mow* is a grimace, a piece of clowning 'for amusement only, not to be taken seriously', which underlines the harmless nature of the character James wishes to play here.[48] Although a real William Mow lived in Dalkeith at the time, and another was an Edinburgh hatmaker,[49] the name is here surely a rhetorical cipher in a coded writing game, an almost carnivalesque, wine-drenched clown king in whom Bacchus meets Bakhtin. James adopts this 'upside-down' identity to soften his admonitory words to a proud favourite with a liking for drink, thus voiding the 'Admonition' of tension in the 'official' world. But James's 'mow' has serious features: the face-pulling court jester is the most versatile mask in the writing game, since a fool by nature can freely shift from satirical to self-mocking modes, all within one and the same rhetorical disguise, and is therefore traditionally allowed the widest range of conciliar and corrective reference at court.

The first of the three names mentioned at the end of the 'Admonition', 'Rob Stene', also partakes of the character of a fool or jester. The name is here applied to Montgomerie (96a). In Montgomerie and Polwarth's *Flyting*, Polwarth calls Montgomerie a fool for trying to compete with him in rhyme: 'Rob Stene, ye raif, foryetting quhom ye mache'.[50] *Rob Stene's Dream*, a dream-vision dealing with topical politics of 1591–92, is attributed both through a colophon and text-internally to 'Rob Stene'.[51] Considering the sensitive nature of the *Dream*, that is unlikely to be its author's real name, and its modern editor thinks Stene 'was being impersonated by a clever poet', his name 'a by-word for a fool' that could be used by, or applied to, anyone.[52] It was perhaps based on George Steuin, jester at Mary's court; her son did not have an official court fool, but poets may have simply modelled an imaginary figure on this earlier fool's name, using 'Rob' as the generic name for an uneducated or rustic figure.

It has been known for some time that there was a real 'Robert Steven' in the Scottish royal household in 1587–88 and in 1599,[53] but payments to him never specified his official duties. To this can now be added a substantial number of references from the unpublished Treasurer's Accounts, recording payments to 'Rob(ert) Stene / Stevin, poet', in 1580, 1582, 1587, 1596, and 1598.[54] There are also payments to 'Rob(ert) Stene / Stevin' *without* the epithet 'poet' in 1580 and, regularly, from 1586 to 1590.[55] These payments indicate that the 'Rob Stevin' who is not identified as a poet was regularly paid smaller sums of money, where 'Rob Stevin, poet', received larger sums of money, but more irregularly. If all references are to one man, it seems he was a daily servitor at James's court who at irregular intervals received extra sums of money that may have involved poetic service. The above-average payment for clothes in October 1589 in connection with Anne's arrival suggests that Stene was indeed called upon to serve his king at high-profile public events in an at least relatively prominent role.[56]

'Rob Stevin' also appears with James Lauder (the musician), William Hudson (the king's dancing master and 'violar'), and William Murray, 'Maister of the Carriage', in payments by James to a group of trusted household servants from December 1598 to February 1599.[57] This is interesting company, and not just because all these men had served James from the early 1580s onwards in the inner household circle, but especially because the wife of William Murray, Maister of the Carriage (that is, the officer in charge of the conveyance of the baggage of an army, or of goods in general), recorded in 1588, was one Christian Lyndsay, so far the only woman of that name found at James's court.[58] Moreover, the CL sonnet is addressed to Robert Hudson, brother to William, and Montgomerie wrote sonnets to an unidentified William Murray and to James Lauder, a Catholic agent and poet who moved among the same people as Montgomerie.[59] This wife of the Maister of the Carriage, therefore, clearly had access to Montgomerie's circles, which makes her a likely candidate to be the CL sonnet's author or ventriloquized speaker. Moreover, the fact that we must now assume that 'Rob Stene' in the 'Admonition' refers to an actual poet makes it more likely that Lyndsay, mentioned in the subsequent stanza, is the name of a real-life author, too.

An inquiry into Stene's reputation as a poet may throw further light on Lyndsay's relationship to literature, and on James's intentions in the 'Admonition'. References to Stene's poetry associate his name with literary utterance that lacks shape and authority. A poem by Stewart of Baldynneis describes itself as:

> Ane new sort of rymand rym,
> Rymand alyk in rym and rym,
> Rymd efter sort of guid Rob steine
> Tein is to purches Robs teine.[60]

The poem to which this is a heading initially seems a largely shapeless cascade of couplets, but on closer inspection its intentions begin to emerge. Stewart's parodic wit adds 'inventioun' to the style of a more pedestrian author, making 'guid' what is otherwise 'bad' Rob Stene by imposing a very complex combination of *rime équivoquée* and *rime enchaînée* on the helter-skelter heroic couplets that *Rob Stene's Dream* also associates Stene with.[61] In *Rob Stene's Dream* Morpheus implies that Stene makes a fool of himself when pretending to write like an educated man:

> Within thy boundis thy self contene.
> Remember thow art bot Rob Stene.
> Thy wit can not win to sic a wark.
> Thow scornis thy self to play the clark. (45–8)

Likewise, Stene wakes from his dream 'as ane with spreits possest and pynd' (696), claiming that Pasquil, who is standing near, caused him to speak out as he did. Stene thus becomes a Scottish Pasquil, whose writings are

> Satyrique all and full of vennum
> And yet maist trew, thocht thay be sair,
> For he the trewth for nane will spair. (701–3)

In terms of both content and style, his reckless 'planenes [may] mak sum folk offendit' (719). Being 'Rob Stene' meant being associated with one who delighted 'to speik despyt / ... and spair no manis names' (*Rob Stene's Dream*, 706–8). That suggests reasons why the *Flyting* and the 'Admonition' apply Stene's name to Montgomerie: their forthright contentiousness made both poets 'Pasquils' to the court.

Just as James annotates his reference to Lyndsay, the Tullibardine MS glosses Polwarth's blunt warning to Montgomerie during their *Flyting* ('Rob Stene, ye raif, foryetting quhom ye mache') with: 'Robert Stene the kingis fuile'.[62] Likewise, when Montgomerie calls Polwarth a bad poet, the latter retorts: 'Ga, drunkin dyvour [*debtor*], the address / Or borrow the Ambassattis brekis' (99.IV.46). Here, the scribe's gloss reads: 'Ambassatis is the name of ane fuill';[63] in other words, these lines tell Montgomerie to 'wear the fool's breeches' when addressing his audience. These are the only two glosses in the Tullibardine MS, which provides the most reliable version of the *Flyting*; it was in the possession of the Murrays, a family with close literary connections to the inner circle of the court as well as to Montgomerie.[64] Apart from the sonnet to William Murray, mentioned above, the CL sonnet itself is immediately followed in the Ker MS by a sonnet 'To M. J. Murray', both poems that reveal personal tensions underly the literary exchange.[65] These glosses that highlight the presence of the rhetorical perspective of a fool therefore carry considerable interpretative weight, as they derive from people with whom Montgomerie was on terms of personal and even intimate acquaintance.

The emphasis in these glosses on the fool as a rhetorical voice at court is a possible clue to Stene's status and may explain why his name is applied to Montgomerie. In the absence of an official court fool, Stene may have occasionally and unofficially functioned in this role. The doggerel satire that the above references clearly associate with Stene matches a fool's status, yet at the same time qualifies Stene for occurring as 'poet' in the accounts. 'Rob Stene' is thus a historical figure as well as a ready-made rhetorical identity to be freely used by anyone. The use of such a figure reflects the coterie's need for a somehow omniscient, ethical authority from within the community who nevertheless always remains an outsider, and distinct from political authority. Such an outsider on the inside (indeed, like a court fool or an ambassador) is thus a very useful, multi-faceted intermediary, as 'William Mow' or Rob Stene were to James, and 'Christian Lyndsay' to Montgomerie. Therefore, 'Christian Lyndsay' or 'Rob Stene' are best read, not as real names or even pseudonyms, but as textually constructed identities used within the rhetorical community as voices from without it that nevertheless have a particular, conventionalized form of authority within it, separate from their historical identities as courtiers, or, indeed poets. James used the name 'Stene' again much later in life: he called the Duke of Buckingham, his favourite in the 1620s, 'Steenie' and 'My sweet Steenie gossip' in his letters to him; Buckingham adopted that nickname himself in his replies.[66] As Goldberg comments, in such name-giving 'all relationships – master and servant, father and son, husband and wife – are replicated in the intensity of feeling',[67] and the parallel with Buckingham suggests that James's application of the label 'Rob Steen' to Montgomerie is evidence of James's feelings of intimate affection for his 'maister poet'.

The 'Admonition' thus shows how James developed the rhetoricized theatre of a literary court as a discourse in which textually constructed authority could regulate relations between courtiers and between courtiers and monarch, making substance arise out of formal playfulness. For poets, this game provided a means of getting the king's ear in a court environment filled with the voices and impersonations of rival courtiers. In such a context, authorship of texts was a multi-faceted tool, which explains the accusations of plagiarism (for example, in the *Flyting*), the denial of authorship, and the habit of impersonation, of adapting disguises in a shadowy tournament of rhetorical fencing. In this royally choreographed rhetorical theatre, Rob Stene, Christian Lyndsay, and William Mow are rhetorical figures that in the 'Admonition' give rise to a composite fourth one, that of James himself as a reprimanding 'wise fool'. In this coterie short-hand, characters have their own particular area of reference, acquiring certain values within the writing game. Casting Montgomerie as plain-speaking Rob Stene, James subsequently inserts Lyndsay's censure of poetic licence as a check on Montgomerie's 'ill … grace' (95) before offering reconciliation in the shape of William Mow. James thus uses Lyndsay and Stene as rhetorical ambassadors to make sure Montgomerie 'mendis … misdeid' (109). Together, these figures constitute a textualized mobbing of Montgomerie by means of a sovereign poet troping his different voices. Montgomerie does exactly the same to Hudson in the Hudson sequence and CL sonnet.

Stewart, in his 'guid Rob Steine' poem, writes: 'Is it not vousting vaine to say ve Men / Mend may all thing by help of guid vemen?' (55–6): the issue of bragging and its mending through the agency of women was clearly a topos in the writing game. In such a male rhetorical universe, it is difficult to hear or recognize a female author speaking in her own voice. Whether she is an object or an agent of discourse, in both cases she has to discard her self in order to be allowed to speak. Paradoxically, of course, this keeps alive the possibility that the CL sonnet was indeed written by Lyndsay herself. Moreover, the references to her suggest she was an individual with a critical mind, holding well-known views about poetry and (its relation to) morality that Montgomerie is accused of having ignored or forgotten (106). However, the fact that James mentions her for her censure of the coterie raises questions about her authorship of the CL sonnet: it is unlikely that a person who criticizes poetry, and Montgomerie's in particular, as a medium of potential untruthfulness, would apply the techniques of that same medium in the name of truthfulness to construct an eloquent attack on the *detractors* of Montgomerie. It seems rather that, in the CL sonnet, Montgomerie performs the female for rhetorical effect, in striking illustration of the claim that 'for a male author to write women … was to refer not to women, but … to the traditions of male textual activity'.[68]

The Hudson sequence

We return to the first sonnet of the Hudson sequence. It opens with an evocation of the brotherhood of the poets who convene at the smoking smithy of the court, thus attaching itself to other poems containing such 'Castalian' signature motifs, such as the CL sonnet. After a self-mocking description of life in rural exile, Montgomerie ends this sonnet by calling on Hudson to seize the 'Castalian' day:

> Your self and I, old Scot and Robert Semple.
> Quhen we are dead, that all our dayis bot daffis,
> Let Christian Lyndesay wryt our epitaphis. (12–14)

Where the four male poets are associated with 'daffis' ('acting playfully or irresponsibly'), Christian Lyndsay, in a richly suggestive contrast, is associated with its rhymed opposite, 'epitaphis'. However ironic the overtones of this concluding couplet may be, Lyndsay is here again pictured as an outsider who is apparently able to assess the literary and – probably related – moral quality of poets, which corresponds to her appearance in the CL sonnet and the 'Admonition'. The obituary nature of the literary and critical activity that the final line attributes to Lyndsay anticipates the CL sonnet itself, which is indeed, as argued above, an 'epitaph' on Montgomerie by 'Christian Lyndsay', again confirming the links between the Hudson sequence and the CL sonnet.

Just as in the 'Admonition', however, Lyndsay is here banned to the margins of the poem in function of male poetic brotherhood. These poems are thus in tune with the Ladyland exchange. Ladyland, after threatening Montgomerie that he might turn nasty if provoked further (9–11), suggests they dissolve any ill will in alcohol and male companionship, having sent the women to bed. In the 'Admonition', too, poetry resides where men come together in 'pen and drinke' (113). Even at this playful end of the literary spectrum, female voices are shut out from passages where power and identity are negotiated. Similarly, the wilful abandon of 'daffis' (13) in the opening sonnet in the Hudson sequence has resonances in Montgomerie's *Flyting* with Polwarth, who responds to Montgomerie's challenge with: 'dastard thow daffis' (99.VIII.10). Evidence from *DOST* shows that the verb was mainly used in the second half of the sixteenth century, and that its meaning was negative rather than neutral. This means that the 'daffis'–'epitaphs' rhyme associates Lyndsay's imagined 'epitaphis' with the judgemental tone of 'daffis', putting her in quite firm opposition to the *carpe diem* Montgomerie proposes to Hudson.

The combined evidence of the references portrays Lyndsay and Stene generally as corrective, even censorious presences in the 'Castalian' rhetorical universe. They have an almost choric presence within the inner circle of the 'Castalian' writing game, interrogating the coterie socially from within, yet poetically still kept outside it. They were instead given rhetorical identities in and by that inner coterie that emphasized aspects of their writing that were at odds with the coterie's conventions. James and Montgomerie used these rhetorical identities to maximum effect. Thus, in the 'Admonition' James, paradoxically, by distancing himself from Montgomerie's critics can afford to criticize Montgomerie. Likewise, in the CL sonnet, Montgomerie can be sharply critical of Hudson by using Lyndsay's censorious voice rather than his own, thus deflecting tension away from the coterie centre in the very act of expressing that tension.

Within this coterie, courtier-poets quickly tried to rise by using the pen, which was, after all, their king's preferred strategy in troping sovereignty and ruling the kingdom as well. In the absence of theatre in Scotland, the writing game offered James scope for 'the royal trope that declares the inherent theatricality of power'.[69] James encouraged the use of textualized identities such as 'Rob Stene' to turn what could become a divisive, potentially destructive form of competition into a metaphysical strategy of shape-shifting. The poem addressed to Robert Hudson that records how poets at James's court turned daggers into 'horns of Ink', quoted earlier, indeed singles out the 'plesant taels / Of formis manifould' of Ovid's *Metamorphoses* as the most appropriate metaphor for 'Castalian' court life.[70] In his *Chamæleon* (1570), Buchanan represents his treacherous opponent as a shape-shifter: the courtly game met with moral objections, and Christian Lyndsay and Rob Stene may have voiced such concerns. English courtiers noted the 'relative informality' and 'easy outspokenness' of the Scottish court and its 'humorous use of trivial shared experience … as a strategy against division, addressing the problem it represents'.[71] The latter is exactly what the CL sonnet and the 'Admonition' do.

In this context, to attribute the CL sonnet unquestioningly (or only) to a historical Christian Lyndsay equals reading literary history backwards, ignoring contemporary coterie poetics that viewed poetry primarily as illocutionary rather than cathartic action. 'Christian Lyndsay' was most likely indeed 'not a textual subject but an object invented by a male author engaged in literary cross-dressing often in order to address other men'.[72] Continued attention to such contemporary poetics will help re-establish, and thus allow us to remove, the masks of revelation so often worn by Scottish Renaissance authors. Otherwise, we risk incurring Montgomerie's own censure, expressed when denying authorship of another poem: 'I wonder of your Wisdomes that ar wyse / That baith miskennis my Method and my Muse'.[73]

Notes

[1] Helena Mennie Shire, *Song, Dance and Poetry of the Court of Scotland under King James VI* (Cambridge, 1969). I am extremely grateful for comments by Professor Alasdair A. MacDonald, Dr Sally Mapstone, and Dr Nicola Royan on earlier drafts of the present article.

[2] Transcribed from Edinburgh University MS De.3.70, fol. 68ᵛ. All other references to Montgomerie's verse are to Volume I of *Alexander Montgomerie. Poems*, ed. by David Parkinson, 2 vols, STS (Edinburgh, 2000). Punctuation is my own; yoghs and thorns have been changed to <y> and <th>, respectively.

[3] Arthur F. Marotti, *Manuscript, Print, and the English Renaissance Lyric* (Ithaca, NY, and London, 1995), p. 160.

[4] The poets discussed in the present paper engaged in responding directly to each other's poetry in ways that can be conveniently summed up as a 'writing game'. The labels 'Castalian' and 'coterie' are here used for ease of reference, applied in a retrospective rather than programmatic manner. The appropriateness of the label 'Castalian' to refer to James's court poets is discussed in Priscilla Bawcutt, 'James VI's Castalian Band: A Modern Myth', *SHR* 80 (2001), 251–9.

[5] *The Poems of Alexander Montgomery. With biographical notices by David Irving*, ed. by David Laing (Edinburgh, 1821), p. 303; *The Poems of Alexander Montgomerie*, ed. by James Cranstoun, STS (Edinburgh and London, 1887), pp. 340–1; Robert S. Rait, *Lvsvs Regivs, Being Poems and Other Pieces by King Iames Ye First* (Oxford, [1901]), p. 13.

[6] Sarah M. Dunnigan, 'Scottish Women Writers, *c.* 1560–*c.* 1650', in *A History of Scottish Women's Writing*, ed. by Douglas Gifford and Dorothy McMillan (Edinburgh, 1997), pp. 15–43 (pp. 15–17).

[7] *Montgomerie*, ed. Parkinson, nos 68.IV.1–3 and 33.8, 40.

[8] Sally Mapstone, 'Invective as Poetic: The Cultural Contexts of Polwarth and Montgomerie's Flyting', *SLJ* 26.2 (1999), 18–40 (p. 29).

[9] *Thomas Hudson's Historie of Judith*, ed. by James Craigie, STS (Edinburgh and London, 1941), p. xi.

[10] *The Poems of James VI of Scotland*, ed. by James Craigie, STS, 2 vols (Edinburgh and London, 1955–1958), I (1955), 81.

[11] Shire, *Song, Dance and Poetry*, p. 97, draws attention to this central metaphor.

[12] *Montgomerie*, ed. Parkinson, nos 72.I.6, 99.II.37, 99.VIII.64.

[13] *Poems of James VI*, ed. Craigie, I, 81; Marotti, *Manuscript, Print*, p. 19.

[14] *The Works of William Fowler*, ed. by Henry W. Meikle *et al.* 3 vols, STS (Edinburgh and London, 1914–1940), III (1940), pp. cli, 10.

15 Patricia Parker, 'Virile Style', in *Pre-Modern Sexualities*, ed. by Louise Fradenburg and Carla Freccero (New York and London, 1996), pp. 201–22 (p. 203).

16 Dunnigan, 'Scottish Women Writers', p. 27.

17 *The English and Latin Poems of Sir Robert Ayton*, ed. by Charles B. Gullans, STS (Edinburgh and London, 1963), pp. 262–6.

18 David Harris Willson, *King James VI and I* (London, 1956), pp. 215–16; James Orchard Halliwell, *Poetical Miscellanies from a Manuscript Collection of the Time of James I*, Percy Society (London, 1845), p. 37; *Poems of James VI*, ed. Craigie, II (1958), 273–4; Curtis Perry, 'Royal Authorship and Problems of Manuscript Attribution in the Poems of King James VI and I', *Notes and Queries* 244 (1999), 243–6. For details of Erskine's life, see *The Scots Peerage*, ed. by J. Balfour Paul, 9 vols (Edinburgh, 1904–1914), V (1908), 84–6.

19 Thomas Maitland, 'The Pretended Conference', in *Bannatyne Club Miscellany* I, part 1, ed. by Sir Walter Scott and David Laing (Edinburgh, 1827), pp. 37–50.

20 I. D. McFarlane, *Buchanan* (London, 1981), p. 393.

21 The sequence attributed to Mary itself talks about 'writings tricked out in a learned tone / That could not be the product of her own brain': *Bittersweet Within My Heart. The Collected Poems of Mary, Queen of Scots*, ed. and trans. by Robin Bell (London, 1992), p. 49.

22 Marotti, *Manuscript, Print*, p. 14.

23 *Montgomerie*, ed. Parkinson, nos 79 and 84 (I and II).

24 *Montgomerie*, ed. Parkinson, no. 95.

25 *Poems of John Stewart of Baldynneis*, ed. by Thomas Crockett, STS (Edinburgh and London, 1913), II (vol I never published), p. 181.

26 Ibid., pp. 141, 118–19; pp. 115–17, 131–4. J. W. Saunders, 'From Manuscript to Print. A Note on the Circulation of Poetic MSS in the Sixteenth Century', *Proceedings of the Leeds Philosophical and Literary Society* 6 (1944–52), 507–28, documents how in sixteenth-century England many women participated in literary circles but initially often left the writing to men.

27 Anne M. McKim, ' "Makand hir mone": Masculine Constructions of the Feminine Voice in Middle Scots Complaints', *Scotlands* 1 (1994), 32–46 (p. 44).

28 Barbara McCarter Bloy, ' "Women's Exercise": Studies in the Female Personae of Elizabethan Miscellanies' (unpublished doctoral thesis, University of Tennessee, 1977), pp. iii, 5, refers to the ability of male poets to impersonate the 'other' as their 'negative capability', particularly visible when that 'other' is female. 'Tudor poets were rhetoricians every one', and practised mimesis as taught by contemporary manuals of rhetoric (pp. iii, 4).

29 *Montgomerie*, ed. Parkinson, no. 75.

30 *Montgomerie*, ed. Parkinson, no. 72.I.12–14. On Sempill's use of 'Maddie', see *Rob Stene's Dream*, ed. by David Reid (Stirling, 1989), pp. 37, 54.

31 This link between gender and genre is a well-known phenomenon: see Gail Reitenbach, ' "Maidens are simple, some men say": Thomas Campion's Female Persona Poems', in *The Renaissance Englishwoman in Print*, ed. by Anne M. Haselkorn and Betty S. Travitsky (Amherst, Mass., 1990), pp. 80–95 (p. 82); Elizabeth D. Harvey, *Ventriloquized Voices. Feminist Theory and English Renaissance Texts* (London and New York, 1992), pp. 140–1. A similarly gendered figure of womanhood is 'Lady Scotland'; versions of her appear in *The Complaynte of Scotland (c. 1550)*, ed. by A. M. Stewart, STS (Edinburgh, 1979) as well as in the 'Complaint of Scotland' and 'The Lamentatioun of Lady Scotland' from the Reformation period: *Satirical Poems of the Time of the Reformation*, ed. by James Cranstoun, 2 vols, STS (Edinburgh and London, 1891–93), I (1891), pp. 95–9, 226–39.

32 Harvey, *Ventriloquized Voices*, pp. 140–1; Lawrence Lipking, *Abandoned Women*

and Poetic Tradition (Chicago, 1988), p. xix. Lipking, p. 129, sees male poets' use of the model of the abandoned woman as a stage of poetic self-definition, while John Kerrigan, in his *Motives of Woe. Shakespeare and 'Female Complaint': A Critical Anthology* (Oxford, 1991), notes (p. 12) that the use of the female voice heightens the notion of the struggle between a narrator's imposition and the speaker's vehemence, the latter trying 'to assert her position as subject', which turns female complaints into 'miniature devices for generating interpretative instability'. See also Bernard Cerquiglini, 'The Syntax of Discursive Authority', *Yale French Studies* 70 (1986), 183–98 (p. 192): loss initiates female discourse, making it 'the register of the lament, a privileged speech-act for the female voice; its signature, in fact, by which it may be heard and identified'.

33 McKim, ' "Makand hir mone" ', p. 33. On the 'male' use of Cresseid, see Felicity Riddy, ' "Abject odious": Feminine and Masculine in Henryson's *Testament of Cresseid*, in *The Long Fifteenth Century*, ed. by Helen Cooper and Sally Mapstone (Oxford, 1997), pp. 229–48.

34 *Works of Fowler*, I (1914), 379–88. S. L. Mapstone, 'The Laste Epistle of Creseyd to Troyalus', in *Sentences. Essays presented to Alan Ward* (Southampton, 1988), pp. 105–17 (p. 105), instances that 'references to *Troilus* and the *Testament* are not infrequent in the Castalian circle in this period', and reminds us that the best complete source text of the *Testament* is in fact a 1593 Edinburgh print. On *The Laste Epistle*, see also Anne M. McKim, 'Tracing the Ring: Henryson, Fowler, and Chaucer's *Troilus*', *Notes and Queries* 238 (1993), 449–51.

35 Reitenbach, ' "Maydes are simple" ', shows that Campion's female persona poems have exactly the same features: strongly delineated speakers that counter Petrarchan conventions by having women speakers use male language ironically.

36 Parker, 'Virile Style', p. 202. On obedience, silence, and piety as prescribed characteristics of women in literature, see Betty S. Travitsky, 'Introduction: Placing Women in the English Renaissance', in *The Renaissance Englishwoman in Print*, ed. by Haselkorn and Travitsky, pp. 3–41.

37 R. D. S. Jack, *Alexander Montgomerie* (Edinburgh, 1985), pp. 38, 70, 84–6; Parkinson, *Montgomerie*, II, p. 5.

38 *Collected Poems of Sir Thomas Wyatt*, ed. by Kenneth Muir and Patricia Thomson (Liverpool, 1969), pp. 163–4 and 146. As with the CL sonnet, authorship is contested here; Muir and Thomson favour Wyatt as author (p. 405).

39 Shire, *Song, Dance and Poetry*, pp. 87–8; *Poems of James VI*, II, 120–31.

40 *Poems of James VI*, I, 80.

41 McKim, ' "Makand hir mone" ', p. 41. The role reversal itself is also noted by Sally Mapstone, *Scots and Their Books in the Middle Ages and the Renaissance* (Oxford, 1996), p. 27.

42 *The Poems of Robert Henryson*, ed. by Denton Fox (Oxford, 1981), p. 271.

43 McKim, ' "Makand hir mone" ', pp. 40–1, outlines this 'patriarchal hegemony' in more detail.

44 Erasmus, *Lingua: On the Use and Abuse of the Tongue*, as quoted in Parker, 'Virile Style', p. 201.

45 Shire, *Song, Dance and Poetry*, p. 88; Rait, *Lvsus Regivs*, p. 19. The elliptical syntax of 108–9 is confusing, but, whether Lyndsay or James speaks these lines, in both cases Montgomerie is criticized for abusing his 'craft'.

46 Rait, *Lvsus Regivs*, p. 19. Neither Westcott, *Poems by James I of England* (New York, 1911), nor *Poems of James VI*, ed. Craigie, mention this striking note.

47 *The True Law of Free Monarchies and Basilikon Doron*, ed. by Daniel Fischlin and Mark Fortier (Toronto, 1996), p. 175.

48 *DOST*, IV, p. 398, 'mow' *n.*

49 Shire, *Song, Dance and Poetry*, p. 88; *Edin. Recs*, IV, p. 525.

50   *Montgomerie*, ed. Parkinson, no. 99.VIII.8.

51   *Rob Stene's Dream*, ed. Reid; pp.18–25 discuss other references to 'Rob Stene' in
     detail.

52   *Rob Stene's Dream*, ed. Reid, p. 24.

53   *Rob Stene's Dream*, ed. Reid, p. 20.

54   NAS E 21 / 61, fol. 69^v (December 1580, £20, no reason specified); E 21 / 63, fol.
     75^r (September 1582, £40, no reason specified); E 21 / 65, fol. 120^r (March 1587,
     collective sums for 'dule clais'); E 21 / 70, fol. 197^v (March 1596, £40, for clothes),
     and E 21 / 72, fol. 79^v (July 1598, £10, 'be his hienes speci[a]ll directioun', possibly
     connected with travelling from Holyrood to Falkland). All but two of the NAS
     references to Stene used in this and the next paragraph are taken from Amy Juhala,
     'The Household and Court of King James VI of Scotland, 1567–1603' (unpub-
     lished doctoral thesis, University of Edinburgh, 2000), pp. 179–80. I am extremely
     grateful to Dr Juhala for providing me with these details. The above dates match
     Montgomerie's life events extremely well, from his rise at court *c.* 1580 to his death,
     shortly before 22 August 1598, but, as Juhala notes, it is unlikely that Montgomerie
     would receive payments from the Scottish court (even under an assumed name)
     after having been put to the horn in July 1597.

55   NAS E 21 / 61, fol. 35^r (July 1580, £10, no reason specified); E 21 / 65, fol. 76^v
     (July 1586, £10, for clothes; he is labelled the king's 'daylie seruitour'); fol. 120^v
     (March 1587, collective payment, for cambric cloth); E 21 / 66, fol. 71^r (July 1587,
     £10, for 'his hous maill and … winter coillis'); E 21 / 67, fol. 105^v (July 1588, £10,
     for clothes); fol. 144^v (May 1589, £10, 'for his support'); fol. 171^r (October 1589,
     £26 13s 4d, 'be his maiesties precept for the furnessing of certane his domestique
     seruitouris to serue thame in cleithing the tyme that his hienes bedfellow wes luikit
     for to arryve'); and fol. 225^r (October 1590, £10, no reason specified).

56   It is worth noting here that *Rob Stene's Dream* contains a lengthy description, with
     many Virgilian echoes, of James's journey to Scandinavia (509–69).

57   NAS E 34 / 48, pp. 1, 4, and 9. On Lauder, see Shire, *Song, Dance and Poetry*,
     passim. (esp. pp. 261–2). On William Hudson, see *Thomas Hudson's Historie of
     Judith*, ed. Craigie, pp. x, xiii, and NAS E 21 / 61, fol. 65^r, where he is paid for his
     'extraordiner panis taikin in teitcheing of his grace to dance' (December 1580). *Rob
     Stene's Dream*, ed. Reid, p. 20, claims that the name of Robert Hudson, the
     musician, rather than William Hudson is found in these documents. If it ever was,
     it is no longer visible; in any case, it cannot be the musician of that name: he died
     in 1596 (*Thomas Hudson's Historie of Judith*, ed. Craigie, p. xi).

58   On 24 August 1588, Christian Lyndsay, 'spouse to Williame Murray, maister of his
     hienes carriage', was granted a yearly pension for providing 'ait kaikis and broun
     breid … to his maiesteis awin mouth': NAS PS 1 / 58, fol. 53^v, listed by Amy
     Juhala, 'Household and Court', 175. Helena M. Shire, in her edition entitled
     Alexander Montgomerie. A Selection from his Songs and Poems (Edinburgh and
     London, 1960), p. 52, without mentioning a source, claims that 'Christian Lyndesay
     …, b. by 1558, of the Crawford family, a cousin of the courtier Bp. of Ross, is other-
     wise unknown'. This is presumably based on the 'Addenda' in *The Scots Peerage*,
     IX (1914), p. 61, which mention Christian, daughter of Robert Lyndsay of Ferne.
     Her father died before 10 May 1558, and his nephew David was indeed appointed
     Bishop of Ross in 1600. The latter was also minister of Leith, a Privy Councillor,
     and extremely popular with James. He married the king to Anne of Denmark in
     Norway and baptized Prince Henry. Moreover, his son married the niece of David
     Lyndsay, the famous poet, a family connection which may have given this Christian
     Lyndsay of Ferne a literary authority of particular ethical standing. See *The Scots
     Peerage*, III (1906), p. 19; Lord Lindsay [Alexander W. Crawford Lindsay], *Lives of
     the Lindsays*, 3 vols (London, 1849), I, pp. 381–95, 413–14; *DNB*, XXXIII, pp.

297–8; Ried R. Zulager, 'A Study of the Middle-Rank Administrators in the Government of King James VI of Scotland, 1580–1603', unpublished Ph.D, Aberdeen University, 1991, pp. 171, 177; James Scott, *A History of the Lives of the Protestant Reformers in Scotland* (Edinburgh, 1810), pp. 216–32. All this projects an image of Christian Lyndsay of Ferne as being on the fringes of literary circles at court; she might be the wife of William Murray, 'Maister of the Carriage', but no connection has yet been found. There was a tradition of naming female Lindsays 'Christian' in the Crawford and Byres lines. A key figure in this is Christiana de Lindsay, cousin of Alexander III, who commissioned a copy of *Le Roman de la Rose*, completed in 1323: see Lindsay, *Lives of the Lindsays*, I, pp. 31 and 413–14; Priscilla Bawcutt, ' "My bright buke": Women and their Books in Medieval and Renaissance Scotland', in *Medieval Women: Texts and Contexts in Late Medieval Britain*, ed. by Jocelyn Wogan-Browne *et al.* (Turnhout, 2000), pp. 17–34 (p. 27).

[59] *Montgomerie*, ed. Parkinson, nos 78, 94.

[60] *Stewart of Baldynneis*, ed. Crockett, II, 149.

[61] James did not consider heroic couplets 'verse': *Poems of James VI*, ed. Craigie, I, 79.

[62] *Montgomerie*, ed. Parkinson, II, p. 150.

[63] Ibid., p. 146.

[64] Parkinson, *Montgomerie. Poems*, II, pp. 8–9. Montgomerie addressed poems to several Murrays: *Montgomerie*, ed. Parkinson, nos 73, 94, and see 51.70

[65] *Montgomerie*, ed. Parkinson, no. 73.

[66] G. P. V. Akrigg, *The Letters of King James VI and I* (Berkeley, 1984), pp. 393–425. I owe this reference to Sally Mapstone.

[67] Jonathan Goldberg, *James I and the Politics of Literature* (Baltimore and London, 1983), p. 144.

[68] McKim, 'Makand hir mone', p. 44, quoting Fisher and Halley.

[69] Goldberg, *James I*, p. xiii.

[70] *Works of William Fowler*, ed. Meikle, III, pp. cli, 3–4.

[71] Sarah Carpenter, 'David Lindsay and James V: Court Literature as Current Event', in *Vernacular Literatures and Current Affairs in the Early Sixteenth Century: France, England and Scotland*, ed. by Jennifer Britnell and Richard Britnell (Aldershot, 2000), pp. 135–52 (pp. 138, 143). The first comment refers to David Lyndsay's poem about two rival court dogs, Bagsche, the old royal favourite, and Bawte, the new one. Montgomerie warns contenders to his poetic throne that 'Quhom Bautie byts he deir that bargan byis' (*Montgomerie*, ed. Parkinson, no. 91.8), which shows how long-standing this practice was at the Stewart court, of negotiating power through the art of the writing game. It also shows Montgomerie saw himself as a 'new' poet.

[72] McKim, ' "Makand hir mone" ', pp. 32–3.

[73] *Montgomerie*, ed. Parkinson, no. 91.1–2.

6

'Kin[g]es be the glas, the verie scoole, the booke, / Where priuate men do learne, and read, and looke' (Alexander Craig, 1604): The Translation of James VI to the Throne of England in 1603

MORNA R. FLEMING

Despite Craig's assertion that kings set the style, in the Renaissance period poets, writers, artists, architects and pageant-makers – in the absence of modern mass media – took on the role of creating the visual imagery and ideology of a monarch's reign. Examination of the descriptions of royal entries, tournaments, entertainments and masques from the fifteenth to the mid-seventeenth century shows that the imagery and iconography of monarchy becomes virtually interchangeable from one country and one ruler to another.[1] In keeping with the *speculum principis* or 'advice to princes' tradition which had been recast for the Renaissance in Erasmus's *Institutio principis christiani* (1516), the monarch is shown in these entries and public entertainments what is expected of a Christian prince who had received a humanist education.

By the time James VI acceded to the throne of England in 1603 he had already been King of Scotland for 36 years (ruling personally since 1579), during which time he had developed fixed notions about the nature of kingship in general and that of his own in particular. *Basilikon Doron*, his book on kingship written for his son and heir, Prince Henry (having been printed originally in Edinburgh in 1599 in a very small print run), was re-published in England in 1603 in an expanded version and on a much wider scale than in Scotland. The book made quite clear what James thought a king should be and how he should be regarded by his counsellors and subjects.[2] This previous, Scottish experience was complicated by the fact that James was entering into government of a realm which had a long-established political iconography and ideology of its own.

Those poets and pageant-makers who were instrumental in creating the physical and verbal expression of royal ideology did have the advantage that James restored the monarchy to patriarchal traditions, with the King as father and husband of his country. Leonard Tennenhouse has compared the accession of James to the restoration of the monarch to his true position at the end of a 'disguised ruler' play, which would imply that Elizabeth had merely been holding the fort until the true ruler returned.[3] And, as is the case in this kind of drama, epitomized by Shakespeare's *Measure for Measure*, the superficial continuities between the rules are more or less subtly undermined by the respective rulers' different exercise of power, which is reflected to some extent in the different reactions of English and Scottish poets in expressing the welcome to James.

However, in spite of these differences, there are common themes: the justification of James's succession; the celebration of the union of the ancient kingdom; the advice to the new ruler about how he should govern his kingdom. Some of this advice is particularly pointed, in the tradition of advice to princes literature, and there is criticism of courtiership that derives from the anti-courtier satires which had proliferated especially in France.[4] In the main, the English accession poems follow a predictable pattern: muted grief for the death of Elizabeth, celebrating her long reign and many achievements, welcoming the new monarch as an already established and known ruler from a land remarkably similar to England rather than from one of the feared Catholic kingdoms of Europe, praising the new king's political (and sometimes also poetical) abilities, and ending with a hope for a renewal – long foretold in the prophecies – of the ancient kingdom of Britain, now poised to take on its rightful role as leader of the world order.

Samuel Daniel in his *Panegyrike*,[5] written in decasyllabic *ottava rima,* a popular form for English pastoral verse, celebrates the spring accession as a new beginning, a time of renewal and revival, a theme taken up by many writers of the time:

> What a returne of comfort dost thou bring
> Now at this fresh returning of our blood,
> Thus meeting with th'opening of the Spring,
> To make our spirits likewise to imbudde?
> What a new season of incouraging
> Beginnes t'inlength the dayes dispos'd to good?
> What apprehension of recouery
> Of greater strength, of more abilitie? (A3ʳ 17:1–8)

What is interesting here is Daniel's use of 'returne' and 'returning' of comfort and blood, a real spring in the sense of rebirth, of natural renewal after winter, which allows him to prophesy a national renascence of power and statecraft. The medieval allegory of the garden of the State, perhaps best known from Shakespeare's *Richard II*, III.4, not only brings a sense of continuity with the past to James's rule but also allows him to claim that, whatever the accident of his birth, he is really an English king. This foreshadows Daniel's contention that, since James is descended from Margaret Tudor, who infused 'the sacred bloud lent to adorne the North' (B1ʳ 48:2) into James's vein through her marriage to his grandfather, James IV, exactly one hundred years before, it is English blood, 'the seede of worth' (48:6), which is now returned 'in periods of vncertaine certainty' (48:8). Significantly, the blood of Mary, Queen of Scots, is not referred to.

That 'vncertaine certainty' rather neatly encapsulates what appeared to be the feeling about James – gratitude that an established ruler had succeeded after the long period of uncertainty when Elizabeth refused to name an heir, and apprehension of what the Jacobean age would bring to the country and its people. As Henry Chettle, adopting the traditional pastoral vein in 'Englandes mourning garment' and speaking as plain Collin, possibly to suggest Spenser's Colin Clout, puts it:

> Euen as a calm, to tempest-tossed men,
> As bread to the faint soule with famine vext;
> As a coole Spring to those with heate perplext,
> As the Sunnes light into a fearefull denne, ...
> One King, one people: blessed vnitie! (F3ᵛ)[6]

Although the King is the panacea for all ills as the long awaited inheritor, the voicing and naming of past troubles makes clear the potential for difficulties ahead, and gives some indication of the expectation that James would have to live up to. The antithesis of mourning the former ruler and celebrating the new is the bedrock of all accession celebrations, but in the case of the succession of James to Elizabeth there is an uneasy surface tension wavering between hope and fear, which is given perhaps its most extreme expression in 'The Lamentation of Melpomene, for the death of Belphoebe, our late Queene. With a Ioy to England for our blessed KING', a poem attributed on its title page to 'T.W. Gentleman'.[7] Although it is also a typographical convention, the fact that the title of this odd poem is in two parts illustrates well the dilemma writers experienced. In T.W.'s mind, the loss of Belphoebe (who, interestingly, was 'chiefest light alone / Of England, Fraunce, Ireland *and Calydoné* [A3ᵛ, emphasis mine]) threatens disaster: '*Caos, not Cosmos* let the world be cleaped' (A3ʳ), a feeling represented by the excessive mourning of the muse Melpomene, too overcome by grief to formulate an appropriately tragic utterance.

What adds interest to this poem, apart from the Spenserian echo of the naming of the Queen, is the fact that T.W.'s Muses are all male. Why this change should have been made is not at all clear, but it could be two-edged. Male muses could have been more romantically or sexually involved with their queen, and certainly the reaction of Melpomene resembles strongly the actions of unrequited lovers in the English Petrarchan sonnet sequences of the 1590s and the literary relationships of courtier poets with the queen. On the other hand, or additionally, James's renown as the leader of a group of poets at the Scottish court, often addressed as their muse as well as their Apollo, may suggest that a literary revival can be anticipated at the Jacobean court in London, bringing a new attitude to poetry. This would appear to be borne out by Melpomene's immediate return to health when he is finally sought out by Terpsichore and told of James's accession, which is the work of the Fates:

> And know, the Fates have seated in her place,
> Though not a Woman, yet of heauenly race,
> A goodly KING, to be earthes Soueraigne:
> Which Iustice, Peace and Vertue, will maintaine. (B4ᵛ)

This could well be the only time that there is an apology for the fact that the ruler is not a woman, throwing into ironic relief the difficulties that the policy-makers had at the beginning of Elizabeth's reign to show that her sex was no bar to the throne and was not providential but rather an accident of birth.[8] Now she has become the ideal sovereign, and excuses have to be made on behalf of those who do not measure up to her, in all senses of that expression. James here, encapsulating all the old prophecies and with the support of the Fates, restores order to the potential chaos, symbolized by the return of the Muses to Parnassus and to their proper lives:

> Where now each Muse enioyes his hartes content,
> Spending the time in wanton meriment:
> Thankes be to those auspicious powers aboue,
> That hath established this concordant loue. (B4ᵛ)

The resonant 'concordant' picks up the theme of union, and also suggests a more Pythagorean harmony of opposites which resolves – by incorporating – the female *versus* male dichotomy of the poem as a whole.

While all English writers celebrate the accession of James as a return of spring, a rebirth for the country, as far as I am aware only John Savile in his 'Salutatorie Poeme' equates the accession of James with the birth of Christ:

> The Angell Gabriell from Iehova sent,
> Told to the Creature, what her maker ment,
> How she a maiden wife should beare a sonne,
> Mankindes sole Sauiour, when wee were vndone,
> This blessed eve of th'blest Annunciation,
> Was first day of your Highnesse Proclamation.
> What hopes, what haps this Proclamation brings,
> Is cause efficient why our Muses sing. (B9ʳ)[9]

Clearly, the proclamation of the accession on 24 March was auspicious to minds accustomed to looking at the calendar for propitious days, and that James would succeed the Virgin Queen made the date doubly significant. It could further be argued that, if Savile knew James's political writings, particularly *Basilikon Doron*, he was appealing directly to the king's belief in divine right, which would undoubtedly give the proclamation of the accession of such a king the force of an Annunciation.

This theme of prophecy fulfilled is one to which all the major poems of congratulation make some reference, as Drayton does in 'To the Maiestie of King James', alluding to prophecies about the reunification of the ancient kingdom:

> An ancient Prophet long agoe foretold,
> (Though fooles their sawes for vanities doe hold)
> A King of Scotland, ages comming on, …
> Two famous Kingdoms seperate thus long,
> Within one Iland, and that speake one tongue,
> Since *Brute* first raign'd, (if men of *Brute* alow)
> Never before united untill now,
> What power, nor war could do, not time expected,
> Thy blessed birth hath happily effected. (133–5; 137–42)[10]

Drayton refers, firstly, to the age-old prophecy of the restoration of the unified kingdom which equates the Scottish Stone of Destiny in Westminster Abbey with Jacob's pillow-stone at Bethel, and which says that a Scottish king crowned on that stone would unite the kingdoms (although according to some reports James and his English courtiers never did 'speake one tongue').[11] Even though Drayton is rather dismissive of the legend of Brutus as the founder of the English kingdom (as was Henry Chettle: 'if that of Brute be true', F3ᵛ) it was extensively used by pageant-makers and phrase-coiners. It was also attractive to James, as is testified by his gift of the Lyte Jewel to Thomas Lyte who drew up the King's genealogy, starting from Brutus.[12] While the references to Brutus resurrect the old controversy about the union between the two countries, dating back to the time of Edward I, in these instances Brutus is not being cited as an argument for the domination of Scotland by England, as was the case earlier, but is being used solely to bolster the new king's Tudor credentials.

What is being established is the legitimacy of James's inheritance and the inevitability of his accession, despite Elizabeth's attempts to deny it for as long as possible. All the long poems spend a considerable time, as was conventional, on James's genealogy, attempting to deal delicately with the vexed question of his mother, put to death at Elizabeth's command. Daniel offers James the chance to forgive those who were involved:

> Th'annoynted blood that staind most shamefully
> This ill seduced state, he lookes thereon,
> With th'eye of griefe, not wrath t'auenge the same. (A4ᵛ 31:5–7)

There is no attempt to expiate the guilt of the execution. Daniel is on fairly safe ground in expecting forgiveness from James, as the latter could hardly now attempt to exact retribution when he, if not actually complicit himself in the execution, had already made his peace with Elizabeth on the subject. Daniel is offering the opportunity for James to show publicly his kingly magnanimity in acknowledging the past with sorrow rather than with a desire for revenge. It may be significant that magnanimity was one of the kingly virtues that Elizabeth had said on her coronation that she, as a woman, could not exercise.[13]

The character of the new king is seen by the English poets as an amalgam of Solomon, Alexander, Jove and – in keeping with current European practice – Astraea, the images of types of the good ruler taken partly from *A Mirror for Magistrates*, contemporary European imagery, Elizabeth's iconography, and James's own writings, respectively. Sir John Davies of Hereford tells his poem to find James on his journey south by looking beyond the outward appearance to 'a judgment grave, and yett a fancy gaye / Joynd with a rich remembrance' (23–4), uncovering 'the sharpest witte and best affected will, / whence floues a streame of vertues' (27–8).[14] The poem in its travels is directed to find out 'if any more then clearly wise, / Or wisely just, or justly valiant bee' (29–30) than the new king. These two lines neatly encapsulate wisdom and justice – personified as Solomon and Astraea in many other poems and in the pageants – simultaneously as both abstract qualities and motivating principles in the king's actions. His legendary wisdom is widely celebrated by Daniel, who congratulates James for bringing to peace a state 'left to thee turbulent' through using 'Princely wisedome' (A6ʳ 43:5–6) just as Henry of Richmond had done at the end of the Wars of the Roses, that other great unification in England's more recent history. Daniel is here referring to the turbulence of the early years of James's reign in Scotland. This is a point he returns to at the end of the poem, warning subjects of the hatred and scorn they may bring upon themselves if they attempt to disrupt harmony within the kingdom, and telling them to rejoice in having a king whose 'iudgement and estate doth free / [him] from these powres of Feare and Flattery' (B4ʳ 73:1–2).

Flattery of the prince by courtiers is, of course, very different from flattery by poets, something most clearly shown in the anti-courtier satires of the Pléiade and their predecessors. The flattery of courtiers could encourage tyrannous behaviour in kings or, as illustrated by the character of Placebo in Sir David Lyndsay's *Ane Satyre of the Thrie Estaitis*, could tempt sovereigns towards luxury, extravagance, and lechery:

> Beleive ye that we will begyll yow,
> Or from your vertew we will wyle you,
> Or with evill consall overseyll yow,
>   Both into gude and evill? (Part One: 227–30)[15]

Similarly, Pierre de Ronsard, in 'Institution pour l'adolescence du Roy tres-chrestien Charles IXe de ce Nom', advised the young king thus:

> Malheureux sont les Rois qui fondent leur appuy
> Sur l'aide d'un commis, qui par les yeus d'autruy
> Voyant l'estat du peuple, et oyent par l'oreille
> D'un flateur mensonger qui leur conte merveille.
> Tel Roy ne regne pas, ou bien il regne en peur
> (D'autant qu'il ne sçait rien) d'offenser un trompeur. (95–100)[16]

In none of these illustrations is it assumed that the new king is unaware of such dangers: it is rather to reinforce the king's disinterested love for his country and its good government that poets reiterate the instructions.

Daniel likewise, in common with many professional writers and moralists, expresses this conventional opinion of courtiers of whatever political or religious persuasion as being self-interested and greedy:

> Especially where mens desires do runne
> A greedy course of eminencie, gaine,
> And priuate hopes, weighing not what is done
> For the Republicke, so themselues may gaine
> Their ends, and where few care who be vndone,
> So they be made. (B2^v 62:1–6)

The Horatian contrast between modest contentment and grasping ambition is combined with the Platonic reference to 'the Republicke', which suggests a correspondence between the ideal state ruled by the most learned men and the marvellous possibilities for the British state under James. The warning against rewarding the undeserving is generalized throughout the panegyrics. Daniel's flattery, comparing James overtly with Jove in the marginal note 'Est Iupiter omnibus idem' that glosses the English line 'And like to *Ioue*, to be alike to all' (B3^v 68:8), is far more subtle and more likely to be rewarded than Drayton's railing against

> The very earthl'est & degenerat'st spirit,
> That is most voyd of vertue, and of merit …
> Those silken, laced, and perfumed hinds,
> That have rich bodies, but poore wretched minds, (161–2, 165–6)

as it could be contended that James would be a poor king indeed if he could not detect such egregious examples.

Individual ambition and place-seeking is an aspect of courtiership that poets frequently warn their Prince about. Drayton, while in search of patronage himself, warns the king: 'But from thy Court (O Worthy) banish quite / The foole, the Pandar, and the Parasite' (167–8), which would suggest that the court is already stuffed with undeservers. This is, however, all part of the traditional vein, in England somewhat differently from in Scotland, where the advice to banish adulterers, witches, and murderers was common.[17] The same can be seen in France, where occult practices of various kinds were associated with courtiers, predominantly as part of Protestant anti-Catholic vituperation.[18]

Whether this independence of the good ruler from flattery should be read ironically is a moot point, as the whole purpose of these poems is to flatter a king who saw himself as Solomon, and it has to be admitted that many of the poems could have been addressed to anyone, as they are hardly specific to James, which is shown most clearly in William Leighton's 1326 lines 'to the King's majesty', celebrating 'Vertue Trivmphant, or A Lively Description of the Foure Vertues Cardinall', that is, Prudence, Temperance, Fortitude, and Justice.[19] In the first three stanzas the poet rehearses the commonplace themes of James as the sun returning to the earth, drying up the 'teares of sorowes raine' (A2^r 1), as the spring that brings plenitude after winter, and as Phoenix reborn from Elizabeth's ashes. He then moves to an encyclopaedic rendering of the four virtues in terms of their earthly counterparts in colours, spices, creatures, and so on, with a description of the various component parts of each of the virtues, similarly glossed. The effect is at times overwhelming in its Ciceronian *copia*, but the poem creates a very telling and detailed picture of the mindset of the time. It moves in a stately circle to end where it began, with the justice of James's rule and the hoped-for prosperity of the reign:

> Iustice brings peace and concord to our land,
> And breeds not warres by off'ring others wrong:
> It knits men fast like faggots in a band,
> In faith and loue, that to one state belong.
>   Religion, loue and vnitie increase
>   Vnder the King whose heart desireth peace. (G1^r 185)

The accession of James, because of his just claim and his personality, will ensure peace to the kingdom, a notion that is reinforced by phrases such as: 'It knits men fast', and by repeated references to 'peace and concord', the 'faggots in a band' adding a homely comparison to counterpoint the lofty sentiments. Leighton hopes that Scots and English will 'to one state belong' in 'vnitie' as opposed to 'warres', which in the pasts of both countries had too often been the result of the death of a monarch. It is seen as significant that, although the two nations of England and Scotland had been forever in enmity if not actually at war, they should now become one through peace rather than conquest. James is not the victorious general, but rather the continuation of Elizabeth by other means, and, of course, is a direct descendant, as 'the bloud of Henrie seuenth' (F4^r 179) flows though his veins. Virtue follows the virtuous, and in Leighton's view Britain is now the seat of virtue, following Assyria, Persia, and the Roman Empire, with James taking on the long-vacant role of Augustus (H1^r 219), embodying and housing kingly virtue.

The idea of empire had been strong throughout Elizabeth's reign, the circumnavigations and colonizing explorations of Drake and Ralegh showing the expansionary aims of Elizabethan statecraft, but writers in 1603 are more concerned with the consolidation of the newly united kingdom, ensuring the integrity of the island state before thinking about Alexandrian conquest. Drayton pictures the length of the kingdom, 'From *Cornwall* now past *Calidons* proude strength' (51), and, after the suppression of Tyrone's rebellion by Essex, even Ireland has been 'brought in subjection to thy glorious hand' (56). Britain is also strong against Continental forces, which are conjured up by the phrases '*German* sea' (54) and 'coast of *Fraunce*' (58). He hopes that James will 'now revive that noble Brittaines name ... / That Scotch and English without difference be' (143, 146), a sentiment echoed by Daniel's 'no Scot, no English now, nor no debate: / No Borders but the Ocean and the Shore' (A1^r 2:4–5).

Ruling the country is one matter; ruling the people could be quite another. Daniel gives warning to James that, despite the legitimacy of his claim, his new people's love will have to be earned:

> God makes thee King of our estates, but we
> Do make thee King of our affection,
> King of our Loue, a passion borne most free,
> And most vn-subiect to dominion. (A1^v 5:1–4)

The word *vn-subiect* is an interesting choice here, as most earlier citations of this word in *The Oxford English Dictionary* relate to religious contexts, with God as the subjecting power. Daniel is arguably asserting the subject's individual rights granted under common law, and warning James against attempting to rule without reference to his subjects. If Daniel had read *Basilikon Doron*, he would know that absolute rule through divine right was James's desire, which would indicate that the English poet was quite deliberately taking the stance of *laudando praecipere* (teaching through praise), tempering his praise and flattery with sound advice. If, in addition, he had read James's *Reulis and Cautelis*, he would also know that this king did not welcome the meddling of poets in affairs of state.[20] The tempering note is to be found everywhere in Daniel's well-considered and measured *Panegyrike*, which is certainly not the case in other poets' celebratory poems. There is perhaps a dig at Drayton in his assertion that the English do 'not haste to runne / Before their time, to an arising Sunne' (A2[r] 9:7–8), and he contents himself with a brief appeal that Elizabeth be honoured in death: 'that no vile tongue may spot her with disgrace, / Nor that her fame become disfigured' (A2[r] 10:3–4).[21]

It is quite clear that the English writers are thoroughly acquainted with advice to princes literature, and they spare no detail in allowing themselves to offer advice to the king who was, after all, firmly established already as a ruler in his own country. Of course, the criticisms of court behaviour do not apply to either England or Scotland, but are only applicable to licentious foreign courts characterized by Daniel as suffering from 'this humour of Luxuriousnesse' (B1[v] 54:8), exemplified in 'ougly Gluttony' (B1[v] 55:4). The criticisms specifically recall the court of Henri III in France, which was notorious for its extravagance and lasciviousness, the king consorting with a succession of *mignons*.[22] Despite the fact that the age is 'full fraught with crime / … [and] all misgouernement' (B2[r] 56:3–4), James, having governed his passions in his youth, has reached his maturity, and his 'chaste Court' (B2[r] 58: 1) will continue that of Elizabeth, who was chastity personified and, in her own characterization as Laura to her courtiers' Petrarch, demanded absolute loyalty to her own person. Queen Anne, as a married woman, will be the object of very much the same kind of disinterested adoration.

All the panegyric in English (as opposed to Scots) of 1603 celebrates the Englishness of the new ruler and through references to his English blood confirms his absolute right to the throne. The descent from Brutus, however fanciful this Trojan ancestor may be admitted to be, awakens the prospect of the long-awaited creation of the British state, something that James deeply desired. Regardless of the new ruler's origins or prospects, however, in their praise of James the 1603 accession celebrations almost inevitably continued what is commonly seen as Elizabeth's iconography, largely owing to the shared characteristics of public representations of sovereignty throughout contemporary Europe. Pageants for Mary, Queen of Scots, in 1561, for James in 1579, and for Anne in 1590 had employed imagery and iconography very similar to that found in the Accession Day tilts in England and in major court ceremonial in Europe. As King of Scotland, James himself had ensured that his reign was seen, internationally, in the context of European Renaissance monarchy and, domestically, in that of Protestant post-Reformation Scotland. Again and again references are made to French practices which James had become familiar with through the Dukes of Lennox, father and son, and which many of his courtiers were familiar with first hand, having travelled on the Continent.[23]

James is welcomed as the rightful heir of Elizabeth through the acceptable female line, but it is being pointed out that this is conditional on his adopting a rather different mode of government than that which he sought to implement in Scotland, accepting the moderating influence of parliament and the nobility rather than ruling personally and absolutely, as was his wish, if not his experience. The smaller, much poorer and less populated northern kingdom could be ruled by a king and council, ensuring a much closer contact between James and his courtiers, which goes a long way towards explaining why Scottish courtiers felt such a sense of abandonment in 1603: their relationship with their monarch had been very much more personal than that of Elizabeth with most of the English nobility. It is to Scotland that one must go to find any expressions of real disquiet at the changes in fortune and the union of the kingdoms.

An ancient Scottish prophecy, predicting that a descendant of Robert the Bruce would unite the kingdoms, finds expression in Alexander Scott's 'Ane New Yeir Gift to the Quene Mary, quhen scho come first hame, 1562':

> Giffe sawis be suth to schaw thy celsitude,
> Quhat berne sould bruke all Bretane be the see?
> The prophecie expreslie dois conclude
> The Frensch wyfe of the Brucis blude suld be:
> Thow art be lyne fra him the nynte degree,
> And wes King Frances pairty maik and peir;
> So be discence the same sowld spring of the,
> By grace of God, agane this gude new yeir. (193–200)[24]

This prophecy reflects a time of Scottish national pride, when the might of the English army was soundly defeated by the Scots. However, the Scots poems of 1603 are very different in tenor, and none of them make reference to this prophecy, perhaps precisely *because* of its discomfiting references both to Mary, Queen of Scots, and to the English defeat. The first awakens the Protestant Catholic tension, while the second smacks of a rather unpleasant kind of triumphalism.

Both William Alexander as courtier and Alexander Craig as aspiring pensioner wrote fairly conventional poems celebrating their king's accession to the joint throne, but their feelings are clearly ambivalent. Courtiers and aspirants could hope for greater reward from the enlarged kingdom, but would have to surrender a good deal of their own national identity to do so successfully. Additional poems attached by both poets to their formal utterances paint quite a different picture of what this accession meant to Scotland, and these two Scots poets follow the example of Robert Ayton (see below) in lamenting the loss of a sovereign rather than celebrating the union of the crowns.

Many of the themes and images already found in the English poems are rehearsed in the Scottish counterparts, such as Alexander's contention that James is greater than all the heroes of history, for he had not *forced* a people to subjection:

> For yee the Potentates of former times,
> Making your will a right, your force a law:
> Staining your conquest with a thousand crimes,
> Still raign'd like tyrants, but obey'd for awe. (13–16)[25]

Perhaps Alexander is here alluding to the concept of divine right in contrast to the power of tyrants of old, who ruled by fear and force rather than by God's right and law, although the syntax seems to say the opposite. James is, in contrast:

> A matchless Monarke whome peace highly raises,
> Who as th'vntainted Ocean of all worth
> As due to him hath swallow'd all your praises. (20–2)

Craig takes up this point, too, his 'To the Kinges Most Excellent Maiestie' referring to Periander's remark that:

> A Monarch's suretie no way stood
> In victories, in warrie broyles, and blood:
> But in the loue of Subiects trust and true. (43–5)[26]

Clearly, to Scots as well as English the fact that the Union had been effected without bloodshed or even much show of resentment on either side was a considerable achievement. It is also clear that the Union is expected to produce a country greater than its constituent parts, as Alexander holds: 'It seemes this Ile would boast, and so she may, / To be the soveraigne of the world some day' (35–6), which picks up the themes of exploration and expansion already noted in Daniel and Drayton and is nicely prophetic of Alexander's own political career.

Advice to the new king is not lacking from Scotland either, with Craig including some eighteen separate pieces of advice to the poem quoted above, most of them eminently sensible and very similar to what was coming from English poets. In this poem, he appears to be adopting a rustic persona, offering 'a friendly counsel from a faithfull heart' (94) in the guise of the countryman who is wiser than he appears, a figure familiar from pastoral poetry. With a mixture of *excusatio* and pride he presents his homely wisdom drawn from classical sources. Situating himself 'farre from *Ioue* and thunder-claps' (95), 'a

Hog, teach[ing] *Minerve*' (98), he directly equates James with this god and goddess and all their joint attributes. Well aware of the classical precedents for such lowly domestication 'while in my tugure (such is my estate) / I take repast of poor vnpeppered Kate' (103–4; *tugure*: hut, cottage), he compares himself with Sinetus, who brought 'cold water in his hollow palme' (110) to Artaxerxes, for which he was thanked and rewarded. This is, of course, the crux of the poem, as Craig is angling for patronage, about which he is quite open: 'right so these riuols of my poore Ingyne, / I heere present, from out this palme of mine' (113–14).

His advice is timely and sensible, and although he follows his normal pattern of finding a classical parallel for every instance of kingly behaviour, which can become somewhat tedious to the modern reader, this does not devalue what he says. Following Herodotus and Pindar, Craig points out that 'kin[g]es be the glas, the verie scoole, the booke, / Where priuate men do learne, and read, and looke' (217–18), but encourages James, in spite of all the classical examples given, to look not to Delphos for advice on how to rule but to the Bible, where he will find that God 'shall giue both Gnom's and Oracles to thee' (226). Craig ends rather abruptly, having made the point that James's own writings (which he cannot spare the time to repeat here) already show that he knows well how kings should conduct themselves, but adding a plea that James should not forget Scottish poets after his move south ('Let vs not want', 256), assuming that 'home-bred *Homers*' (249) refers to English poets.

This last point reveals the fears not only of Scots poets, but of courtiers and Scots at large, namely that they would be deserted once the king found himself ensconced in luxury in the London palaces. Scotland was being left in the care of a council which would govern with the King's authority, but there was a distinct feeling that of James himself little more would be seen.[27] The most concise yet fully formulated expression of this fear is Robert Ayton's sonnet on the River Tweed ('Faire famous flood, which sometyme did devyde'), which perhaps inspired William Alexander to write his poem on the River Devon.[28] The river imagery may well derive from Ovid's 'Flumina senserunt ipsa quid esset amor', which was a theme used by Ben Jonson in his part of the Coronation pageant.[29] The Tweed, that 'faire famous flood' (1), was the traditional boundary between the two countries, but is now seen as the link, joining 'two Diadems in one' (2). However, this is no cause for celebration; instead, the river, appointed 'trinchman of our mone' ('spokesman for our distress', 4), seems filled by the tears of Scotsmen lamenting their loss, carrying the tale of their lament out to sea. The uneasiness of the sight-rhyme 'one' / 'mone', which only rhymes at all when read in Scots as 'ane' / 'mane', underlines the unhappiness of the poet's position. The rather Petrarchan overtone of the river consisting of the tears of those left behind is very much in tune with the language that was commonplace in writings by English courtiers like Ralegh and Essex to Elizabeth and by the Scots poets and courtiers Alexander Montgomerie and William Fowler in praise of King James, while the alternative meaning of 'trinchman' as 'go-between', like Pandarus, suggests the need for an artificial conduit between two people who once could communicate directly.

The imagery is extremely complicated, although superficially very straightforward, the rhyme and alliteration serving always to heighten the emotional impact of the simple words. Although nominating the Tweed as 'trinchman', Ayton is really taking on that role himself, as he was, by a piece of spectacularly bad timing, in France at the time of the accession and had to enter into competition with all the other would-be courtiers, both Scots and English. This sense of lost opportunity is found in Alexander's poem also, and, as Alexander's court position was secure, this shows that there was more than personal status at stake for these men. Whether it is fear of a dissolution of identity or of national integrity is unclear, but a definite loss is imminent, and there is little hope of restoration.

The river, once it reaches the sea, becomes part of the ocean, analogous to Scotland's becoming part of the greater British union. The image of Neptune handing over the keys of the oceans to James is a recurrent theme in English congratulatory poems, although this particular image takes a rather interestingly different form in the Scottish poems.[30] In Ayton's mind the Tweed retains its integrity even in the waters of the sea, remaining identifiably itself. Because James has crossed the river to go south, it retains a remembrance of 'our Captaines last farewell' (6), the adjective intensifying the feeling that this is a finished kingdom that will never see its 'Captaine' again. Not only the King and his whole court have left, but those who have remained behind might be dead and gone as well, something the following line already subtly anticipates: 'when wee are gon' (7). The river will carry the memory of an independent nation with it as it flows to the sea, where 'perhapps your Lord the Sea will it reveale' (8). This is one of the most problematic lines in a difficult poem: what will perhaps be revealed, and what has the sea to do with it? The 'it' is the 'last farewell' of line six, which becomes 'that courtesye' of line seven, and what seems to be intended is that, rather than making the Tweed's waters part of the amorphous mass of the ocean, that special trait, the memory of what used to be which the river carries, will remain with it, holding it as one stream which the sea will be proud to carry without attempting to break up. In this way, it arguably expresses the hope that Scots customs and mores will be maintained at the English court, rather than being dissolved and dissipated, which would be an extremely ironic use of the water imagery. Here, too, rhyme intensifies the meaning of the words, as the apparently unrhyming 'farewell' / 'reveale' does in fact rhyme perfectly when spoken in Scots, echoing the plea for Scottish integrity and identity.

Ayton's use of the Scottish interlaced rhyme scheme of the sonnet not only underlines the poem's Scottish vantage point but also further intensifies the sense, as it mirrors the sliding and interlacing movement of the waters, and allows Ayton to point the rhymes in significant ways. At the end of the octave, where in an English form of the sonnet the second movement of the sestet would begin, the Scottish form retains one of the rhymes of the previous quatrain, creating a rhyming couplet over lines eight and nine to oppose 'reveale' of line eight to 'conceale' of line nine, a juxtaposition further intensified by 'and' at the beginning of line nine:

> And you againe the same will not conceale,
> But straight proclaim't through all his bremish bounds,
> Till his high tydes these flowing tydeings tell. (9–11)

The river will protect the integrity of its message and will spread the latter as it flows and thus – a sentiment expressed in a lovely pun on 'tydes' and 'tydeings' (11) – carry the news with it. The use of enjambment here hastens the pace and echoes the flow of the water to the high tide mark, which in this case is 'that Religious place whose stately walls / Does keepe the heart which all our hearts inthralls' (13–14). Once again, the images and ideas multiply in small space, as the river has now clearly become the Thames, replacing Scottish by English water washing up to 'that Religious place'. The latter must refer to Westminster, the 'stately walls' implying that statecraft is practised there. That James 'all our hearts inthralls' gives him the status of a beloved as well as a king, and conveys additionally the idea that there had been some kind of enchantment at the Scottish court which has now been lost.

Although a very short piece, and certainly the shortest of the 'celebratory' poems studied, this has more matter in it than many a poem ten times its length or more. The poem in each quatrain uses rhymes that are perfect only when pronounced in Scots, which highlights the uncertainty and sense of incompleteness felt by Scots at the time of James's departure, and the very fact that Ayton is writing in English with a Scottish accent in terms of both diction and rhyme epitomizes his own ambivalence. That national identity should be seen in terms of something as literally fluid and changeful as a river's waters shows clearly the Scots fears regarding their national integrity. The Tweed is no Rubicon whose crossing is symbolic of a change of status, but a reservoir of national pride.

William Alexander, in his companion poem to the one quoted above, also takes a river to symbolize his feelings of loss, and once again this river is imbued with nationalistic sentiment of its own – the natural world revolts against the change in status. The poet has written a short poem in alternately rhyming quatrains 'by reason of an inundation of Douen, a water neere unto the Authors house, whereupon his Maiestie was sometimes wont to Hawke', according to the superscription.[31] The association of the King's presence with the river appears to be recognized even by the insensible waters, as they are now in revolt against their unaccustomed neglect. The river is compared to the Tiber, flooding a Rome which is now past its days of glory:

> As *Tiber*, mindefull of his olde renowne, …
> And greeu'd to glide through that degener'd towne,
> Toyles with his depthes to couer their disgrace. (13, 15–16)

The comparison is apt, as the river's 'wonted honour' (18) is that 'to that great Prince whilst he afforded sport, / To whom his *Trident Neptune* hath resign'd' (19–20). Once again the image of James as ruler of the seas, noted in several of the English accession poems, is used, and this image may also underlie Ayton's hope that the outflow of the river Tweed will maintain its integrity in a sea ruled by a Scottish king rather than by the impartial Neptune.

Having compared the Devon to the Tiber, the allegory is made clear in the next stanzas, where the Scots are described as 'creatures of this orphand boundes' (25). The King is seen as the only reason for fame; now that he is removed, his subjects in Scotland 'in a corner of the world obscure, / … Rest vngrac'd without the bounds of fame' (31–2). This is interesting as Alexander, who did have a place at court, feels the same kind of abandonment as the ordinary people left behind, who probably had little hope or prospect of ever seeing their King again. They have been plunged into a permanent night by the departure of their sun:

> And since our Sunne shines in another part,
> Liue like th'Antipodes depriu'd of light:
> Whilst those to whom his beames he doth impart,
> Begin their day whilst we begin our night. (33–6)

Where the English poets seem to look no further than the boundaries of the united kingdom, Alexander is taking a global perspective to intensify the Scots feeling of loss. The King might as well be going to the other side of the world, so desolate does Scotland feel. The repetition of 'whilst' in lines 35 and 36 suggests the older Scots parallel structure: 'Quhyles ioy rang, / Quhyles noy rang', quoted by James in *Reulis and Cautelis* as an example of successful and functional decoration in Scots that carries in its balanced opposition a kind of unchangeable harmony.[32] There is no sense in Alexander's poem that Scots and English can rejoice at the same time.

Benighted, Alexander's persona cannot think of writing, which was where he opened the poem, referring to his 'abortiue scroules' (4) as his 'high-bended minde / … Still in doale my drouping Muse arrayes' (37–8). The use of oxymoron in 'high-bended' neatly encapsulates the contrast between the ideal, eagle-like flight of the persona's Muse towards the highest subjects and the drooping reality of his present feelings. Only seeing the King again can restore the speaker's poetic gift, 'which if my *Phoebus* once vpon me shin'd, / Might raise her flight to build amidst his rayes' (39–40). It would not take much to restore him, but the conditionals 'if' and 'might', although in keeping with Petrarchan expressions of hopeful anticipation, suggest that even this little is not likely to happen soon, if at all. The kingdom will remain in darkness, and the poetic endeavours of the King's circle will cease, further darkening the land. This type of diction and imagery is of course very reminiscent of Petrarchan love poetry, and highlights the personal sense of desolation which conveys the rather more private nature of these Scottish accession poems.

Alexander Craig takes a different tack in his poems of complaint, using words from his own earlier poetry to describe his feelings. In 'Scotlands Teares' he bitterly laments the departure of the King, describing the country as 'maymed *Scotland* thou made Orphane from delight, / Whom all the hosts of heauens abhor with vndeseru'd despight' (9–10).[33] This is much stronger than the resigned melancholy of Ayton and Alexander, and suggests that Scotland is actually injured by the loss of her King, as well as being unfathered. In his sonnet to Queen Anne, included in this collection of accession-related poems, Craig identifies her with Scotland by describing her, too, as 'Orphane from delight' (2) when separated from James before following him south.[34] Craig is clearly afraid that Scotland will be diminished by the departure of the monarch to London.

The death of Elizabeth has caused mourning in England, but, as has already been noted above, the English poets could celebrate the peaceful union of the kingdoms. Scotland, in Craig's view, now has far more cause to mourn:

> But *Scotland* if thou rightly looke thou has more cause indeede.
> They for a *Dian* dead, *Apolloes* beames enioy,
> And all their straying steps allace, our *Titan* dooth tonnoy,
> Now dawn's their glorius day with *Phoebus* rayes bespred,
> And we are but *Cymmerian* slaves with gloomy clouds
>   ou'rcled. (22–6)

The imagery long associated with both Elizabeth and James is here brought into skilful play to echo Alexander's complaint that Scotland is being thrust into unnatural darkness. Clearly, England is getting by far the best of the deal, the three different classical names for the sun-god vastly outweighing the single moon-goddess that England has lost.

Neatly filching James's own lines from his 'Complaint of his mistressis absence from Court', and borrowing the same imagery that Ronsard had used to lament the departure of Mary, Queen of Scots, from France, Craig complains: 'Our Garland lacks the Rose, our chatton tins the stone, / Our Volier wants the *Philomel*, we left allace alone' (29–30), which places James firmly at the very centre of Scottish life, now simply a gaping void.[35] The land is losing its identity and humanity:

> What art thou *Scotland* then? no Monarchie allace,
> A oligarchie desolate, with straying and onkow face,
> A maymed bodie now, but shaip some monstrous thing,
> A reconfused chaos now, a countrey, but a King. (31–4)

The ruling council left behind to govern in James's absence is not seen as a protection but rather as a curse, a many-headed monster which cannot but return Scotland to barbarous internecine feuding. Where England's potential chaos following the death of Elizabeth was brought to order and control by the accession of James, Scotland must suffer the opposite.

What is noticeable about Craig's poems, in contrast to those of Ayton and Alexander, is that they are determinedly Scots, and not simply Scots-accented English. To a certain extent it could be said that Ayton and Alexander had already accepted English domination of letters, if not of the crowns, as they were in the process of Englishing their work, presumably in the hope of a wider audience and in an attempt to re-align their own situation with that of their king. Craig would quickly learn to do the same, but at the present time it suited his purpose to maintain a strongly Scots vocabulary and idiom.

What a study of the poems of the accession period shows is that in the main, English poets accepted James as one of their own, adopting the conventions of advice to princes literature to frame their expressions of welcome. The Scots, writing more personally and more poignantly because they sensed more keenly the loss of their sovereign, approached closer the truth of what the accession would mean to Scotland, and saw James as 'the booke' which they would have to learn to 'read, and looke' at from afar.

Notes

[1] The following, among others, detail festivals and rituals of monarchy in Britain and Europe during the late sixteenth and early seventeenth centuries: David M. Bergeron, *English Civic Pageantry 1558–1642* (London, 1971); Graham Parry, *The Golden Age Restored: The Culture of the Stuart Court 1603–42* (Manchester, 1981); Roy Strong, *Art and Power* (Woodbridge, 1984); Frances A. Yates, *Astraea: The Imperial Theme in the Sixteenth Century* (London, 1975); Michael Lynch, 'Court Ceremony and Ritual during the Personal Reign of James VI', in *The Reign of James VI*, ed. by Julian Goodare and Michael Lynch (East Linton, 2000), pp. 71–92. I am extremely grateful to Michael Lynch for showing

me a draft version of this now published chapter while I was originally writing this article.

2   James Craigie, in his edition of *The Basilicon Doron of King James VI* , 2 vols, STS (Edinburgh and London, 1944–50), II, pp. 143–5, draws attention to the fact that the 1603 print was done in a considerable hurry, and that it is unclear whether it was published both in London and Edinburgh, or just in London.

3   Leonard Tennenhouse, 'Representing Power: *Measure for Measure* in its Time', in *The Power of Forms in the English Renaissance*, ed. by Stephen Greenblatt (Norman, Okla., 1982), pp. 151–3.

4   Pauline M. Smith, in *The Anti-Courtier Trend in Sixteenth Century French Literature* (Geneva, 1966), argues that, while the anti-courtier tradition in literature had been a feature of neo-Latin and medieval writing, from the 1540s onwards attacks were triggered by Baldesar Castiglione's increasingly influential ideal portrait of the courtier, while in the last quarter of the sixteenth century the actual events observed in the courts of Henri III and Charles IX inspired a more mordant criticism which would lead in a straight line to Molière and the criticism of *préciosité* in language and dilettantism generally.

5   Samuel Daniel, *A Panegyrike Congratvlatorie* (London [1603], included in Samuel Daniel, *A Panegyrike with a Defence of Ryme*, facs. repr. Menston, 1969), A1ʳ–B4ʳ.

6   Henry Chettle, 'Englandes mourning garment: worne here by plaine shepheardes; in memorie of their mistresse Elizabeth. To which is added the manner of her funeral. [And] the shepheards spring-song, for entertainment of king James.' [Partly in verse.] (London, 1603) [*STC* 5121].

7   'The lamentation of Melpomene, for the death of Belphoebe, our late Queene. With a Ioy to England for our blessed KING. By T. W. Gentleman' (London, 1603) [*STC* 24918].

8   David Norbrook, *Poetry and Politics in Renaissance England* (London, 1984), p. 114, refers to the treatise by John Aylmer which describes Elizabeth's reign as natural by right of legitimacy and hereditary succession, that is, having authority thus conferred through the bloodline rather than as a divinely-ordained exception.

9   John Savile, 'King James his entertainment at Theobalds with his welcome to London, together with a salutatorie poeme' (London, 1603) [*STC* 21784].

10 *The Works of Michael Drayton*, ed. by J. William Hebel, 5 vols (Oxford, 1931–41), I, pp. 471–4.

11 Antonia Fraser, in *King James VI of Scotland, I of England* (London, 1994), comments on the opposition between James's desires for a united kingdom and the lukewarm response of his English subjects, pp. 92–7.

12 Ibid., p. 92.

13 Norbrook, *Poetry and Politics*, p. 114.

14 *The Poems of Sir John Davies*, ed. by Robert Krueger (Oxford, 1975), pp. 228–30.

15 Sir David Lindsay, *Ane Satyre of the Thrie Estaitis*, ed. by Roderick Lyall (Edinburgh, 1989), p. 8.

16 *Ronsard. Œuvres Complètes*, ed. by Jean Céard, Daniel Ménager and Michel Simonin, 2 vols (Paris, 1993–94), II, pp. 1006–11 (1009). All references are to this edition. 'Unhappy the kings who rely too heavily on an advisor, seeing the state of the people through the eyes of others and hearing through the ear of a lying flatterer who tells them fairy-tales. Such a king does not rule, or rather he rules in fear (to the extent that he is unaware of it) of offending a deceiver.' The translation is my own.

17 Alexander Montgomerie, in 'Shir, clenge ȝour Cuntrie of thir cruell crymis', mentions just these abuses in his catalogue of 'cruell crymis, / Adultries, witch-craftis, incests, sakeles bluid' (1–2): *Alexander Montgomerie. Poems*, ed. by David

Parkinson, STS, 2 vols (Edinburgh, 2000), I, p. 103.

18   Pauline M. Smith, *The Anti-Courtier Trend*, p. 199, refers to the preoccupation with sorcery, necromancy, and other occult practices that were the subject of Henri Estienne's *Apologie pour Herodote* (Geneva, 1566), which makes the point that blasphemy was then regarded among courtiers as an essential elegance.

19   William Leighton, 'Vertue Trivmphant, or A Liuely Description of the foure Vertues Cardinall' (London, 1603) [STC 15435], is written in 221 common verse stanzas 'to the King's majesty', but appears rather to be a piece 'from the bottom drawer' which has no real specificity at all.

20   *The Poems of James VI*, ed. by James Craigie, STS, 2 vols (Edinburgh and London, 1955–58) I, pp. 67–83.

21   Michael Drayton raced headlong to Scotland to be the first to present James with a celebratory poem, but he did not in fact find favour with James, losing out to Daniel and Ben Jonson.

22   Pauline M. Smith, *The Anti-Courtier Trend*, p. 158, cites Pierre de L'Estoile commenting on the minions: 'Le nom de *Mignons* commença, en ce temps, a trotter par la bouche du peuple, auquel ils estoient fort odieux, tant pour leurs façons de faire, qui estoient badines et hautaines que pour leurs fards et accoustremens effeminés et impudiques, mais surtout pour les dons insensés et liberalités, que leur faisoit le Roy.' [The people, at that time, began to use the name 'Mignons' to show how hateful they found them, as much for their behaviour, which was playful and haughty, as for their effeminate and immodest painting and dress, but above all for the extravagant and generous gifts which the King made to them.]

23   Michael Lynch, 'A Royal Progress', details the increasing Europeanization of the Scottish court during the last years of the sixteenth century.

24   *The Poems of Alexander Scott*, ed. by James Cranstoun, STS (Edinburgh and London, 1896). See pp. 111–13 for the origins of this prophecy.

25   'SOME VERSES Written to his Majestie by the Author at the time of his Maiesties first entrie into England', included in *The Poetical Works of Sir William Alexander, Earl of Stirling*, ed. by L. E. Kastner and H. B. Charlton, STS, 2 vols (Edinburgh and London, 1921–29), II: *The Non-Dramatic Works* (1929), pp. 535–6.

26   'To the Kinges Most Excellent Maiestie. *Epistle Congratulatorie & Pæranetic*' in *The Poeticall Essayes of Alexander Craige Scotobritane* (London, 1604), pp. 9–16, included in *The Poetical Works of Alexander Craig of Rose-Craig 1604–1631*, ed. by David Laing, Hunterian Club (Glasgow, 1873).

27   Arthur H. Williamson, in *Scottish National Consciousness in the Age of James VI: The Apocalypse, the Union and the Shaping of Scotland's Public Culture* (Edinburgh, 1979), pp. 130–4, describes the feeling of abandonment associated with the loss of king and court, and the apparent dismissal of past outrages perpetrated against the Scots by a king who should have seen England as 'accessory' to his responsibility to Scotland. Similarly, Gerard Carruthers and Sarah M. Dunnigan, in ' "A reconfused chaos now": Scottish Poetry and Nation from the Medieval Period to the Eighteenth Century', *Edinburgh Review* 100 (1999), 81–94, comment on the Scots' feelings of bereavement and of the subjugation of the Scottish sovereignty by 'an insensitively imperious England', the feminized northern country forced into exactly the kind of wedlock proposed by the 'rough wooings' of earlier centuries (p. 85).

28   *The English and Latin Poems of Sir Robert Ayton*, ed. by Charles B. Gullans, STS (Edinburgh and London, 1963), p. 167.

29   'Rivers although inanimate become sensible of passion or emotion.' The use of river imagery in the poetry of the period is examined by David Quint in *Origin and Originality in Renaissance Literature* (New Haven, CT, 1983), pp. 150–6.

30 This reference may relate to the sense that, now that the two neighbouring countries are joined in one, the surrounding sea can be seen as a true defence for the country, whereas before there was always border warfare to create a point of instability. Alternatively, this Neptune image could be a representation of the King's bounty, boundless as the ocean. Neptune shows his bounty in handing over the keys of the ocean, and the King will then reciprocate to his subjects.

31 'SOME VERSES Written shortly thereafter by reason of an inundation of Douen, a water neere vnto the Authors house, wherevpon his Maiestie was sometimes wont to Hawke', in *The Poetical Works of Sir William Alexander*, II, 537–8.

32 *The Poems of James VI* I, pp. 65–83. This particular example of the figure of 'Repetitioun' in *Reulis and Cautelis* is found on p. 78.

33 'Scotlands Teares', in *The Poeticall Essayes of Alexander Craige*, pp. 18–20.

34 'THE MOST VERTVOVS / And accomplished Prince ANNA, Queene of / *Britaine, Fraunce*, and Ireland; Complaineth / the absence of her Lord and Spous / *IAMES*, King of the / foresayd Realmes', in *The Poeticall Essayes of Alexander Craige*, p. 17.

35 Ronsard's 'Elegie [sur le départ de la Royne d'Escosse]', in *Le Premier Livre des Poêmes, dedié à tresillustre et tresvertueuse princesse Marie Stuart, Royne d'Escosse*, includes the lines: 'Comme un beau pré despouillé de ses fleurs / … Et un anneau sa perle precieuse: / Ainsi perdra la France soucieuse / Ses ornemens, perdant la Royauté / Qui fut sa fleur, sa couleur, sa beauté' (1, 7–10) ('Like a beautiful meadow plucked of its flowers / … And a ring [which has lost] its precious stone / Thus careful France will lose / Her adornments, losing the majesty / Which was its flower, its colour, its beauty.') (See *Œuvres Complètes* II, pp. 668–71 (668)). James's lines from 'Complaint of his mistressis absence from court' (*Poems of James VI*, II, pp. 80–1) are:

> The Court as garland lackes the cheefest floure
> The Court a chatton toome that lackes her stone
> The Court is like a volier at this houre
> Wherout of is her sweetest Sirene gone. (50–3)

7

Scottish Students and Masters at the Faculty of Law of the University of Bourges in the Sixteenth and Seventeenth Centuries

MARIE-CLAUDE TUCKER

In the fifteenth and sixteenth centuries attempts were made to provide facilities for the study of law in Scottish universities, but these were not successful until the eighteenth century, and Scottish students had to go abroad as they had done since the Middle Ages, to Italy, to France, and later to the Low Countries.[1] From its creation in 1265, the University of Paris had always been the most popular centre with Scottish students who left home for the continent to study theology and the arts.[2] However, the Faculty of Law in Paris was of limited attraction to these students, because only canon law was taught in the capital until 1657.[3] Roman civil law was not taught in Paris following a decision of Pope Honorius III in 1219, and for their legal studies students had to go to Orléans, situated one hundred kilometres south of Paris. From its foundation in 1235, the School of Law of Orléans had been the most renowned centre for teaching Roman civil law in France.[4] It attracted Scottish students to such an extent that a separate Scottish nation existed in the university from 1336 onwards, playing a very important part in university life until it was dissolved in 1538. This date is highly symbolic, because from then on the teaching of law in Orléans was on the decline and students left for Bourges, a hundred kilometres further south. Subsequently, the University of Bourges became famous throughout Europe, and its Faculty of Law attracted many foreign students, especially from German-speaking countries, but also including a contingent of Scottish students.[5] Bourges was not the only law faculty in the country. There were others: Angers, Poitiers, and Toulouse, and all had Scottish students. For our period, roughly between 1538 and 1628, Angers had eight Scottish students, Orléans six, Poitiers twenty-seven, and Toulouse nineteen. Bourges had forty-one between 1538 and 1628; over the whole of the sixteenth and seventeenth centuries, it had forty-five Scottish students.[6]

One has to remain cautious in promoting such statistics; even when they do exist, relevant university registers are very incomplete, because the period under investigation predates the introduction of compulsory university registers which started in 1679, after the reforms in legal studies promulgated

          Marie-Claude Tucker

by Colbert.[7] For Bourges, we have registers for short periods: graduation records for 1577–1606 – bachelors in canon law only (*nomination des bacheliers en droit canon*) – and for 1583–85, all graduations – *réceptions aux grades de bacheliers, licenciés et docteurs*, from which pages are missing. There are also the matriculation registers for 1656–65, and again from 1680–1705. In many cases, the student would attend lectures without proceeding to a degree, and thus avoid paying fees and registration. Therefore, I had to refer to other means of documentation and glean information from other sources, which I give in full for each student in my doctoral thesis. The incompleteness or lack of records means that it is impossible to give a complete list, although enough information has come to light to permit a fairly accurate picture of students' attendance.

The University of Bourges was founded in 1463 by Louis XI. It had four faculties: arts, theology, medicine, and law, but only the last was developed, under the direction of Marguerite, duchess of Berry (1492–1549), better known as Marguerite de Navarre and beloved sister of King Francis I.[8] She called in eminent masters in law: the first one was Andrea Alciati from Milan, soon followed by a group of dynamic masters, François Le Douaren, Eguinaire Baron, François Baudouin, Hugues Doneau, François Hotman, and Jacques Cujas, who created the School of Law of Bourges, overshadowing Orléans. Two lines cannot do justice to the School of Bourges, but, in short, the above-mentioned legal humanists applied new philological and chronological kinds of analysis to the ancient texts, and their contribution helped develop an interest in comparative legal studies. Most of their books were written while they were in Bourges, too.[9] Bourges was thus at the height of its fame exactly at the time when in Scotland the Court of Session was established in Edinburgh (1532) and there was consequently a need for more trained lawyers, both as judges and advocates.

However, the University was a centre of avant-garde ideas in more ways than one. As early as 1525, Lutheran doctrines had infiltrated the town and the school. John Calvin himself studied law there in 1530–31. All the members of the historical school of law, as developed by Andrea Alciati, were sympathetic to the reformed religion, and the Faculty was an 'exciting place'.[10] Thus, the devoted Catholic William Barclay enjoyed lessons from two famous Protestant masters, François Hotman and Hugues Doneau, and the Catholic Alexander Scot published Cujas's complete works. The School nearly came to a halt in 1572 with the flight of prominent Huguenot teachers during the Massacre of St Bartholomew's Day, and the death of Cujas in 1590 meant the end of the golden age of Roman law scholarship in France, and certainly in Bourges. However, the lessons given by Cujas were endlessly repeated all through the first half of the seventeenth century, when the Jesuit Edmund

Mérille was at the head of the Faculty. The University, and especially the Faculty of Arts, was then run by Jesuits. Protestant Scottish students still attended the Faculty, for the town councillors had always made a point of preserving the ideas of tolerance and progress within the university establishment.

Important from a Scottish point of view was the fact that the four-year course at Bourges was based on the twin studies of civil and canon law. Even if civil law was deemed the superior study, students graduated *in utroque iure* and were examined in both parts of the course; indeed, teachers at Bourges taught both disciplines. A knowledge of Roman law was essential for a full understanding of the Church canons and essential for lawyers in areas of common law (*droit coutumier*). Scrimgeour, Henryson, Barclay, Boyd, Scot, and Mackenzie were doctors in both laws, David MacGill, John Logie, and Malcolm MacGregore graduated *in utroque.*

The civil law course comprised the textual study of the collections of the sixth-century emperor, Justinian. Professors lectured on the *Institutes*, the *Code* and the *Digest*. The *Novellae*, Justinian's own imperial constitutions, were also discussed. Canon law teaching, too, was textually orientated, the core of the course being the five books of *Decretals* and the *Decretum*. For Scots, canon law remained equally important even long after the Reformation; thus, Malcolm MacGregore in 1703 was proud to obtain his licence *in utroque,* defending theses on the *Institutes*, and being examined on the *Digest* and the *Decretals.* The first of these he again defended for admission as an advocate in Edinburgh in 1706, after which he did not fail to point out that 'both laws hath a Reciprocal Dependance of each other'.[11]

For the proper understanding of the law, one needed a knowledge of correct and elegant Latin, and a method of interpretation founded upon historical analysis. This foregrounds a point worth making: Scottish students who proceeded to the study of law at Bourges had already studied at a home university and had qualifications in arts, either at bachelor's or a more advanced level, obtained at St Andrews, Aberdeen, Glasgow, or, later on, at Edinburgh. Two students, Scrimgeour and Henryson, had even taken a second arts degree at Paris before they came to Bourges.

The Scottish attendance at Bourges is remarkable in several ways. First of all, although the university had four nations from the beginning (France, Berry, Aquitaine, and Touraine), the Scots did not belong to any of these, nor did they belong to the German nation which was founded later, in 1625. Only one Scot is mentioned in the pages of the registers of the German nation, and the name is crossed out.[12] As such, the Scottish contingent remained unobtrusive and appears as a transient element that did not play a significant role in the life of the university. Nevertheless, a large number of Scottish students attended

Bourges over the years, as indicated above, and these can be divided into two groups according to the period and style of attendance: the first from 1538 to 1588, the second from roughly 1616 to 1628.

With regards to the period before 1538, only sixteen years after the very first lecture was given at the Faculty of Law do we notice the presence of the first Scot. He was Alan Levenax, elected rector on 1 January 1479, then re-elected two years later.[13] Being a rector was a position of honour and responsibility, demanding qualities of scholarship and organization. Unfortunately, I have not been able to trace either his origins or his subsequent career. After this date there is a gap of exactly forty-eight years before another Scottish student appears at Bourges. Even the nomination of Andrew Foreman in 1513 at the head of the diocese of Bourges failed to attract Scottish students. On the other hand, the archbishop came back to St Andrews with a French master, Jean Charpentier, known as John Carpenter.[14]

However, this changed in 1538, when Henry Scrimgeour reached Bourges and its Faculy of Law.[15] He was the first of a group of thirteen Scots who attended the Faculty one after the other, in a constant though thin flow for fifty years. It is clear that this first period of attendance corresponds exactly with the period of prosperity of the Faculty. The Scots were, as always, attracted by the reputation of the doctors in place. This group includes students who were in due course to become distinguished figures in Scotland and on the Continent. For example, Henry Scrimgeour was followed in 1543 by Edward Henryson, both setting out on fascinating careers on the Continent and in Scotland. Scrimgeour settled in Bourges quite happily and developed a life-long friendship with his patron, Bochetel[16] (for Henryson's career, see below). William Skene was certainly there in the early 1550s, when he obtained his *licence* in both laws. Back in Scotland, in the Reformation period, he became Professor of Law at St Andrews.

James Boyd, the first tulchan bishop in Glasgow (appointed 1573), spent two years in Bourges under Cujas. He preceded his nephew Mark Alexander Boyd, who also attended Cujas's lectures some thirty years later, between 1581 and *c.* 1584, when an outbreak of plague drove him to Lyons. From there, he visited Italy, but returned to France in 1585, where he remained until 1595. He wrote a dissertation dedicated to Baudouin, as well as a commentary on the *Institutes* dated 1591 and an essay in French entitled *Discours civiles sur le Royaume d'Ecosse.*[17]

Alexander Arbuthnot on his return to Scotland was elected principal of King's College, Aberdeen, in 1569. Later he was one of the commissioners to inquire into the financial condition and educational efficiency of St Andrews University. He was an important figure in the Reformation movement in Scotland and was twice Moderator of the General Assembly. Apart from a

Latin treatise on church law, three poems by him in the vernacular and an account of the Arbuthnot family also survive.[18]

John Logie became advocate at the Court of Session immediately after his return from Bourges, where he had just passed his degree in both laws. In 1563, he was the first post-Reformation applicant.[19] James McGill, son of Sir James McGill, Clerk Register, came to Bourges in the 1570s, accompanied by Patrick Adamson. Melville reports that Adamson spent nine months hidden in an inn studying law at the time of the massacre of St Bartholomew's Eve. This Archbishop of St Andrews is famous enough; it may suffice to add here that he also became Chancellor of St Andrews University.[20]

When Nicol Dalgleish attended the university in Bourges, he was accommodated by Madame Monbirneau, whose husband accompanied Esmé Stuart when he left Berry to go to Scotland on the invitation of his beloved cousin, King James VI.[21] David McGill obtained his degree in civil law on 21 July 1579. His diploma is the only one of any of these Scottish students that has been preserved; it is now in the National Archives of Scotland and is signed by Jacques Cujas.[22] Once he was back in Scotland, David was admitted advocate in 1586.

The last Scot of this 'first period of attendance', Alexander Scot, was a student under Cujas before he went to Avignon and then Carpentras, where he spent the rest of his life as a judge and in charge of the college there. Scot married a French lady and had ten children, two of whom became advocates in Avignon themselves. Scot published his *Oraisons de Cicéron* in two volumes in 1588–89 before his well-known *Universa Grammatica Graeca* was published in Leyden in 1593. Scot was appointed principal regent of the College of Carpentras, where he attracted a significant number of pupils. He was still there in 1601, but by 1608 he had left the College and is attested as *juge mage* at the major Court of Carpentras, a position which he still held in 1611. He collected and brought to light Jacques Cujas's unpublished works in four volumes under the title *Opera priora et posthuma* (Lyons, 1614). His activities as a writer on law and on grammar suggest that he is an important figure in the story of learned Scots in France; as yet, however, very little has been published about him.

It appears that no Scot ever established himself as a master at Bourges for more than a very few years, and Scottish students therefore had no immediate reason to go to the university there. Still, of this first group of Scottish students at Bourges, three became teachers: Edward Henryson, William Barclay, and Alexander Arbuthnot. Henryson had left Bourges in 1547 only to come back again in 1553, when he was appointed teacher of civil law. He stayed in Bourges until 1556, probably expecting a chair (which he did not get), and then returned to Edinburgh to start lecturing in law and letters (Greek and Hebrew).

Later, Henryson became an extraordinary Lord of Session and member of a commission set up to revise and print the laws and acts of the Parliament of Scotland. Dempster mentions that students at Bourges remembered the Greek scholar fifty years after his departure.[23] Whilst at Bourges, he published several works on Roman law which received high praise. 'Henri Edouard Ecossais' also remained famous for another, less commendable reason, namely the meagreness of his wages, which were a mere 45 *livres* a year. As a matter of comparison, Baudouin's wages were 920 *livres*.[24]

Arbuthnot taught in Bourges between 1565 and 1566, a fact l'Estoile mentions in his *Journal*.[25] William *alias* Guillaume Barclay taught at Bourges immediately after he obtained his doctorate in both laws in 1575. He was chosen *Lecteur des Institutes* in March of the same year. The register of the town accounts refers to his wages as 70 *livres* per year. Because he felt underpaid, the town raised his wages to 100 *livres* per annum from July of that same year.[26] Barclay taught for one year in Bourges, then left for Pont-à-Mousson to teach law in the new Jesuit faculty, where he wrote his *De Regno*, published in Paris in 1600. He ended his career in the University of Angers, where he died in 1608, and where he was buried.

We have no record of the method and contents of the teaching of these Scottish teachers in Bourges. It would seem that they followed Alciati's historical method, but there was nothing conspicuous about their teaching, nor anything particularly substantial about their contribution to the development of law at Bourges. However, by participating at this level in the study and the teaching of the historical method, the Scots at Bourges belonged to a new school of legal thought which would come to influence approaches to the law at home.

In the first decades of the seventeenth century, Scottish attendance underwent a social transformation, following the evolution of the Faculty itself and the general trends of legal studies at that time. The poet William Drummond of Hawthornden heralded the new trend of attendance. From Paris, he came to Bourges in 1607 and spent sixteen months there. During his stay, Drummond became an enthusiastic theatre-goer and attended around twenty plays over several weeks. Crucially, he left notes on the plays performed in Bourges and on the comedians involved in these performances, which provides one of the few sources of evidence for theatre in Bourges at this time.[27] During his stay, he bought a large number of books, many of which survive in Edinburgh University Library.

From 1616 to 1628, a second cluster of names of Scottish students appears at Bourges, twenty-eight in all, young men on their Grand Tour. They eventually attend university lectures, but also practise fencing with the local master-of-arms, Guy Faitot dit Labiche. They nearly all had a degree in arts from Edinburgh University and were young members of the aristocratic elite: the Earl of Angus; Lord Pitcur; Lord Pitmillie; the Earl of Roxburghe; Archibald Douglas, baron of Spott; William Douglas, Earl of Morton; Stewart of Traquair; and Patrick Hume of Polwart. To this group also belonged the Earl of Mar's sons, Henry and Alexander Erskine, grandsons of Esmé Stuart, seigneur of Aubigny. During their stay in Bourges, they paid a visit to their French grandmother, Esmé's wife, Catherine de Balsac d'Entragues. Other students belonged to well-established families of jurists: MacGill, Burnet, Gibson, Hay, Hope, Heriot, Lyndsay, Graham, and Kerr are familiar names on the registers of the Faculty of Advocates in Edinburgh. On 22 December 1617, Henry and Alexander Erskine wrote to their father complaining that there were too many Scots in Bourges, that these disturbed the lessons and prevented them from learning the French language, and that they would rather leave for the Protestant academy of Saumur, even if law was not taught there.[28] They had spent nine months in Bourges. Lord Pitmillie and the Earl of Roxburghe died while students at Bourges; they were buried in Sancerre.[29] As mentioned above, the last Scottish student connected with Bourges is Malcolm MacGregore.

Special reference has to be made to one particular student: George Mackenzie of Rosehaugh graduated *in utroque* in 1658. Thirty years later, he remembered his landlady in Bourges because she had given him flesh to eat in Lent, and he was himself still remembered some twenty-six years after his graduation there by his teachers, who praised his work on eloquence.[30] Mackenzie was certainly the youngest Scottish student at Bourges, at the age of sixteen, and he spent two years there, which is attested in the registration book of the faculty.[31] The Lord Advocate's career is sufficiently well-known, but he is of special interest to us as the Dean of the Faculty of Advocates in Edinburgh, which he promoted as a learned body, and for the foundation and development of the Advocates' Library. For him, the library's function was to facilitate the practice of law, and he gave priority to Roman law in the library's classification system. The library contained books that represented the school of Bourges well, notably through its copies of the works of Alciati, Baron, Doneau, Le Douaren, Hotman, and Jean Domat. Mackenzie himself donated to the library the complete works of Cujas, published in Paris in 1658, together with an edition of the *Novellae* by Henry Scrimgeour, published in 1558. Hector MacQueen has remarked that Mackenzie's work as Dean of the Faculty 'helped pave the way for the establishment of legal education within the Scottish universities'.[32] Indeed, *The Institutions of the Laws of Scotland* (1684) was of prime importance in Scottish legal history, because for almost a century, it was the means of introducing entrants to the legal professions, and it was a text book used for examination as well, with nine editions up to 1758.[33]

All in all, three students remained on the continent: Scrimgeour, Barclay, and Scot. The others returned to public life in Scotland, pursuing careers in the spheres of education, the church, or statecraft. The present paper is not the place to investigate these individual careers themselves in detail; instead, it clearly shows that, even though any conclusion is of necessity impressionistic, the Scottish attendance at Bourges in the sixteenth and seventeenth centuries is noteworthy not so much in terms of size but for its quality.

Notes

[1] The material in the present article is based on my doctoral thesis, M.-C. Tucker, *Maîtres et étudiants écossais à la Faculté de droit de l'Université de Bourges (1480–1703)* (Paris, 2001). On the study of law before the eighteenth century in Scotland, see J. W. Cairns, 'The Law, the Advocates and the Universities in Late Sixteenth-Century Scotland', *SHR*, 73 (1994), 145–64. I am indebted to John W. Cairns who guided my research on the legal side. On Scots going abroad to study, see W. Caird-Taylor, 'Scottish Students in Heidelberg 1382–1662', *SHR* 5 (1908), 67–75; A. I. Dunlop, *Scots Abroad in the Fifteenth Century*, Historical Association Pamphlet 124 (London, 1942), 3–24; J. Durkan, 'The French Connection in the Sixteenth and Seventeenth Centuries', in *Scotland and Europe 1200–1850*, ed. by T. C. Smout (Edinburgh, 1986), pp. 19–44; J. Durkan, 'Notes on Scots in Italy', *IR* 1 (1950), 12–18; R. J. Lyall, 'Scottish Students and Masters at the Universities of Cologne and Louvain in the Fifteenth Century', *IR* 36 (1985), 55–73; R. J. Mitchell, 'Scottish Law Students in Italy in the Later Middle Ages', *Juridical Review* 39 (1937), 19–24; H. Stewart, 'The Scottish "Nation" at the University of Padova', *SHR* 3 (1906), 53–62; K. van Strian and M. Ashmann, 'Scottish Law Students in Leiden at the End of the Seventeenth Century', *Lias: Sources and Documents of the Early Modern History of Ideas* 19 (1991), 271–330, and 20 (1993), 1–65; Jean Plattard, 'Scottish Masters and Students at Poitiers in the Second Half of the Sixteenth Century', *SHR* 21 (1924), 82–6; W. A. McNeill, 'Scottish Entries in the Acta Rectoria Universitatis Parisiensis, 1519–*c*. 1633', *SHR* 43 (1964), 67–86; *History of the University in Europe*, ed. by H. de Ridder-Symoens, 2 vols (Cambridge, 1992–96), I: *Universities in the Middle Ages* (1992), and II: *Universities in Early Modern Europe 1500–1800* (1996).

[2] J.-B. Coissac, 'Les Universités d'Écosse depuis la Fondation de l'Université de St-Andrews jusqu'au Triomphe de la Réforme (1410–1560)', doctoral thesis, University of Paris, 1914, pp. 10–16, and also J.-B. Coissac, 'Les étudiants écossais à l'Université de Paris', *Revue Internationale de l'Enseignement* 17 (1917), 22–33.

[3] D. B. Smith, *An Introductory Survey of the Sources and Literature of Scots Law by Various Authors*, Stair Society (Edinburgh, 1936), p. 185; J. Verger, *Histoire des Universités en France* (Toulouse, 1986), p. 164.

[4] J. Kirkpatrick, 'The Scottish Nation in the University of Orléans 1336–1538', *Miscellany of the Scottish History Society* II (Edinburgh, 1904), pp. 47–102.

[5] See R. Gandilhon, *La Nation germanique de l'Université de Bourges et le Liber Amicorum de Yves Dugué* (Bourges, 1936); W. Dotzauer, *Deutsche Studenten an der Universität Bourges, Album und Liber Amicorum* (Melsenheim am Glan, 1971); W. Frijhoff, 'Matricule de la Nation germano-néerlandaise de Bourges; le second registre (1642–1671) retrouvé et de nouveau transcrit', *Lias: Sources and Documents of the Early Modern History of Ideas* 11 (1984), 83–116. No complete study has ever been undertaken on the subject of Scottish students at

Bourges, despite the historical connection between Berry and Scotland. The presence of Scottish students at Bourges was first mentioned in Francisque Michel, *Les Écossais en France, les Français en Écosse*, 2 vols (London, 1862), II, 261–6; then in a two-page essay: J.-Y. Ribault, 'Les Écossais à l'Université de Bourges', in *Souvenirs écossais en Berry* ([n.p.], 1973), and in Durkan, 'French Connection', pp. 25–6 and pp. 37–8.

[6] Figures from Angers, Orléans, Poitiers, and Toulouse are from Durkan, 'The French Connection', pp. 37–43; figures for Bourges are from my thesis, pp. 20–36.

[7] D. Julia, J. Revel, and R. Chartier (eds), *Les Universités Européennes du XVIème au XVIIIème siècle* (Paris, 1986–), II: *Histoire sociale des populations étudiantes* (Paris, 1989), p. 397.

[8] L. Raynal, *Histoire du Berry, depuis les temps les plus anciens jusq'en 1789*, 4 vols (Bourges, 1844–47), III (1846), 349–67.

[9] R. Pillorget, 'Le rôle universitaire de Marguerite de Savoie', in *Culture et Pouvoir au temps de l'Humanisme et de la Renaissance* (Paris, 1978), pp. 207–22; J.-Y. Ribault, 'Le rayonnement européen de l'Université de Bourges (XVIe–XVIIe siècles)', in *L'Europe des Universités*, Actes du Colloque, Bourges 1991 (forthcoming); D. R. Kelley, *Foundations of Modern Historical Scholarship: Language, Law and History in the French Renaissance* (New York and London, 1970), pp. 100–15.

[10] Kelley, *Foundations of Modern Historical Scholarship*, p. 101.

[11] J. W. Cairns, *Legal Education in Eighteenth-Century Edinburgh* (forthcoming). I am grateful to Professor Cairns for letting me see his work in draft.

[12] Bibliothèque Nationale, MSS Lat. 9088.

[13] See N. Catherinot, *Annales Académiques du Cher* (1684), pp. 10–20.

[14] J. Durkan, 'The Cultural Background in Sixteenth-Century Scotland', in *Essays on the Scottish Reformation 1523–1625*, ed. by David McRoberts (Edinburgh, 1962), p. 285.

[15] J. Durkan, 'Henry Scrimgeour, Renaissance Bookman', *Edinburgh Bibliographical Society Transactions* 5.1, (1971–87), 1–31.

[16] On Bochetel, see J.-Y. Ribault, 'Le séjour de Jacques Amyot à Bourges (1534–1546)', in *Fortunes de Jacques Amyot*, ed. by Michel Balard (Paris, 1986), pp. 105–22. For Skene, see Tucker, *Maîtres et étudiants*.

[17] See I. C. Cunningham, 'Marcus Alexander Bodius, Scotus', in *A Palace in the Wild: Essays on Vernacular Culture and Humanism in Late-Medieval and Renaissance Scotland*, ed. by L. A. J. R. Houwen, A. A. MacDonald, and S. L. Mapstone (Louvain, 2000), pp. 161–74 (pp. 164–5). I am greatly indebted to Ian Cunningham for sending me notes on Mark Alexander Boyd in advance of the publication of his essay.

[18] The poems are 'On Love', 'The Praises of Women', and 'The Miseries of a Poor Scholar'; the family history is in manuscript still, and is entitled 'Origines et incrementi Arbuthnoticae familae descriptio historica' (*DNB*, I, pp. 531–2).

[19] NAS Books of Sederunt, CS 1/2/1, fol. 79.

[20] On Adamson, see *DNB*, I, pp. 112–15.

[21] See my essay, 'Jacques VI, roi d'Écosse et les Stuarts seigneurs d'Aubigny (1579–1625)', *Études Écossaises* 6 (1999), 105–14.

[22] NAS GD 135/2717; a full transcript of the diploma is included in my thesis.

[23] Thomas Dempster, *Historia Ecclesiastica Gentis Scotorum*, 2 vols, Bannatyne Club (Edinburgh, 1829), II, p. 349.

[24] See S. Catherinot, *Le Calvinisme de Berry* (1684), pp. 35–40.

[25] *Mémoires-Journaux de Pierre de l'Estoile*, ed. by G. Brunet and A. Champollion, 12 vols (Paris, 1875–96), IX: *Journal de Henry IV 1607–1609* (1881), pp. 28–9.

[26] Archives municipales de Bourges, BB8 fol. 128.

[27] See R. H. MacDonald, 'Drummond of Hawthornden: The Season at Bourges 1607', *Comparative Drama* 4.2 (1970), 89–109.

[28] NAS GD124/15/32, fol. 8.

[29] NAS GD124/15/34, fol. 2.

[30] A letter survives in the NAS from teachers at Bourges complimenting him on the publication of his book on eloquence, *Idea eloquentia forensis hodiernae una cum actione forensic ex unaquaque juris parte* (Edinburgh, 1681). The letter is signed by three teachers, one of whom, Pierre de la Chapelle, had taught Mackenzie twenty-six years earlier (NAS RH9/2, fol. 20). See also G. Mackenzie, *The Works of that Eminent and Learned Lawyer Sir George Mackenzie of Rosehaugh*, 2 vols (Edinburgh, 1716–22), I: *Moral Essays* (1716), p. 55.

[31] To prove that he has spent two years there studying law, Mackenzie wrote the following lines: *ego Giorgius Mackenzie Scoto britannus, studiosorum utriusque juris matriculae nomem meum inscripsi hodie 24 february 1658 studium juris aggressus mense novembris 5ta anni 1656* (I, George Mackenzie, Scoto-briton, wrote my name today, 24 February 1658, matriculated in the study of both laws, having entered the study of law on 5th November 1656). See Archives départmentales du Cher, AD9, fol. 5^{v}.

[32] H. L. MacQueen, 'Mackenzie's Institutions in Scottish Legal History', *Journal of the Law Society of Scotland* 29 (1984), 498–501 (p. 499)

[33] *The Best and Fynest Lawers and Other Raire Bookes, A Facsimile of the Earliest List of Books in the Advocates' Library, Edinburgh, with an Introduction and a Modern Catalogue*, ed. by M. Townley (Edinburgh, 1990), pp. 11–19; J. W. Cairns, 'Advocates: History of the Faculty of Advocates to 1900', in *The Laws of Scotland. Stair Memorial Encyclopedia*, XIII (Edinburgh, 1992), pp. 499–537; T. I. Rae, 'The Origins of the Advocates' Library', in *For the Encouragement of Learning: Scotland's National Library 1689–1989*, ed. by P. Cadell and A. Matheson (Edinburgh, 1989), pp. 1–22.

8

After 'The Backward Look': Trials of a Gaelic Historian

WILLIAM GILLIES

This paper is about the impact of 'modern' ways of thinking about the past on an historiographical tradition which was not entirely at one with Western European post-Renaissance thinking about the nature of history, and about its justification and purpose. For in some respects the Gaelic historical tradition in the Early Modern period embodies a medieval or at least pre-modern attitude to the past. Our question, concerning the way in which the past as envisaged by historians at a given time can change in the face of new challenges and demands, has naturally attracted scholarly attention, and there have been notable contributions relevant to our enquiry from both Scottish and Irish historians.[1]

My aim in what follows is to subject a historical work from Scotland's Gaelic tradition to scrutiny in the light of this general question.[2] To be precise, I am interested in the Highland family histories that appear in considerable numbers in the seventeenth and eighteenth centuries, and more particularly in the Clanranald History which is found in the so-called Red and Black Books of Clanranald.[3] In this latter history the poet *cum* historian *cum* scribe Niall MacMhuirich has left us with an interesting, and in several ways unusual manuscript history of a Highland clan – the Clanranald branch of the Clan Donald – which he apparently put into its present form in the last years of the seventeenth century.[4] My work on this text has forced me to confront Niall's eccentricities, and led me to view the Clanranald History in the context of similar activities regarding other Highland families; and, more widely, in the Scottish and pan-Gaelic historiographical contexts. Some interesting conclusions emerge, and I hope that I have identified a suitable framework within which to describe Niall's activities and their end-product, and to make some observations with a more general applicability.[5]

The 'backward look' in my title echoes Frank O'Connor's famous survey of Irish literature bearing that title.[6] It signifies the traditional (here as opposed to the 'modern') outlook, with its implications of acceptance and continuation, respect and imitation. In O'Connor's usage it captured the simultaneously enriching and deadening legacy of orally transmitted, professionally maintained lore (Early Modern Irish *seanchas*) which existed when the arrival of

Christianity and literacy gave rise to the Gaelic literary tradition as we know it; a legacy which, in O'Connor's words, 'imposed itself' upon the imagination of subsequent generations of literati, as an 'obsession with the past'.[7] 'The backward look' is certainly an element that needs to be taken account of in any assessment of the Clanranald History. But it was not the whole story; for contemporary preoccupations and reactions can also be identified. It was the competing pressures of the timeless and the contemporary that I have termed the 'trials' of our Gaelic historian.

We may begin with some remarks on the Gaelic learned tradition in general, before discussing certain features of the Clanranald History that seem to show Niall MacMhuirich reacting to the competing demands of his profession and his circumstances. In the Gaelic world in the late Middle Ages learning was a serious matter, in the hands of professional, hereditary poets, historians, genealogists, lawyers, and medical doctors. When talking about the learned order it is sometimes expedient to emphasize the specialization, and the distinctions between the several professions involved. On other occasions it is more appropriate to stress the unity of this 'mandarin' class, as when we find members of a learned family contributing to more than one professional field, or individuals showing competency in more than one branch of learned activity. For they were united by their literacy and by a common platform of basic training in the Early Modern Gaelic literary language and its literature.[8]

The most solemn duty of a chief's poet was, of course, the composition of formal bardic panegyrics and elegies.[9] But this visible manifestation of his function was underpinned by several categories of historical expertise. The bodies of knowledge he was expected to maintain and draw on included the legends and myths, genealogy and territorial lore of his clan. He would, moreover, have had to know the grand apparatus of pseudo-historical lore that defined the position of his patron's family in relation to all the others in the 'ramifications of the Gael'. He was, in fact, an authority in all the domains of *seanchas*. This authority depended on what one seventeenth-century Scottish poet revealingly defined as *slán croinice*, 'the guarantee of chronicle', together with *béal suadh*, 'the lips of sages', which I take to include the written and oral aspects of the training and work of the learned poet-historians.[10]

Historical writing in the medieval Gaelic tradition manifested itself in monastically based annals and chronicles, and in ultimately secular compilations of genealogical material, legalistic privileges, and origin legends, including the 'national' origin legend *Leabhar Gabhála Éireann* ('The Book of the Seizing of Ireland', or 'The Book of Conquests').[11] By the end of the Early Modern period, the fuller Irish record shows how the Gaelic literati had developed the early categories and blurred the older categorial distinctions in various ways. These activities lie behind the work of Geoffrey Keating, whose continental training also gave him linguistic and intellectual access to the post-Renaissance European, English, and Scottish historians. His *Foras Feasa ar Éirinn*, 'Basis of Knowledge about Ireland', completed *c.* 1632, set out to synthesize native historical, myth-historical, and literary works in a critical and hence defensible way to tell Ireland's story in pre-Christian and Christian times for a Catholic, Irish-speaking readership, at a time when war and plantations and social upheaval threatened the viability of traditional Irish society.[12]

We should at the very least be on the look-out for similar or comparable phenomena in Gaelic Scotland. For while the sometimes profoundly different political, social, and religious experiences of Scotland and Ireland warn us against making facile equations between their respective Gaelic traditions, the well-authenticated visits of Irish poets to Scotland, and the examples of Irish bardic families serving Scottish chiefs, not to mention their surviving compositions, show that there was a ready channel for communication at this specialized, self-consciously cohesive level.[13] Although Niall MacMhuirich lived near the end of the bardic period, he was a 'paid-up' member of that world, as can be judged from his participation, along with northern Irish poets, in the many-handed poetic controversy known as the 'Contention of the Red Hand', and from the evidence he himself provides (see below) for his own travel in Ireland.[14] It is therefore appropriate to look out in Niall's work for echoes of, or parallels to, the 'ideologies and *mentalités*'[15] of his Irish colleagues or counterparts.

On the other hand, one of the differences sometimes cited between the Scottish and Irish literati is the fact that the degree of professional specialization appears to have been less in Scotland than in Ireland. Certainly, a review of the known activities of Niall MacMhuirich shows him to have functioned as a poet, scribe, genealogist, historian, and story-teller. Indeed, the 'official' view of the duties of a MacMhuirich bard is set out in a tack granted by Allan of Clanranald to Niall's nephew Donald MacMhuirich, in 1707: Donald was to be Clanranald's 'bard and seanachie'.[16] Equally, we should bear in mind that Niall in his old age composed vernacular elegies for his chief on the latter's death in 1715 after the Battle of Sheriffmuir. Living and working, as he did, in the second half of the seventeenth century and at the start of the eighteenth, he would have partaken of a whole spectrum of Gaelic views of history and of the past, ranging from the doctrines of the Classical poets, historians, and genealogists through to popular tradition and folk-belief. Considerations like these should caution us against making casual extrapolations from Ireland to Scotland, for fear of begging questions of constitutional difference between the two traditions.

We may now pose our first question about Niall MacMhuirich's understanding of the past – with a certain degree of anticipation but with no fixed expectations. I suggest we may catch him with his guard down in the following passage in the Clanranald History, where he breaks off from his chronicle-based account of the Lordship of the Isles and its aftermath, to talk about the stirring events of 1644–46.[17]

> I treat (now) of certain of the events that have taken place during my own lifetime. The king at the time of my earliest recollection was Charles I, son of James VI of the House of Stewart. Here are some of the chiefs who ruled over the Gaels loyal to the King at that time: Raghnall Óg son of Raghnall Arannach; Gilleasbuig Caoch son of Gilleasbuig Gruamach; Sir Lachlan Maclean, Laird of Duart; John of Moydart, Captain of Clanranald; John son of Ruairidh Mór MacLeod of Harris; Sir Donald, lord of Sleat and Trotternish, a great courtier of King Charles's; Neill MacNeill of Barra; Lachlan Mackinnon of Strath; Iain Garbh MacLeod of Raasay; Iain Garbh, Laird of Coll; Murchadh of Lochbuie; Donald, chieftain of Glengarry, an old warrior at the time of my earliest memory, and his grandson then in captivity in Edinburgh; and Ailein, chieftain of Clan Cameron, and his grandson a young man, namely Ewen son of John, who is still alive; and George, Earl of Seaforth; and Donald Mackay, chief of the Clan Mackay; and many other gentlemen who were chieftains at that time, with the proviso that only the men whom I have seen personally, and of whose deeds I have some knowledge, are listed here.

In a sense, this is the past as seen by a Gaelic tradition-bearer and genealogist down to the present day: a tapestry formed by combining vertical sequences of generations in genealogies with horizontal linkages between contemporary individuals. In Niall's case, of course, it taps into a quite venerable formalization of that 'warp and weft' principle: the matrix of regnal successions and synchronisms which the medieval Gaelic literati had elaborated to control both the recent, fully historical past and remote legendary times.

But other ways of viewing the past were represented in the Gaelic tradition. By Niall's day the Gaelic literati had a millennium of experience of operating with firm dates within an absolute chronological framework: that is, in terms of Years of the World or Years of Our Lord. This quite different principle was explicit in an annalistic tradition which had become established in monastic centres like Iona and which (equally strikingly) remained a feature of the later Middle Ages.[18] Thus the Clanranald History starts, without beating about the bush, with the following words:[19]

> The Age of the World when the Sons of Míl came to Ireland (was) 3500. These are the names of the sons of Míl of Spain ...

In later sections the annalistic under-pinning of Niall's account is unmistakable. But, although the idea of using absolute dating as a means of organizing the past was familiar to the literati from the annalistic tradition, dates did not feature powerfully outwith that specific milieu; and the locating of historical events by position in a date-free temporal sequence, or by reference to synchronous events, remained ubiquitous in oral contexts and powerful in the genealogical tradition. Thus, Niall must have been confronted with a certain degree of choice as to the nature of the past, even within the Gaelic tradition. His position was further complicated by factors originating outside the Gaelic world.

While it is perfectly in order to talk of 'traditional Gaelic concepts of the past', we must beware of assuming that someone like Niall MacMhuirich existed in a hermetically sealed Gaelic continuum, insulated from the outside world. The rhetoric of bardic panegyric certainly suggests that, but the reality must have been quite different. Interaction between the Highlands and Lowlands gathered pace during the sixteenth and seventeenth centuries, not least in connection with efforts by the Crown to bring the Highlands properly within its jurisdiction. Things happened more slowly in some parts than in others, and differing causes were prominent in different areas. At the upper end of the social scale, the attractions of Edinburgh and the Scottish court became gradually more obvious to Highland chiefs and their ladies. Lowland education, in the form of schools and Universities, was open to their sons; indeed, a Lowland schooling had been mandatory since the beginning of the seventeenth century in the case of their eldest sons and heirs. Military service outside the Highlands became increasingly fashionable when the same lads came of age.

The cumulative effect of these and similar factors was to create a drift towards Anglicization in the Highland gentry at least. With their Lowland experiences and contacts, and, in some cases, their European experience and attendance at court, they became open to intellectual stimulation from outside the Highlands. Political or religious or literary trends and issues, no less than fashions in dress, percolated through at certain social levels to the Highlands, just as they did to other landward and maritime parts of Scotland. Even where, as in the case of the Clanranald MacDonalds, the chiefly family continued to cultivate Gaelic arts and ways, such novelties would have been discussed at home amongst the gentlemen, the officers, and the ministers – and in the hearing of anybody else who frequented the chief's table. However gradually and marginally at first, people in the Highlands, as elsewhere in Scotland, would have become exposed to the intellectual climate of post-Renaissance, post-Reformation Scotland.

This would have impacted, in due course, on the likes of Niall MacMhuirich. I would stress two particular reasons for this. In the first place,

people who read Boece and Buchanan would have been reminded of the place
of Gaelic learning in earlier Scottish history, and would have had questions to
ask contemporary exponents of the bardic trade. One can see this curiosity
powerfully at work at the end of the seventeenth century in the correspondence of Edward Lhuyd and his associates and informants.[20] In the second
place, and contemporary with the general scientific enquiries of Lhuyd, there
was a great upsurge in curiosity about the origins of the Scottish nobility and
gentry, and a fashion for compiling family histories. It has been associated
with far-reaching changes in the make-up of Britain as a whole. Where trained
bards and shennachies were available, they would doubtless have been the
target of enquiries as to the genealogy and history of their patrons' family,
and in some cases would have had to cope with challenges to their Classical
Gaelic understanding of the facts: for example where a Norman pedigree was
pretended.[21]

Amongst the welter of written family histories which emanated from the
Highlands at this time, which formed a distinct genre within the wider awak-
ening of antiquarian interest in Scotland as a whole, we find accounts of the
Mackenzies, the Macraes, the Mathesons, the House of Argyle, and of course
the MacDonalds. There are interesting variations amongst them in respect of
their language (Latin, Scots, or English for the most part), and in their authorship, approach, and content. They are all more or less explicable as the
products of the polarities and tensions we have described. Some of them have
a critical, thoroughly 'written' feel about them, while others represent rather a
written adumbration of a nucleus of traditional tales and lore. The existence
of this pattern of activity would, I suggest, have constituted an additional challenge to someone in Niall MacMhuirich's position. We should be alive to the
possibility that its impact may be detectable in the Clanranald History.

It will be helpful to recall the contents of the Clanranald History at this
point. It may be divided up into five sections, as follows:

(1) 'Prehistoric' section ('1000 BC' to 12th century AD)
(2) The rise of Clan Donald and the Lordship of the Isles (12th to early
    16th century)
(3) The history of the Clanranald branch of Clan Donald (15th to end of
    16th century)
(4) The Montrose Campaigns in the Wars of the Covenant (1644–46)
(5) The history of the Clanranald branch of Clan Donald resumed (mid-
    17th century to 1686)

There are important differences of texture and in the level of detail given in
these sections, though I argue elsewhere that one can discern consistent
threads of authorial purpose.[22] We may start with the passage quoted already,

in which Niall identifies the Highland chiefs of his early boyhood. It occurs at the beginning of what I have termed section (4). Niall's wording is significant. He begins by emphasizing that the events in question took place 'during my own lifetime', more specifically 'at the time of my earliest recollection'. The chiefs, it is stressed, were those who ruled 'at that time', and that emphasis is repeated before the end of the paragraph. Donald of Glengarry was an old warrior 'at the time of my earliest memory', and his grandson Ewen 'is still alive'. In case we have not got the message, he adds for good effect: 'Only the men whom I have seen personally, and of whose deeds I have some knowledge, are listed here.' There is here an unmistakable effort to emphasize the authority of the narrator, by appealing to the incontrovertibility of personal memory.

Similar messages can be extracted from the other sections. Thus, in section (2), when sketching in the Irish 'cousins' of Clan Donald, Niall is at pains to establish his credibility as a witness, on the basis of personal travels and acquaintance:[23]

> It was Gilla-Adhamhnáin [i.e. the grandfather of Somerled] who erected the monastery of Screen in Tireragh in Co. Sligo … and his name is commemorated there, and there are written chronicles of his times there yet, and if it was to my purpose I could recall the time when I was in that territory …

Similarly, when talking about the expedition mounted by Giolla-Brighde, Somerled's father, to recover his patrimony from the Norse, which in Niall's account began with a call to his Maguire 'cousins' in Co. Fermanagh, Niall adds this comment:[24]

> I have seen the fort, and people who were demonstrating that four or five hundred men drawn up in order and rank could fit into it.

Again, when relating the progress of the Battle of Alford in section (4), he closes his description of the *mêlée* and confusion of the central stage of the battle as follows:[25]

> Alasdair son of Ranald son of Allan was a witness to that, for he and Allan Og, grandson of Alasdair, were the officers of the Clanranald on that occasion.

It seems likely that Niall's extended treatment of the Montrose campaigns was a bard's and shennachie's response to the *jours de gloire* of his older contemporaries who had fought with Montrose and Alasdair Mac Colla. Where first-hand recollection failed, the second-hand testimony of a named witness was the next-best thing.

The reasons for Niall's care over establishing authority bring us into contact with his motive and purpose in writing the History. The following statement is clear in that respect:[26]

> I could have found plenty to write about the deeds of the time [i.e. Montrose's campaigns] if I had set myself that task; but what spurred me to write even the amount that I have done was the way I saw that the writers who deal with the period make no mention of the Gaels, who did all the grafting.

In fact, not only is the 'service' of the Gaels underplayed in Niall's estimation, but they are the subject of unjust vilification. With reference to John of Moydart, a contemporary of Mary, Queen of Scots, he complains:[27]

> There was a troubled time during [John's] chieftaincy, for the Kingdom of Scotland was divided into factions, and the historians[28] find it easy to speak harshly of anybody who is not of the same faction as themselves. And I hear that they speak (thus) of John of Moydart, and especially Buchanan. But ask Sir George how he wishes to speak of the Princess to whom John of Moydart owed loyalty [i.e. Mary, Queen of Scots]. But whoever reviles the head does not usually praise the limbs.

Like a bard whose patron has been satirized, Niall knows it is his place to ward off the insult and restore the good name of the patron's family by rebutting it. Even in reference to much earlier times we can pick up this sense of the need to set the record straight. When assessing the career of Somerled, Niall first concedes that the Scottish Crown was worried by Somerled's final expedition to the Clyde, but then continues:[29]

> His own people say that it was not to make war on the King that [Somerled] made that expedition, but to obtain peace; for he subdued the enemies of the King more than he waged war on [the Crown].

The presence of these and similar explicit demonstrations of concern with questions of authority and correctness of record and interpretation suggests that it is worth looking afresh at the several sections of the History as a whole and asking how far this sense of challenge and desire to vindicate may have coloured his whole enterprise.

The first section, containing the fictitious pre-history relating to the Sons of Míl of Spain, may appear initially unpromising. But I have argued elsewhere that the use Niall makes of the mass of material at his disposal, in the Book of Invasions and associated genealogies and origin legends, was discriminating and purposeful.[30] Certainly, it would have been difficult for him as an exponent of the Classical tradition to ignore it. But he picks his way selectively through the genealogical thickets, following a tightly stretched line of information. It is suggestive that the only divagations he permits himself are to interject notes on Irish 'cousins' of the Scottish Clan Donald, that is, families claiming descent from the Three Collas.[31] It seems legitimate to suspect an element of demonstration in the way this information is deployed: in a sense, the message is: 'The Maguires (or whoever) are our cousins, and the fact that they really exist over yonder tends to prove that the genealogical account is valid.'

Whereas I would not want to make too much of this last point, when we move on to sections 2 and 3 we are on firmer ground. In the first place, Niall has clearly used Gaelic annalistic sources as the framework for his account of the Lordship of the Isles: as I would argue, this is in order to impart credibility to his story.[32] In the next example, if we set aside the problem of the actual date mentioned, we can see the *slán croinice* at work:[33]

> Let it be known to you that Raghnall and his power was the greatest [help] which King Alexander had against the king(s) of Norway at the time when he took the Isles from the Norsemen. And after that, having received a cross from Jerusalem, and after partaking of the body of Christ and receiving extreme unction, [Raghnall] died and was buried in Relic Oran in Iona in the year 12 …[34]

A common feature in the obits in Gaelic annals is the addition of an honorific quatrain – sometimes, no doubt, a quotation from a bardic elegy or some learned source, but sometimes simply an *ad hoc* composition designed to look as though it were taken from such a source. Here is an example from the Clanranald History.[35]

> This Ailein son of Ruairidh, having attended on the King and having received a charter to his patrimony from King James IV in 1509, died in Blair Atholl, and his body was interred in the local monastery:
>
> > A thousand years and nine to boot, / (and) five hundred years to tell,
> > from the One who succoured every land / to the death of Ailín son of Ruairidh.

There are complex agendas at work in items like these, of course. The reference to Ailín's receipt of a royal charter is not there casually, but to make a point on behalf of the family. Many obits similarly make reference to the munificence of the Clan Donald chiefs to the Church. Here we may surmise that the original annalist's purpose may have been to make a point on behalf of the Church, but that in Niall's account, in changed times, the point was being made on behalf of the chiefly family. Many obits demonstrate an additional concern to portray the chiefs of Clan Donald and Clanranald as enjoying prosperous and untroubled reigns, and as men of peace as well as war.[36]

> Donald son of Allan took the Lordship (of Clanranald) after [Allan], and there was every prosperity during his reign, and he died in Caisteal Tioram in the year of the Age of Christ, 1617. And Ranald son of Allan died in Canna in the year 1636 and his body was buried in Howmore in the same year.

Mention of the power of poetry brings us to another source of authority: bardic elegies. Although the edition in *Reliquiae Celticae* obscures the picture by removing the elegies from the body of the work, and although Christopher Beaton, author of the copy of the History in the so-called Black Book of Clanranald, simply eliminated them as he went along, one of the striking innovations of Niall's work is the insertion, at the correct point in the narrative, of the official elegies of many of the chiefs. The way Niall introduces them suggests to me that here, too, his motive was to cite evidence to lend authority to his account. Here are a couple of examples:[37]

> Ranald left his son Dugald in the Lordship; but I shall leave it to someone else to recall how he spent and ended his life …

> Great was the sadness and the gloom which the death of this fine man brought over the Isles, as is demonstrated in his elegy …

It seems altogether plausible to regard the inclusion of official poems of this sort as invoking the authority of the poets (i.e. *cuimhne druadh*, the oral counterpart to *slán croinice*), and thus illustrating both Niall's motivation and his respect for the poetry.

On a different tack, it is also possible to regard Niall's work as being characterized, for most of the time, by a significant measure of restraint and self-control. We may compare Niall's treatment of an episode from the twelfth century with that of Hugh MacDonald, the 'Sleat shennachie'. Here is Niall's description of the death of Somerled:[38]

> (Somerled) spent part of his time in war and part in peace, until he went with an army to the vicinity of Glasgow, where his own page murdered him, and took his head to the king in the year 1180 [*sic*].

Hugh MacDonald's account is more circumstantial and better motivated:[39]

> As the most of kings are commonly led by their councillors, the king himself being young, they contrived Sommerled's death in another manner. There was a nephew of Sommerled's, Maurice MacNeill, his sister's son, who was bribed to destroy him. Sommerled lay encamped

> at the confluence of the river Pasley into Clyde. His nephew taking a
> little boat, went over the river, and having got private audience with him,
> being suspected of none, stabbed him, and made his escape.

Despite their differences, these accounts would seem to draw on the same
traditional account. The suspicion that Niall's reticence is deliberate is reinforced by certain remarks at other points in his narrative. Thus, when referring
to Somerled's great-grandson, Angus Mór (*ob.* 1294), the father of Angus Óg
who fought with Bruce at Bannockburn, Niall remarks – tantalizingly, to us –
that 'there is much to be written about this Angus which is not written here'.[40]
Again, Niall merely mentions the Battle of Harlaw (1411), while recognizing its
significance and acknowledging that 'a great deal of martial exploits and deeds
are set down in writing' about Donald of Islay.[41]

It looks to me as though Niall is aiming at a 'sober', factual account, free from
the taint of anything anecdotal or fabulous. This does not mean he is free of bias.
His accounts of the end of the Lordship of the Isles ('[John] lived a year after
[Angus Og] and all the territories submitted to him; however, he gave many of
them to the King') and of the Battle of Philiphaugh ('The Marquis of Montrose
marched with part of his army heading for England to give relief to the King …
and he was defeated at Philiphaugh and was unable to give support to the King')
take the laconic style so far that they make his narrative disingenuous.[42] Yet I
believe it can be maintained that one of his aims is to distance himself from tale
and legend, and also (as will appear in a moment) from *literary* excess.

It must be admitted that not all sections of Niall's work are equally consistent. The Montrose Wars section contains accounts of the battles of
Inverlochy, Auldearn, Alford, and Kilsyth, and there are interesting differences
between them. As we know from other Gaelic sources, and most conspicu-
ously in the poetry of Iain Lom, the Keppoch bard, Inverlochy was seen as a
climactic victory for the MacDonalds and their allies over the Campbells. Yet
Niall's account is determinedly objective and factual in tone, with none of
Iain's triumphalism:[43]

> The two (skirmishing) parties engaged. It was not long before that party
> of the Earl of Argyll's army was routed and driven unwillingly into its
> own main force. The main body of the army became disorganized as a
> result of that, the (command to) advance on them was given, (and) they
> were all routed. The majority of the host were killed: very many of them
> were drowned at Nevis foot.

However, when we come to the later battles in the campaign, the accounts are
not only fuller and more minutely circumstantial, but also more literary, in their
style and diction, and in the fact that they contain rhetorically constructed
speeches.[44]

> The trained, bright-weaponed battalions of the Gaels were drawn up
> facing their enemies and the right wing was assigned to the bright-lively
> Gordon cavalry and to their Lord, and the command of the body of the
> army to the high-spirited magnanimous Marquis of Montrose, and Sir
> Alasdair of the reddened weapons and the numerous deeds of valour,
> namely the brave warrior son of Colla Ciotach son of Gilleasbuig son
> of Colla son of Alasdair son of Eóin Cathanach, took the left wing of
> the army facing the enemy right …

These concessions to the inflated style of romances and encomiastic prose are
at first sight a problem for the sort of explanation I have espoused, which
seeks to play up the positive, deliberate, consistent aspects of the History, and
argues for restraint and avoidance of literary, legendary, and folkloristic
material as a matter of policy. However, it may be misguided to view the
History as a finished work in the modern sense; for I would also wish to recognize in it a dynamic, inchoate quality, as though we have captured a work which
is in a process of evolution towards unity by the synthesis of disparate sorts of
source material.[45] On that reading, it may be argued that we see in these richly
drawn battle-scenes materials prepared in another context and not properly
assimilated into the style of the present work, or perhaps familiarity with
literary genres infecting the historian's writing. If so, we should have here
evidence for another sort of 'tide-rip', another type of trial for our poet-
historian.

In order to establish this last point it is worth quoting briefly from a piece
of prose encomium taken from a type of prose-verse miscellany which Niall
included in the 'Red Book', though not within the body of the History. It is
described in *Reliquiae Celticae* as 'The Arming and Army of John, Earl of
Ross, Lord of the Isles', and begins as follows:[46]

> It was then that the wise, woven-worded, close-reasoning, excellent-
> counselling, noble, substantial, famous, lively-of-exploits, high-spirited,
> golden-armed warriors of the Fair Foreigners [i.e. the men of the
> Hebrides] came, namely the conspicuous, successful, silk-bannered,
> excellent, fierce-lively Macleans, and the warlike spirited-brave tribe of
> Mac Iain …

This inflated style was in fact the norm for Early Modern prose, occurring in
such disparate texts as the 'historical' *Cogadh Gaedheal re Gallaibh* ('The War
of the Gael against the Foreigners') and *In Cath Cathardha* ('The Civil War',
a version of Lucan's *Pharsalia*), in the biographical *Beatha Aodha Ruaidh
Uí Dhomhnaill* ('Life of Hugh Roe O'Donnell') and in the hagiographical
Beatha Choluim Chille ('Life of Columba'), not to mention the many literary
romances.[47] Viewed from that perspective, the Clanranald History may well

have seemed frankly experimental. As I have suggested above, some of Niall's experimentation was apparently too much for his Beaton colleague who made the copy which has survived in the 'Black Book'. Specifically, this seems to be why he eliminated the 'pen-portraits' in the form of the bardic elegies which Niall had inserted. On the other hand, he followed Niall pretty faithfully in regard to the inflated battle-descriptions, confining his editorial activities there to excising some minute details relating to the doings of individual members of the Clanranald company, which Niall had doubtless got in the form of oral testimony and included in the name of authenticity.[48] We are entitled to conclude that the Clanranald History was a pretty unusual piece of writing; however much it drew on traditional sources, it adapted these into something quite different.

Why did Niall do this? Innovation was not a notable characteristic of the Classical Gaelic poets. Moreover, Niall's extant poetry, although competent and more, does not show evidence of a particularly radical and original mind.[49] The motivation suggested above – vindication of the Gael against the criticisms or dismissiveness of non-Gaelic historians – is clearly an important part of the answer. Yet Niall's references to Buchanan and other 'writers' do not involve rebuttal or debate, but seem to have a superficial, almost perfunctory air about them.[50]

I believe we need at this point to acknowledge the presence and challenge of historiographical activity much nearer home. The MacDonald History associated with 'the Sleat Shennachie' is comparable in its scope to the Clanranald History, despite the fact that it was written in English and not Gaelic, more anecdotal and less learned in tone, more argumentative and less didactic. The same may be said of the fragmentary Antrim MacDonald History, which in a couple of places shows significant (though not complete) resemblance to Niall's work.[51] We may refer also to the 'Black Book' itself as another Antrim-based product of this historiographical activity. For one thing, it contains an original account (in English) of some adventures of the Earl of Antrim, together with other historical texts relating to the 1640s;[52] while at the same time Christopher Beaton's version of Niall's account, with its omissions and additions and tonal changes, may arguably be classed as a contribution in its own right.[53]

We may be justified, then, in seeing Niall as a representative of the Highland poetic order becoming involved in a field of activity that also involved non-professional Gaelic historians, who could have formed a conduit to the wider world of Scottish historiography. In that respect, the Clanranald History can take its place amongst the traditional Highland and Scottish clan and family histories that flowered in the late seventeenth and early eighteenth centuries. It appears odd in many ways when set beside them, but I would argue that its oddity is a function of the materials and modes of discourse available to Niall when he, as a member of an ancient bardic family, asked the same questions as the more typical clan historians were asking themselves.

Finally, these common questions arose from the growth of new ways of accessing, rationalizing, and drawing lessons from the past, which in their turn reflected the far-reaching socio-political developments of the times. In the case of the Clanranald History we may detect faint but tell-tale signs of the presence of these factors. First, there is a muted but recurrent emphasis on the rightness of honourable (sometimes 'noble') action. Second, this is often linked with loyalty to the King (or the Queen or the Crown). And third, there is in the concluding section of the History a sense of pessimism about the ever-present burden of debt on the Clanranald family.[54] It would be my contention that the uncertainties of the Jacobite era may have contributed to Niall's motivation to write his History, as may also those prefigured by the family's recurrent financial difficulties in the late seventeenth century. These would have combined with the more strictly professional challenge Niall felt to produce a history that would answer contemporary questions about his patron's family and their race, to form the crucible out of which his innovative, imperfect, remarkable History emerged.

Notes

1   On the Scottish side see, for example, the papers from the 1996 Edinburgh Conference 'Writing Scotland's history' published together in *Scottish Historical Review* 76 (1997), and further works referred to there. On the Irish side, see, for example, Marc Caball, *Poets and Politics: Continuity and Reaction in Irish Poetry, 1558–1625* (Cork, 1998); B. Cunningham, *The World of Geoffrey Keating: History, Myth and Religion in Seventeenth-Century Ireland* (Dublin, 2000); J. T. Leerssen, *Mere Irish and Fíor-Ghael: Studies in the Idea of Nationality, Its Development and Literary Expression Prior to the Nineteenth Century* (Amsterdam and Philadelphia, Pa., 1986); M. MacCraith, 'Gaelic Ireland and the Renaissance', in *The Celts and the Renaissance: Tradition and Innovation*, ed. by G. Williams and R. O. Jones (Cardiff, 1990); B. Ó Buachalla, *Aisling ghéar: Na Stíobhartaigh agus an t-aos léinn* (Dublin, 1996); Michelle O Riordan, *The Gaelic Mind and the Collapse of the Gaelic World* (Cork, 1990); K. Simms, *From Kings to Warlords: The Changing Political Structure of Gaelic Ireland in the Later Middle Ages* (Woodbridge, 1987).

2   An earlier and more general treatment of this topic formed the subject matter of the Vernam Hull Memorial Lecture which I gave at Harvard University in 1995. I wish to acknowledge the helpful comments I received on that occasion, and also the work of Dr Martin MacGregor, whose own research in the area of Highland family histories has expanded our knowledge and understanding considerably, and who kindly let me see a draft of his forthcoming paper, 'The genealogical histories of Gaelic Scotland'.

3   Respectively MCR39 and MCR40 in the Royal Museum of Scotland. For a useful account of the history of these MSS see R. Black, 'In Search of the Red Book of Clanranald', *Clan Donald Magazine* 8 (1979), 43–51. I am working on a new edition of the Clanranald History for the Scottish Gaelic Texts Society, and the

portions of text quoted below contain my translations of my text of the History. For convenience's sake, however, I give references to the edition contained in A. Cameron (ed.), *Reliquiae Celticae*, 2 vols (Inverness, 1892–94), II, 138–309 (hereafter referred to as *RC*), which provides the only currently available English version of the Clanranald History. Both the text and the translation in *RC* have to be treated with caution.

4 The last date mentioned in the body of the History is 1686 (*RC* 208 / 9). Since it refers to the death of Charles II, one may surmise that a little time had elapsed between the event and the writing of the entry.

5 See further W. Gillies, 'The Clanranald Histories: Authorship and Purpose', in *Origins and Revivals: Proceedings of the First Australian Conference of Celtic Studies*, ed. by G. Evans, B. Martin, and J. Wooding (Sydney, 2001), pp. 315–40; 'Leabhraichean Chlann Raghnaill', *Clan Donald Magazine* 12 (1991), 20–5; and ibid., 13 (1995), 49–50; 'Oral and Written Sources and Effects in the Clanranald Histories', in *Orality, Literacy and Modern Media*, ed. by D. Scheunemann (Columbia, SC, 1996), pp. 27–43.

6 Frank O'Connor, *The Backward Look: A Survey of Irish Literature* (London, 1967).

7 *The Backward Look*, p. 2. See also F. J. Byrne, '*Senchas*: The Nature of Gaelic Historical Tradition', *Irish Historical Studies* 9 (1974), 137–59.

8 See, for example, D. S. Thomson, 'Gaelic Learned Orders and Literati in Medieval Scotland', *Scottish Studies* 12 (1968), 57–78; W. Gillies, 'Gaelic: The Classical Tradition', in *The History of Scottish Literature*, ed. by Cairns Craig, 4 vols (Aberdeen, 1987–88), I: *Origins to 1660*, ed. by R. D. S. Jack (Aberdeen, 1988), pp. 245–62. For Ireland, see K. Simms, 'The Brehons of Later Medieval Ireland', in *Brehons, Serjeants and Attorneys: Studies in the History of the Irish Legal Profession*, ed. by D. Hogan and W. N. Osborough (Dublin, 1990), pp. 51–76.

9 See P. Breatnach, 'The Chief's Poet', *Proceedings of the Royal Irish Academy* 83 C (1983), 37–79.

10 From *Triath na nGaoidheal Giolla-easbuig*, ed. by W. J. Watson, *Scottish Gaelic Studies* 3 (1931), 141–51 (st. 34). Compare also, from the same poem, st. 16, *cuimhne druadh*, 'the memory of druids' (= 'men of traditional learning'), and st. 31, *seanchas*, '(traditional) history', beside st. 32, *ughdair*, '(especially written) authorities'.

11 *Lebor Gabála Érenn*, ed. by R. A. S. Macalister, 5 vols (London and Dublin, 1938–56).

12 See B. Ó Buachalla, 'Introduction' to second edn (1987) of G. Keating, *Foras Feasa ar Éirinn*, ed. by D. Comyn and P. S. Dinneen, 4 vols (London and Dublin); Cunningham, *World of Keating*. Compare An Dubhaltach Mac Fhir-Bhisigh's introduction to his *Book of Genealogies*, written in 1652: 'Its time [of writing] is the period of the religious war between the Catholics of Ireland and the Heretics of Ireland, Scotland and England ... The cause of writing the same book is to increase the glory of God, and to give information to everyone generally' (T. Ó Raithbheartaigh, *Genealogical Tracts* I (Dublin, 1932) p. 2).

13 For an up-to-date re-statement of the 'one Gaeltacht' position see M. Ó Mainnín, ' "The Same in Origin and in Blood": Bardic Windows on the Relationship between Irish and Scottish Gaels, *c.* 1200–1650', *Cambrian Medieval Celtic Studies* 38 (Winter 1999), 1–52. A searching fresh appraisal of the evidence is contained in Wilson McLeod's forthcoming *Divided Gaels: Gaelic Scotland and Ireland, 1200–1650* (Oxford, 2002).

14 See A. Hughes, 'The Seventeenth-Century Ulster / Scottish Contention of the Red Hand: Background and Significance', in *Gaelic and Scots in Harmony*, ed. by D. S. Thomson (Glasgow, [1989]), pp. 78–94.

15   Caball, *Poets and Politics*, p. 1.
16   Printed in A. MacDonald and A. MacDonald, *The Clan Donald*, 3 vols (Inverness, 1896–1904), II, 790–801.
17   *RC* 175 / 6–77 / 8. For identifications of the characters named, see D. S. Thomson, 'The Poetry of Niall MacMhuirich', *Transactions of the Gaelic Society of Inverness* 46 (1970), 281–307.
18   See B. Ó Cuív, 'The Irish Language in the Early Modern Period', in *A New History of Ireland*, ed. by T. W. Moody, F. X. Martin and F. Byrne, 9 vols (Oxford, 1976–), III: *Early Modern Ireland 1534–1691* (1976), pp. 509–43.
19   *RC* 148 / 9. Since the world was held to have been created in 5200 BC, this puts the coming of the Milesians to Ireland in 1700 BC.
20   See J. L. Campbell and D. S. Thomson, *Edward Lhuyd in the Scottish Highlands* (Oxford, 1963), pp. xiii–xxiv.
21   See e.g. M. Lynch, *Scotland: A New History*, rev. edn (London 1992), pp. 247–56; MacGregor, 'Genealogical Histories' (n.2). For an example of conflict between Classical and post-Classical understanding of a family's early history, see David Sellar, 'The Earliest Campbells – Norman, Briton or Gael?', *Scottish Studies* 17 (1973), 109–25, and W. Gillies, 'Heroes and Ancestors', in *The Heroic Process*, ed. by B. Almqvist, S. Ó Catháin and P. Ó Héalaí (Dublin, 1987), pp. 57–74.
22   Fuller discussion of the sections and related issues is in 'Authorship and Purpose'.
23   *RC* 659 (cf. 152 / 3).
24   *RC* 659 (cf. 154 / 5).
25   *RC* 194 / 5.
26   *RC* 202 / 3.
27   *RC* 170 / 1.
28   Niall here uses the plural form of *scríbhneóir*, literally 'writer'.
29   *RC* 154 / 5.
30   See again 'Authorship and Purpose'.
31   Thus, when giving the Clan Donald pedigree from Colla Uais down to Somerled, Niall reaches the generation of Niallgus son of Gothfraidh and pauses to say: 'You should know, reader, that there are many roots extending from the tree which will not be written down here; yet one may as well set down a certain portion of them' (*RC* 659 and 152 / 3).
32   The question of Gaelic annalistic sources, raised also in 'Authorship and Purpose', needs to be investigated further. For the present it is enough to record (1) the probability that an Iona-based or at least Iona-oriented chronicle has been used, whether directly or indirectly, for the period of the Lordship, and (2) the possibility that an annalistic *style* rather than an annalistic *source* may need to be reckoned with later on. (Cf. 'Oral and Written Sources', p. 39.)
33   *RC* 156 / 7.
34   For the problem about the date, see A. B. MacEwen, 'The Death of Reginald Son of Somerled', *West Highland Notes and Queries* 2nd series no. 6 (September 1990), 3–7.
35   *RC* 168 / 9.
36   *RC* 172 / 3.
37   *RC* 170 / 1 (given as 1514, but synchronized with Flodden, i.e. 1513) and 208 / 9 (given as 1686, but synchronized with the death of Charles II, i.e. 1685). The elegies are printed separately at *RC* 216–49.
38   *RC* 154 / 5.
39   See 'History of the MacDonalds', in *Highland Papers*, I, ed. by J. R. N. MacPhail (Edinburgh, 1914), pp. 2–72 (p. 9).
40   *RC* 158 / 9.
41   *RC* 160 / 1.

42   *RC* 162 / 3, 202 / 3.

43   *RC* 184 / 5.

44   *RC* 186 / 7. The translation does not do justice to the alliteration and rhythmic balance of the original. Cf. 'Oral and Written Sources', pp. 40–1, for a comment on the questions raised by the speeches.

45   The principal evidence for this statement is (1) material contained in RB but outside the actual History, and material contained in other MSS written by Niall, which could have been in the History but is not; and (2) stylistic and similar 'gear changes' at several points in the narrative, including differences in the textual basis. For (1) see 'Authorship and Purpose'; for (2) see brief references in *Études Celtiques* 29 (1992), 459–60, and in 'Leabhraichean Chlann Raghnaill' (see n. 5 above).

46   *RC* 258 / 9–60 / 1.

47   See J. E. C. Williams and P. K. Ford, *The Irish Literary Tradition* (Cardiff and Belmont, Mass., 1992), ch. 3; E. Poppe, 'The Early Modern Irish Version of Beves of Hamtoun', *Cambridge Medieval Celtic Studies* 23 (Summer 1992), 77–98 (pp. 82–7).

48   See, for example, *RC* 188 / 9.

49   Cf. Thomson, 'Poetry of Niall MacMhuirich', pp. 286–93.

50   The complaint against Lowland historians may have been a commonplace, since it recurs in the Sleat Shennachie (MacPhail, 'History', pp. 9–10), who, however, gives the impression of having actually seen the criticisms, and in the fragmentary Antrim history (see next note), p. 282, which is reminiscent of Niall's tone.

51   For the Antrim history, see A. MacDonald, 'A Fragment of an Irish MS History of the MacDonalds of Antrim', *Transactions of the Gaelic Society of Inverness* 37 (1934–36), 262–84 (pp. 282–3).

52   The Clanranald History begins at fol. 53. 'Antrime's Trophee', a group of panegyric texts composed to welcome the Earl of Antrim to Scotland in 1646, begins at fol. 122^r. 'A brief Relation of the Earle of Antrimes first escape out of Carrickfergus' begins at fol. 165^r and is followed by a similar account of Antrim's 'second escape' at fol. 180^r.

53   Sometimes the alteration was merely a matter of taste. Where Niall says of Donald of Harlaw, 'He died thereafter in Islay, and his full noble body was buried in the south side of his church of Oran', Beaton emends to what he may have felt was more in keeping with Niall's generally austere style: 'He died thereafter in Islay, and was buried in his church of Oran' (*RC* 162 / 3). Again, Beaton could be irritated by Niall's occasional slackness, as where he copies 'They continued in that manner for thirteen or fourteen days without respite' as 'They continued in that manner for a fortnight without respite' (*RC* 198 / 9). But sometimes his changes are more substantial, as when he suppresses the details of Domhnall, son of Eóin Múideartach's expedition to Ireland in 1648. Some of these changes would appear to spring from impatience with detailed discussion of northern Hebridean affairs, and others from respect for the sensitivities of an Antrim MacDonald view of the actions concerned.

54   The same 'moral' under-current and a similar analysis of present troubles are present in the Antrim history: see pp. 282–3.

9

Dreams in the Clear Light of Day: Older Scots Poetry in Modern Scotland

David J. Parkinson

From the sixteenth through the eighteenth centuries, it might be argued, Scottish literature predicts, enacts and then mourns its loss of autonomy. Modern Scottish narratives dwell inventively and memorably on the separation of a former age from the present. That former age is irrevocable and decisive, uncompletable and finished, a bogle haunting the present, still to be 'recognized by the present as one of its own concerns'.[1] For Scottish writers at the end of the eighteenth century, the older literature of their nation possesses an untidy energy with a troubling whiff of the macabre.[2] Access to the past of their literature gradually enables these writers to attain a doubleness of implication on various grave and exalted subjects.[3]

In the eighteenth and early nineteenth century, Scottish poets and novelists allude to their vernacular past affectionately, but often patronizingly. They do so in depictions of humble domesticity, wild merrymaking, or supernatural onset: in the homely scene, singing the old songs and reading the old books bespeaks poverty, piety, and cultural conservatism; in the tavern, a suspicious, often alienating, tendency towards the grotesque. The kirkyard arouses strong suspicions about the threat of the past as the inversion of the present. Thus Burns, quoting Gavin Douglas's prologue to Book Six of his Scots *Eneados*, gives 'Tam o'Shanter' the epigraph 'Of Brownyis and of Bogillis full is this buke'. Riding 'thro' dub and mire, / Despising wind, and rain, and fire', towards the ruined Kirk of Alloway, Tam o'Shanter tries to keep his spirits up by 'crooning o'er some auld Scots sonnet' (81–2, 84).[4] At first, Tam's lore hardly protects him but adds to his danger: his choice of lyric may only provoke the diablerie he wishes to avert.[5]

Likewise, it is a few pages from the *Works* of the sixteenth-century Sir David Lyndsay rather than Holy Scripture that the serving-men con over before tending to their master's corpse in *Redgauntlet*: 'down the carles sat ower a stoup of brandy, and Hutcheon, who was something of a clerk, would have read a chapter of the Bible; but Dougal would hear naething but a blaud of Davie Lindsay, whilk was the waur preparation'.[6] Recourse to an old but familiar Scottish book seems to animate and invite what was to be kept reverently still and remote, the world of the dead. The later spectacle of Sir Robert

Redgauntlet in hell suggests that his 'values are both rejected and sanctioned by the narrative', Hell itself being depicted as 'an underworld version of the family mansion. There is little suffering here. The place seems, indeed, to have about it a festive atmosphere'.[7] As with Burns's 'Tam o'Shanter', narration has the air of being 'good-humoured' and 'finding "entertainment to a philosophic mind" in rural superstition'.[8]

Depicted thus, the former age of Scottish literature begins to assume a double face: underlying their references – eulogizing or patronizing – to aspects of bygone national culture, late eighteenth-century writers are employing 'new rhetoric' and 'new narrative strategies and perspectives' to indicate a 'degeneration of national archetype'.[9] Allusions to old Scottish songs and books point towards the Gothic. Associated with the eldritch, that mingling of the domestic and the fantastic, the everyday and the otherworldly, the risible and the terrifying, that had long been one of its prevailing topics, the relics of the Scottish past generate élan at the expense of gravity.[10]

To trivialize discourse thus is to dye it fast. In 1706–07, during the final stages of debate over the Treaty of Union between Scotland and England, advocates of Union were adept at such trivialization. Late one November afternoon in 1706, for example, Lord Belhaven, a 'rough, fat, black, noisy man, more like a butcher than a lord', but also 'widely read and accomplished', has just sat down after delivering the first of his speeches in the Scottish Parliament against the motion for dissolution.[11] It has been an impassioned, visionary oration on a Caledonia, murdered like Caesar by supposed friends, and glimpsed in a dark anaphora of vignettes – sentence after sentence beginning 'I seem to see' – evoking the disorder, poverty, and humiliation the nation's institutions and inhabitants will suffer if Parliament accedes now to Union.[12] Who will speak from the other side in defence of the motion? The Earl of Marchmont rises; he is a namesake descendant of that Patrick Hume of Polwarth who flyted with Alexander Montgomerie over a century before, at the court of the young James VI. What happens next is unexpected. According to Daniel Defoe – in Edinburgh as an English propagandist – the Earl of Marchmont uncorks one flippant sentence by way of retort to Belhaven: 'Behold, he dreamed, but lo! when he awoke, he found it was a dream'. Defoe comments that 'this answer, some said, was as satisfactory to the members, who understood the design of that speech, as if it had been answered vision by vision'.[13] Marchmont's characterization of dream as deceptive but fleeting draws on one biblical type: 'He [the wicked hypocrite] shall fly away as a dream, and shall not be found: yea, he shall be chased away as a vision of the night' (Job 20.8); 'As a dream when one awaketh; so, O Lord, when thou awakest, thou shalt despise their image' (Ps. 73.20). Prophetic vision becomes its burlesque double: 'a vision or rhapsody of nonsense'; false, insubstantial

                    David J. Parkinson

dream.[14] As John Erskine, Earl of Mar, noted, Belhaven's speech 'was made pretty ridiculous'.[15]

The second anecdote is simpler than the first, but more famous. It is the first of May, 1707, a day, according to the Jacobite George Lockhart, 'never to be forgot by Scotland; a day in which the Scots were stripped of what their predecessors had gallantly maintained for many hundred years'.[16] Having signed the engrossed exemplification of the Act of Union, Chancellor James Ogilvy, first Earl of Seafield and a prominent broker of the Union, hands it to the clerk 'in the face of Parliament, with this despising and contemning remark, "Now there's ane end of ane old song" '.[17] Like Marchmont reducing Belhaven's grim vision of the Scottish future to at best a day-dream, Seafield compresses the Scottish past to something outmoded and petty: that future and this past are both insubstantial, dreams to be disregarded. Again it is the advocate of Union who gets off the cleverest witticism, and again that brilliance draws on burlesque of Scripture: Babylon falls, a new Jerusalem arises, and 'I heard the voice of harpers harping with their harps: And they sung as it were a new song' (Rev. 14.2). Despite the harsh colours in which Lockhart depicts the event, one may still wonder what sort of old song Seafield was thinking of, and whether it might have sounded like the one historian Rosalind Mitchison had in mind when she wrote that 'the Border eventually succumbed to law and order, but it went down with song'.[18] This voices the notion that, however stirring or soothing they may have been regarded, such songs had to end. They were barbarous at best; in the workaday new world (hardly a new Jerusalem), only beggars sing thus for a living. Only the drunk, destitute, and disabled sing in the streets, and their voices are to be heard with mingled admiration and complacency.[19] With their epigrammatic punchlines, these anecdotes locate the emptying of meaning from song and dream at the time of Union. The scar left by the Earl of Seafield's verbal incision has become a defining mark of Scottish culture.[20]

In fact, much sinew connects early seventeenth with late eighteenth-century culture. For instance, the reading habits of eighteenth-century Scots deserve attention: the vernacular past, broadly comprising texts in both English and Scots, provides material for various activities, among them the curriculum for primary school instruction in 'English'.[21] Modernized versions of old books appear: Hary's *Wallace*, Douglas's *Prologues*, Lyndsay's *Works*, Montgomerie's *Cherrie and the Slae*.[22] These books are not antiquarian projects like Allan Ramsay's *Ever Green* (1724), nor may it be accurate to characterize them, as both *Ever Green* and James Watson's *Choice Collection* (1706–11) have been, as politically partisan ventures.[23] Instead, they have been selected, revised, and reprinted to form a canon, eloquent and venerable in their articulation of a heritage and inculcation of its values and stances. In this sense, the line between the early seventeenth century and the end of the eighteenth is direct.[24]

Participants in seventeenth-century Scottish culture were adept at finding coherence in arrays of potentially significant motifs, on the pages of books as on the ceilings of churches and great houses. According to Henry Peacham, 'Who hath ever seene more wittie, proper, and significant devises, then those of Scotland?'[25] Understanding such devices enables the skilled reader to resolve the enigmatically emblematic text and not become ensnared by 'the whorish ornam[ents] of affected eloquence', 'an vnsutable ornament to garnish pure Truth'.[26] As the English Jesuit Robert Southwell argues in his prefatory Epistle to *Saint Peter's Complaint,* a book reprinted in seventeenth-century Scotland, poetry may grow utterly corrupt, and still offer 'skilfuller wits' the means to avoid 'the errours of their Workes'.[27] Taken emblematically, the poem, always vulnerable to the charge of infectiveness, deceitfulness, and impoverishment, is redeemed. Readers from all sectarian positions may look herein for signs of the immanence of divine grace. A strong reader places a poem with one ideology beside one with another, and transforms both.

Nowhere does such reading come into play more fully than in the dream vision. The Scottish dream vision may be epitomized as a visionary dialogue in a place that is by turns blissful and horrible; with these emphases, the genre attains its characteristic resilience. Such destabilization of authorship and sovereignty acclimatizes the latter to Scottish political and cultural realities. As reprinted in 1579, while Morton tottered, Lennox triumphed, and James VI assumed his majority, Gavin Douglas's *Palice of Honour* revitalizes dream vision as an allusive, labyrinthine genre that befits a time of heightened faction, intrigue, and scrutiny. One way to demonstrate the suitability of *The Palice of Honour* to these circumstances is to investigate its transitions between glorious and infernal scenes, and between didacticism and farce. On one level, the encyclopedism of the *Palice* represents literature as pedagogical and monitory, strengthening the prince and hence the nation in faith and wisdom; on another, its farce undermines such ideals. For two or three decades after its reprinting in 1579, this book is often imitated, and from contrary political positions.

The year 1579 marks the last extant reprinting of the *Palice*.[28] Two other books rise in its place to gain a remarkable hold on the attention and memory of generations of Scottish readers: Sir David Lyndsay's *Dialog betuix Experience and ane Courteour* (?1552, 1554, 1558, 1559 etc.) and Captain Alexander Montgomerie's *Cherrie and the Slae* (1584, 1597, [1615?], 1636, etc.).[29] Both are the major works in books as notable for what they omit as for what they include. Neither *Squyer Meldrum* nor the *Satyre of the Thrie Estaitis* appear in Lyndsay's *Works,* which is dominated instead by the *Dialog.* Likewise, Montgomerie's book is similarly largely devoted to the augmented, completed second version of *The Cherrie and the Slae.* Both books teach their readers to comport themselves wisely in a place and time in which the source of authority must be sought within.

Lyndsay's *Dialog betuix Experience and ane Courteour* principally concerns the fall of Adam and Eve, the punishment of wicked humankind in the Flood, and the multiplication of human fallenness under the first age of kingship, at Babylon. Three more 'monarchies' are rapidly surveyed before Experience, the principal speaker of the poem, castigates the papacy as the fifth and worst monarchy, and memorably envisions divine restitution in the apocalypse. It is a very long poem, over sixty-three hundred lines; throughout, energy is doom-laden, and rest is the proper goal:

> We se the gret Gloube of the Firmament
> Continuallie in moueying maruellous.
> The Sewin Planetis, contrary thare intent,
> Ar reft about, with coursse contrarious.
> The wynd, and See, with stormys furious,
> The trublit Air, with Frostis, Snaw, and Rane,
> On to that day thay trauell euer in pane. (6253–9)

The original contrast between Edenic bliss and the usually chaotic labour of fallenness now encompasses the universe, all of which awaits recreation. The *Dialog* turns out to be a recasting of *ars moriendi* in the guise of an ultimately redemptive history, in which fear gives way at last to hope.[30]

There is a link between the *Dialog* and the *Cherrie*: the first part of Lyndsay's poem was adapted into a song in fourteen-line stanzas, to be sung to a famous tune, 'The Banks of Helicon'. A copy of this lyric appears in the Bannatyne Manuscript, where it is ascribed to Sir Richard Maitland; the stanza form is the quatorziem of Montgomerie's poem, and its tune is that upon which the composer Andrew Blackhall based his setting of the *Cherrie*. At some stage, both poems served as songs. Stanza and tune enable the reader to become a performer of versions of each of these poems.[31]

Song likewise endowed the reader of the *Dialog* with a performer's power to move as well as instruct. In his Diary, the reformer James Melville writes that during a return to the family home in 1569, he was consoled by reading 'David Lindsayes book', which his eldest sister Isobel 'wald reid and sing, namlie, concerning the letter judgment, the peanes of hell, and the joyes of heavin, wherby sho wald caus me bathe greit and be glad' (*letter*: last; *peanes*: pains; *bathe*: both; *greit*: weep).[32] Lyndsay's *Works* were frequently reprinted between 1568 and 1776. The editor of Lyndsay adduces proverbial sayings, anecdotes, and allusions to prove that 'those many editions … were printed for reading by the peasant, the farmer, and the humbler townsman'.[33] By 1681, along with *Bruce* and *Wallace*, Lyndsay's book is on a par with ballads and romances: *Gray-Steel, Bevis of Hampton*, 'Adam Bell', 'Johnny Armstrong's Last Goodnight', and 'Chevy Chase'.[34] By 1721, Lyndsay keeps company with *Pilgrim's Progress*, 'Davie Dallas', and *Wallace*.[35] Lyndsay does not sit unopened on the common Scottish shelf: learning passages from the *Dialog* locks them into the common memory.

With its store of useful material – proverbs and witty retorts – *The Cherrie and the Slae* makes demonstrably similar demands on memory. It may be Montgomerie's most famous poem, but few readers now would describe it as their favourite: its descriptions are both idealized and localized, its stanza complexly tuneful, and its allegory unresolvably enigmatic.[36] The longer version of *The Cherrie and the Slae*, the version known through the seventeenth and eighteenth centuries, may be summarized thus: in the pleasant place, the narrator encounters Cupid, who tempts him to borrow his wings and his bow and arrows; having done so, the narrator wounds himself and falls to earth, where he sees two possible remedies for his injury, a remote cherry tree and an accessible sloe bush. A debate ensues between those qualities of mind committed to climb for the cherry (Courage, Will, Hope) and those deprecating the goal as too difficult (Dread, Danger, and Experience), with Reason tending towards the latter group. Disputation advances from the old question of dream dialogue, 'What constitutes right action?', towards the more fundamental 'What constitutes identity?'. It is only after hope has been admitted to be an element of identity that the attempt on the cherry can be planned and effected.

All the many reprints of the augmented *Cherrie* include a cluster of shorter poems ascribed to Montgomerie; of these poems, three are attested to be his in independent sources. These three are the sonnet 'Supreme essence', and the lyrics 'The Solsequium' and 'Captain Alexander Montgomerie his Lamentation' (elsewhere entitled 'A Godly Prayer'). There is much to say about the way these lyrics – along with the other inclusions, less securely attributed – teach the reader how to read the *Cherrie*. For instance, 'The Solsequium' reduces the alternation of hope and despondency in existence to the diurnal cycle: it traces the emotional crests and troughs while the object of the singer's desire repeatedly approaches and withdraws. This process comes to seem as inevitable as the day it traces. Even if the speaker does not realize it, the whole cycle, dwindling in its recurrence, is draining of meaning:

> O happy Day, go not away; *Apollo* stay
> The Cart from going down into the West,
> Of me thou makes thy *Zodiack*, that I may take
> My pleasure to behold whom I love best,
> Her presence me restores from Death to rise,
> Her absence also shores to cut my Breath,

> I wish in vain thee to remain,
> Since *Primum Mobile* doth say me nay;
> At least thy Wain, hast so again,
> Farewell with patience perforce till Day.[37]

As existence loses meaning in its recurrence, so does experience. The lyric heightens longing for some better life than such loss. *The Cherrie* deliberates over the form this life might take, and the way to achieve it. The seventeenth-century reprints of Montgomerie's work prepare the reader to relate its conflicts of longing and discouragement to personal experience; that this association is located within the capacities of the individual may explain the enduring pertinence of this book.

The second *Cherrie* has particular importance for Scottish literature: it addresses a long-standing problem therein, namely the unresolvable instability of meaning. Those aspects of sixteenth-century Scottish poetry currently regarded as most intriguing have to do with transition: the pleasant place as lyric setting for something prized, adorable, now absent; invective as the push into *purteth* – poverty, homelessness, disease, sterility, decay. Style-shifting dynamizes the most memorable of these texts, in which moral seems to hover detached from narrative surface.[38] The second *Cherrie* encourages the reader, not the author, to resolve this dilemma of style. The reader occupies the avid, faceless protagonist's place, and has the opportunity to identify the emblem upon which the poem depends, the inaccessible but finally generous cherry tree. To read the poem is to work towards a balance of the specialized, limited, conflicting aspects of one's own mind. In the penultimate stanza, mental toil is subsumed:

> As *Reason* ordain'd, all obey'd;
> None was o'er-rash, none was afraid,
>   our Counsel was so wise:
> As of our Journey *Wit* did note,
> We found it true in every Jot,
>   God bless our Enterprise.
> For ev'n as wee came to the Tree,
>   which, as ye heard mee tell,
> Could not be clumb, there suddenly
>   the Fruit for Ripeness fell:
>   Which tasting, and hasting,
>   I found my self reliev'd
>   Of Cares all, and Snares all,
>   which Mind and Body griev'd. (1569–82)[39]

All is resolved: the yearning of the dreamer to possess the cherry and of the reader to possess the multivalent emblem of and in the text. It is a decisive outcome to be contrasted with the congested, unresolved moment in which Henryson's Troilus, struggling to understand whom he has encountered, tosses jewels 'with a swak' into the lap of the defaced Cresseid. The cherries fall; freed from orbit around an unattainable goal, the dreamer hastens to taste them and be 'reliev'd' thereby. Consumed in the act of reading, ideally the poem is reborn: when the cherries fall, the moment is, among other things, a bestowal on that conceivably educable, redeemable being, the Scottish reader.

On the title page of the earliest extant edition of the second *Cherrie* (1636) appears the emblem of a crude phoenix, derived from a recurrent design of the pelican in her piety.[40] This roughly reconfigured phoenix is a significant emblem of this version of the *Cherrie*, both celebrating rather than achieving the values of harmonious consumption and rebirth. The second *Cherrie and the Slae* emblematizes two ways of reading: one, to seek meaning ready-made in the matter of the text, and thus to be frustrated and impoverished; the other, to regard the reading of the text as the meaning of the text, which may liberate. What is being read is the reader's own experience of learning. If the reader shows initiative, this *Cherrie* reveals itself as a repository of situations in which bad experience, partial argument, and incomplete reasoning can be completed and resolved.

The conjunction is revealing between the second *Cherrie* and the makeshift phoenix on its earliest extant title page. Iconographically, the phoenix is unique – it is peerless but also solitary – and reborn.[41] Authenticity, stability, permanence – a series of perfect replicas unto infinity – these in fact are the values claimed by the printers of the poem as they convey it from decade to decade across two centuries. *The Cherrie and the Slae* survives into the eighteenth century because it is complete, eloquent, and ethically oriented; its allegory and that of the lyrics that accompany it is tolerable because it teaches the reader to seek good morality within a homespun fiction.[42] By the nineteenth century, the poem has grown obsolete, the certitude it had come to represent no longer compelling.

It may be worthwhile, therefore, to end with an episode from James Hogg's *Private Memoirs and Confessions of a Justified Sinner* (1824). Hogg represents the last generation of those for whom Scottish texts were curricular, and for him the dream vision is significant less for its content and more for its open-endedness.[43] Hogg's novel, it has been argued, hinges upon the reader's capacity to 'glimpse something "beyond [our] depth", to admit that life is "boundless and unfathomable", and irreducible to rational or religious theories'.[44] Fugitive from the family estate he has dishonoured, the title character Robert Wringhim finds work at the Edinburgh printing house of the real-life James Watson, printer of *The Cherrie and the Slae* in his *Choice Collection*. Emulating Bunyan's *Pilgrim's Progress* and learning what he can about presswork, Wringhim works to justify his life into print. Meantime, learning that devils are haunting his shop, Watson reads Wringhim's self-justfying pamphlet 'and thereupon flew into a great rage, called my work a medley of lies and blasphemy, and ordered the whole to be consigned to the flames'.[45] As the master-printer condemns the false book, so God will condemn the false author.

All along, Wringhim has insisted that his name is eternally 'written in the Lamb's book of life'. Intending to find for it an earthly permanence, he claims a place for it, significantly, in personification allegory, a genre with a distinguished Scottish pedigree that he nevertheless associates with its best-known English example, Bunyan's *Pilgrim's Progress*. Often reprinted in late seventeenth-century Scotland, this book appealed to a middle-class audience with its growing taste for 'a contemplative brand of Calvinism'.[46] It may be relevant that a prominent publisher of Bunyan in Scotland was Agnes Campbell, widow of the printer Andrew Anderson and embattled holder of the title of Queen's Printer despite the efforts of James Watson, Episcopalian and Jacobite, to wrest it from her.[47] It need not be entirely trivial to wonder whether Watson's fury may have had something to do with professional rivalry: his best-known book is the important three-part anthology of Scottish literature popularly known as *Watson's Choice Collection*, in which prominence is given to the best-known Scottish personification-allegory, Montgomerie's *Cherrie and the Slae*. Tempting as it is to dwell on the possibility that Watson hurls Wringhim's pamphlet into the flames because its author preferred Bunyan to Montgomerie, Hogg's irony extends further. In the hands of the Justified Sinner, a once-prestigious, avidly read genre, allegorical vision, has become deceptive, even corruptive. With a Calvinist, English exemplar and a self-serving, deceitful author, Wringhim's work – the narrative that comprises the bulk of the second half of Hogg's novel as well as the abortive pamphlet that appears to have been an earlier form of that narrative – is wholly culpable. Unlike Hogg's ironic, multi-voiced novel, Wringhim's allegorical vision burns because it all too readily conveys influence – the diabolic Gil-Martin's, that is – and self-serving authorial intention. It fails to give the reader scope to work out meaning.[48] Wringhim the would-be author abuses his national culture, and has no choice but to experience its revenge.

The vernacular past sustained generations of Scottish readers. The books that convey that past into the eighteenth century – Douglas, Lyndsay, Montgomerie, and the rest – are not superficial reading, but instead enliven interpretation and response. Having been taught, moved, and entertained herein, Scottish readers are challenged to exercise their powers of deliberation upon matters of great importance. Given the durable jumping-off places they afford, these perennial books may have traceable links with the infernal visions of false identities and destinations, hallucination and addiction, recurrent in nineteenth-century Scottish fiction. Even when they stereotype the national literature of the past as whimsical, rustic, superstitious, and irrelevant, later Scottish writers are also drawing upon its deeper resources to make some of their most characteristic, implicitly powerful utterances, 'shot through with chips of Messianic time'.[49]

Notes

[1] Walter Benjamin, *Illuminations*, ed. by Hannah Arendt, trans. by Harry Zohn (New York, 1968), p. 257.

[2] On the untidiness of the past, for example, Allan Ramsay's 'purging and pruning' of Scottish literary tradition 'to suit contemporary tastes', see Alexander M. Kinghorn, 'Ramsay the Antiquary', in *The Works of Allan Ramsay*, ed. by B. Martin *et al.*, 6 vols, STS (Edinburgh, 1951–74), IV, ed. by A. M. Kinghorn and A. Law, pp. 147–8; on the supernatural and its obsolescence, James Kerr, *Fiction Against History: Scott as Storyteller* (Cambridge, 1989), p. 117.

[3] E.g. Mary Jane Scott, 'James Thomson and the Anglo-Scots', in *The History of Scottish Literature Volume 2: 1660–1800*, ed. by A. Hook and C. Craig (Aberdeen, 1987), pp. 81–99 (pp. 93, 95); cf. Kenneth Simpson, *The Protean Scot* (Aberdeen, 1988), p. 6.

[4] *The Poems and Songs of Robert Burns*, 3 vols, ed. by James Kinsley (Oxford, 1968), II, pp. 557–64.

[5] Cf. Carol McGuirk, 'Scottish Hero, Scottish Victim: Myths of Robert Burns', in *History of Scottish Literature 2*, pp. 219–38 (p. 221).

[6] Sir Walter Scott, *Redgauntlet*, ed. by G. A. M. Wood and David Hewitt (Edinburgh, 1997), p. 91.

[7] Kerr, *Fiction Against History*, p. 118.

[8] Kinsley, *Poems and Songs of Robert Burns*, III, p. 1351.

[9] Douglas Gifford, 'Myth, Parody and Dissociation: Scottish Fiction 1814–1914', in *The History of Scottish Literature Volume 3: Nineteenth Century*, ed. by D. Gifford and C. Craig (Aberdeen, 1988), pp. 217–59 (p. 240).

[10] On the context and larger significance of the eldritch for eighteenth-century Scottish writers, see Simpson, pp. 36–40, and F. W. Freeman, *Robert Fergusson and the Scots Humanist Compromise* (Edinburgh, 1984), pp. 140–1.

[11] *Memoirs of the Secret Services of John Macky, Esq.* (London, 1733), p. 236; quoted by P. Hume Brown, *The Legislative Union of England and Scotland* (Oxford, 1914), p. 117.

[12] John Hamilton, Lord Belhaven, 'The Lord Belhaven's Speech in Parliament, Saturday the Second of November, On the Subject-Matter of an Union Betwixt the Two Kingdoms of Scotland and England' (Edinburgh, 1706), in *Scotland and the Union*, ed. by David Daiches (London, 1977), pp. 147–9; Daniel Defoe, *The History of the Union Between England and Scotland, With a Collection of Original Papers Relating Thereto*, ed. by George Chalmers (London, 1786), pp. 317–28; Iain Gordon Brown, 'Modern Rome and Ancient Caledonia: The Union and the Politics of Scottish Culture', in *History of Scottish Literature 2*, pp. 33–49 (p. 37).

[13] Defoe, p. 328; on Defoe's response to Belhaven, see Leith Davis, *Acts of Union: Scotland and the Literary Negotiation of the British Nation, 1707–1830*

14 (Stanford, CA, 1998), pp. 19–45.

Daniel Defoe, *A Seasonable Warning or The Pope and King of France Unmasked*, quoted by P. W. J. Riley, *The Union of England and Scotland: A Study in Anglo-Scottish Politics of the Eighteenth Century* (Manchester, 1978), p. 289; Marchmont has misread his source, the end of *Pilgrim's Progress*.

15 *Report on the Manuscripts of the Earl of Mar and Kellie*, Historical Manuscripts Commission (London, 1904), p. 309.

16 George Lockhart of Carnwath, *The Lockhart Papers: Containing Memoirs and Commentaries Upon the Affairs of Scotland From 1702 to 1715*, ed. by Anthony Aufrere, 2 vols (London, 1817), I, p. 222.

17 Lockhart, I, p. 223.

18 Rosalind Mitchison, *A History of Scotland* (London, 1982), p. 185.

19 Cf. Sir Philip Sidney: 'Certainly, I must confess my own barbarousness, I never heard the old song of Percy and Douglas that I found not my heart moved more than with a trumpet; and yet is it sung but by some blind crowder, with no rougher voice than rude style; which, being so evil apparelled in the dust and cobwebs of that uncivil age, what would it work trimmed in the gorgeous eloquence of Pindar?', 'A Defence of Poetry', in *Miscellaneous Prose of Sir Philip Sidney*, ed. by Katherine Duncan-Jones and Jan van Dorsten (Oxford, 1973), p. 97.

20 Daiches, *Scotland and the Union*, pp. 186–7; Murray G. H. Pittock, *The Invention of Scotland: The Stuart Myth and the Scottish Identity, 1638 to the Present* (London, 1991), pp. 54, 87; Douglas Gifford, 'Introduction' to *The History of Scottish Literature Volume 3*, p. 4; cf. Thomas Crawford, *Society and the Lyric: A Study of the Song Culture of Eighteenth-Century Scotland* (Edinburgh, 1979), p. 9; and R. D. S. Jack, 'Which Vernacular Revival? Burns and the Makars', *SSL* 30 (1998), 9–17.

21 John Strong, *A History of Secondary Education in Scotland* (Oxford, 1909), pp. 111–12, 141, 143, 146, 161–9; James Scotland, *History of Scottish Education*, 2 vols (London, 1969), I, pp. 65–6; William Ferguson, *Scotland 1689 to the Present. The Edinburgh History of Scotland Volume 4*, ed. by Gordon Donaldson (Edinburgh, 1968), pp. 98–9; A. M. Kinghorn, 'Biographical Introduction', in *The Works of Allan Ramsay*, IV, p. 6; Hugh Ouston, 'Cultural Life from the Restoration to the Union', in *History of Scottish Literature 2*, pp. 11–31 (pp. 19–20).

22 E.g. *A New Edition of the Life and Heroick Actions of the Renoun'd Sir William Wallace*, trans. by William Hamilton of Gilbertfield (Glasgow, 1722); Gavin Douglas, *A Description of May*, trans. by Francis Fawkes (London, 1752); Gavin Douglas, *A Description of Winter*, trans. by Francis Fawkes (London, 1754); *Select Works of Gawin Douglass* (Perth, 1787); *The Works of the Famous and Worthy Knight, Sir David Lindsay of the Mount* (Glasgow, 1754); *The Works of the Famous and Worthy Knight, Sir David Lindsay of the Mount* (Edinburgh, 1776–77); Alexander Montgomerie, *The Notable and Antient History of the Cherry and the Slae: Being a Young Man's Love and Courtiship [sic] to Two Young Girls by Him, the One the Cherry and the Other the Slae* (Edinburgh, [1775–85]).

23 *James Watson's 'Choice Collection of Comic and Serious Scots Poems'*, ed. by Harriet Harvey Wood, 2 vols, STS (Edinburgh, 1977; Aberdeen, 1991), II, p. xvii; on Ramsay's 'sentimental Jacobitism', see Kinghorn, 'Biographical Introduction', pp. 12–17.

24 For evidence of early nineteenth-century decline in curricular use of Scottish texts at parish and burgh schools, see Hugh Miller, *My Schools and Schoolmasters* (Edinburgh, 1869), pp. 27–30, 39; also J. V. Smith, 'Manners, Morals and Mentalities: Reflections on the Popular Enlightenment of Early Nineteenth-

Century Scotland', in *Scottish Culture and Scottish Education 1800–1980*, ed. by Walter M. Humes and Hamish M. Paterson (Edinburgh, 1983), p. 44.

[25] *Minerva Britanna* (London, 1612), sig. A3; quoted by Michael Bath, *Speaking Pictures: English Emblem Books and Renaissance Culture* (London, 1994), pp. 97–8.

[26] Sir William Mure of Rowallan, 'To the Reader', *The Trve Crvcifixe for True Catholickes* (Edinburgh, 1629), sig. *2.

[27] Robert Southwell, *Saint Peter's Complaint,* (Edinburgh, 1634), sig. A2v.

[28] For bibliographical information regarding *The Palice of Honour*, see *The Shorter Poems of Gavin Douglas*, ed. by Priscilla Bawcutt, STS (Edinburgh and London, 1967), and Gavin Douglas, *The Palis of Honoure*, ed. by David Parkinson (Kalamazoo, MI, 1992).

[29] See *The Works of Sir David Lindsay*, ed. by D. Hamer, STS, 4 vols (Edinburgh, 1931–36), IV, pp. 15–122; *The Poems of Alexander Montgomerie*, ed. by J. Cranstoun, STS (Edinburgh and London, 1887), pp. xxvi–lvii; *Poems of Alexander Montgomerie – Supplementary Volume,* ed. by George Stevenson, STS (Edinburgh and London, 1910), pp. vii–lxv; and *The Poems of Alexander Montgomerie,* ed. by D. Parkinson, 2 vols, STS (Edinburgh, 2000), I, pp. xiii–xviii.

[30] Regarding the end of the *Dialog*, Lyndsay's editor notes a similar emphasis on hope: Hamer, *The Works of Sir David Lindsay*, III, p. 482.

[31] See *Music of Scotland 1500–1700*, ed. by Kenneth Elliott and Helena M. Shire (London, 1957; 3rd, revised edn, 1975), no. 49; Helena Mennie Shire, *Song, Dance and Poetry of the Court of Scotland under King James VI* (Cambridge, 1969), pp. 34–7.

[32] *The Autobiography and Diary of Mr James Melvill*, ed. by Robert Pitcairn (Edinburgh, 1842), p. 18.

[33] Hamer, *The Works of Sir David Lindsay*, III, pp. 243–4.

[34] Samuel Colvil, *Mock Poem or Whiggs Supplication*, 2 parts (London, 1681), part 2, p. 9; quoted in Hamer, *The Works of Sir David Lindsay*, III, p. 244.

[35] Alexander Pennecuik, *Streams from Helicon* (Edinburgh, 1720), p. 74; quoted in Hamer, *The Works of Sir David Lindsay*, III, p. 244.

[36] Alasdair MacDonald, 'The Sense of Place in Early Scottish Verse: Rhetoric and Reality', *English Studies* 72 (1991), 12–27; Ian Ross, 'The Form and Matter of *The Cherrie and the Slae*', *Texas Studies in English* 37 (1958), 79–91; Shire, *Song, Dance, and Poetry*, pp. 165–73.

[37] Wood, *James Watson's 'Choice Collection'*, I, part 1, p. 127.

[38] One of the most far-reaching and perceptive studies of these ideas continues to be Ian Jamieson, 'Some Attitudes to Poetry in Late Fifteenth-Century Scotland', *SSL* 15 (1980), 28–42.

[39] Wood, *James Watson's 'Choice Collection'*, I, part 1, pp. 123–4.

[40] *A Dictionary of Printers and Booksellers in England, Scotland and Ireland, and of Foreign Printers of English Books 1557–1640*, ed. by Ronald B. McKerrow *et al.* (London, 1968), pp. 301–2; for antecedents to the emblem, see Ronald B. McKerrow, *Printers' and Publishers' Devices in England and Scotland 1485–1640* (London, 1949), pp. 45–6, 85–6, illustrations 123, 125a–b, 225, 228.

[41] *The English Emblem Tradition (Index Emblematicus)*, ed. by Peter M. Daly *et al.*, 2 vols (Toronto, 1988–93), I, p. 276; II, p. 75; Peter M. Daly, *Literature in the Light of the Emblem: Structural Parallels between the Emblem and Literature in the Sixteenth and Seventeenth Centuries* (Toronto, 1979), p. 23.

[42] E.g. Freeman, *Fergusson*, pp. 10–11, 81; in his 'Preface' to *The Ever Green*, Ramsay characterizes the former age of Scottish poetry as one in which 'we had not yet made Use of imported Trimming upon our Cloaths, nor of Foreign Embroidery in our Writings': *The Works of Allan Ramsay*, IV, p. 236.

43   Thomas Crawford, 'James Hogg: The Play of Region and Nation', in *History of Scottish Literature 3*, pp. 89–106 (p. 103).

44   David Groves, 'Introduction' to James Hogg, *The Private Memoirs and Confessions of a Justified Sinner*, ed. by David Groves (Edinburgh, 1991), p. xiii; Emma Letley, *From Galt to Douglas Brown: Nineteenth-Century Fiction and Scots Language* (Edinburgh, 1988), p. 27.

45   James Hogg, *Confessions of a Justified Sinner*, p. 182; Groves comments perceptively on this episode in *James Hogg: The Growth of a Writer* (Edinburgh, 1988), p. 127; Regina B. Oost, ' "False Friends, Squeamish Readers, and Foolish Critics": The Subtext of Authorship in Hogg's *Justified Sinner*', *SSL* 31 (1999), 86–106 (p. 103).

46   Michael Lynch, *Scotland: A New History* (London, 1991), p. 259; on Scott's use of Bunyan, see Gifford, 'Myth, Parody and Dissociation', p. 221; n. 14 above.

47   *James Watson's 'Preface to the History of Printing', 1713*, ed. by James Munro (Greenock, 1963), pp. 10–13; Wood, *James Watson's 'Choice Collection'*, II, pp. xii, xix; Ouston, 'Cultural Life', p. 29; Harriet Harvey Wood, 'Burns and Watson's *Choice Collection*', *SSL* 30 (1998), 19–30 (p. 21).

48   Groves, *James Hogg: The Growth of a Writer*, pp. 150–1.

49   Benjamin, *Illuminations*, p. 265.

Lennox, Esmé Stuart, Duke of, Seigneur
d'Aubigny 99–100, 141
his companions to Scotland 115
his grandsons 117
his wife 117
letters, use of the term x, xxi, xxii, xxiii, xxiv,
xxvi n.1
Levenax, Alan, rector at Bourges 114
Lhuyd, Edward 126
Lindsay of Pitscottie, Robert 23
literary periodization x–xi, xv
Lithgow, William xxiv
Lock (Lok), Anne xix, 38
her sonnet sequence xix, xxviii n.32
Lockhart, George, of Carnwath 140
Logie, John, student at Bourges 113
Advocate at Court of Session 115
Lok, Anne *see* Lock, Anne
Lom, Iain 131
Lordship of the Isles 124, 131
Louis XI, king of France 112
Lowis, John of 63
Luther, Martin 42
Lutheran doctrines 112
Lydgate, John
The Fall of Princes 22
Scottish manuscript of xvii
Lyndsay, Christian 69–85, 88–9 n.58
sonnet attributed to her xiii–xiv, xix, 69–89
Lyndsay, David x, 2, 22–34
*The Answer quhilk Schir Dauid Lindesay
maid to the Kingis Flyting* 1
The Complaint … of Bagsche 89 n.71
*Ane Dialog Betuix Experience and ane
Courteour* 23, 41, 141–2
one of his works owned by Countess of
Mar xix
and Protestant ideology xii, xiii, xvii, xix,
30–1
Ane Satyre of the Thrie Estaitis 95–6,
141
Squyer Meldrum 141
The Testament of the Paypyngo 18 n.17
The Tragedie of the Cardinall xii–xiii,
22–34
welcome to Mary of Guise xxviii n.34
Works xxv, 138, 141, 142–3
lyric xvii, xxiii, 71
lyrical voice 75–6, 143–4

Machiavelli, Niccolò, *Clizia* 56
Mac Colla, Alasdair 127
MacDonald, Hugh 'Sleat Shennachie' 130–1,
133
McGill, David, student at Bourges 113, 115,
McGill, James, student at Bourges 115
MacGregore, Martin, student at Bourges 113,
117

Mackenzie, George, of Rosehaugh xxiv, 117,
120 n.31 *see also* Advocates' Library
The Institutions of the Laws of Scotland
117
MacMhuirich, Donald, tack granted to 123
MacMhuirich, Niall xv, xxx n.47, 121–37
approach to historiographical authorities
126–30
Clanranald History 121–37
comparison with Hugh MacDonald 130–1
historiographical approach, 124–34
motivations 128, 133–4
poetry 133
sources 126–34, 136 n.32
style 131–3, 137 nn.45, 53
Maitland Folio and Quarto manuscripts, xxiv,
17 n.2, 20 n.38
Maitland, Richard, 'The Banks of Helicon' 142
Maitland, Thomas, 'The Pretended
Conference' xvi, xix, xxv, 73
Maitland, William, of Lethington 63
mannerist xi
Mar, Marie Stewart, Countess of xviii–xix,
xxviii nn.28–9
The Countesse of Marres Arcadia xviii
her books xix
Mar,
John Erskine, Earl of (16th C) xvi
John Erskine, Earl of (18th C) 140
Marchmont, Lord 139–40
Margaret Tudor, wife of James IV, king of
Scotland xiii, 92
Marguerite of Navarre, duchess of Berry 112
marriage, 4, 54, 56, 57–9, 69, 61, 63
dominion in 38, 40, 42–3, 46–7
martyrdom, 27, 29, 30
Mary I (Tudor), queen of England xiii, 35–8,
44–7, 48 n.15, 49 n.17, 50 n.61
Mary of Guise (Marie de Guise), wife of
James V, king of Scotland xxviii n.34, 35–6,
44, 47
Mary Stuart, queen of Scots 67 nn.33, 41, 79,
92, 94–5, 99, 100, 107, 128
as queen 36, 37, 42, 46
her education in France xx, xxi
her library xvii, xxi, 60
her marriage 46, 60–3, 68 n.44,
her writing 73, 86 n.21
masculinity 35, 38–45, 74, 77, 83
male voice 70, 73, 75, 77, 85
de Medicis, Catherine, *see* Catherine de Medicis
medieval literature x, xv
Melville, James 115, 142
metafiction xv, xxvi, 77–8
Metaphysical poets xxiii
Mirror for Magistrates 34 n.40, 95
misogyny 35–51